£2

STRAIGHT & NARROW?

Compassion & Clarity in the Homosexuality Debate

Thomas E. Schmidt

InterVarsity Press
Downers Grove, Illinois

InterVarsity Press® is the book-publishing division of InterVarsity Christian Fellowship®, a student movement active on campus at hundreds of universities, colleges and schools of nursing in the United States of America, and a member movement of the International Fellowship of Evangelical Students. For information about local and regional activities, write Public Relations Dept., InterVarsity Christian Fellowship, 6400 Schroeder Rd., P.O. Box 7895, Madison, WI 53707-7895.

All Scripture quotations, unless otherwise indicated, are taken from the New Revised Standard Version of the Bible, copyright 1989 by the Division of Christian Education of the National Council of the Churches of Christ in the U.S.A., and are used by permission.

Cover photograph: Alinari/Art Resource, NY: Detail of the Doriphoros. Vatican Museums, Vatican State.
ISBN 0-8308-1858-8

Printed in the United States of America ∞

Library of Congress Cataloging-in-Publication Data
Schmidt, Thomas E.
    Straight and narrow?: compassion and clarity in the homosexuality
debate/Thomas E. Schmidt.
       p.   cm
    Includes bibliographical references (p.) and index.
    ISBN 0-8308-1858-8
    1. Homosexuality—Religious aspects—Christianity.
    2. Homosexuality—Moral and ethical aspects.   3. Evangelicalism.
    I. Title.
    BR115.H6S35   1995
    241'.66—dc20   95-6429
                                                CIP

| 17 | 16 | 15 | 14 | 13 | 12 | 11 | 10 | 9 | 8 | 7 | 6 |
| 09 | 08 | 07 | 06 | 05 | 04 | 03 | 02 | 01 | 00 | | |

In memory of
Kenneth N. Hansen
1919-1994
And every work that he undertook
in the service of the house of God
and in accordance with the law and the commandments,
seeking his God,
he did with all his heart, and prospered.

2 CHRONICLES 31:21

Acknowledgments —————————————————————— 9

1 About Me, About You —————————————————— 11

2 What All the Fuss Is About —————————————— 25

3 Sexuality from the Beginning ———————————— 39

4 Romans 1:26-27: The Main Text in Context ————— 64

5 From Sodom to Sodom ————————————————— 86

6 The Price of Love —————————————————————— 100

7 The Great Nature-Nurture Debate ———————————— 131

8 Straight & Narrow? ———————————————————— 160

Postscript: A Letter to a Friend ——————————————— 176

Notes ————————————————————————————— 181

Bibliography ———————————————————————— 219

Index of Subjects ———————————————————— 237

Index of Scripture References ———————————— 238

Index of Other Ancient Writings —————————— 240

Acknowledgments

The names of many people should appear on the cover of this book, like credits at the end of a film. The "producers" are David and Judy Neuneubel, without whom the book would have appeared years later—if at all. David's support took many forms, including ambitious fundraising efforts to provide a teaching leave. The Neuneubels' "associate producers" are a group of twenty supporters who gave of their means to see this project completed. The "director" is InterVarsity Press editor Rodney Clapp, who was prompt and helpful at every point in the publishing process.

The "supporting cast" performed their various parts superbly. Dean Bud Blankenbaker helped greatly with the arrangements for my leave. Walter Hansen graciously taught classes in my absence and received rave reviews from the students. Connie Tappy is thanked for having been the corrector of awful sentences like this one in the first three chapters before the baby was born. Library gofers Kimi Moran, Steve Baker and Rosalee Velloso saved untold hours with their tedious work of fetching and photocopying. Ned Divelbiss was quick to acquire interlibrary loan materials. El Montecito Presbyterian Church kindly loaned an empty office to save me from the distractions of home and campus. Lois Gundry performed a hundred favors to simplify my transient existence vis-à-vis the college. Jonathan Wilson made helpful comments on theological matters, and several physicians (whose names I choose to withhold) made helpful comments on medical matters.

These people and many others offered prayers and encouragement during an intensive period of writing. Throughout that time I enjoyed an unusual ability to concentrate and to work long hours. I regret my temporary one-dimensionality—but not nearly as much as do those closest to me, who undoubtedly look forward to my finding something else to talk about.

I dedicate this book to the memory of Kenneth R. Hansen, who died just after it went to press. Ken supported this project, as he did a hundred others, briskly, generously and prayerfully. He was one of the great warriors.

1
ABOUT ME, ABOUT YOU

I sit staring at a computer screen looking for words to introduce a moral issue, an issue so important that it increasingly appears to be the battleground for all the forces seeking to give shape to the world of the next century. What appear before me, however, are not words but faces. For after the politicians and school boards and courts have shaped public policy, after the denominations have interpreted Scripture and tradition, after the educators and scientists and psychologists have explained phenomena, after the media have tailored everything for mass consumption—after all of this, people, one at a time, still desire to love and to be loved. Some seek love with members of their own sex.

These are people with faces, people with names, often Christian people, and whatever we conclude about the larger issues their stories represent, we must never lose sight of their individual struggles, their individual pain, their faces. If we neglect faces, we neglect the gospel. The gospel is powerful medicine, but ultimately it is not administered by volumes or votes or verdicts.

It is administered by a single trembling hand holding up a spoon before the willing face of another.

In my mind's eye I see Jim—one of my best friends in high school, highly popular, a natural leader, a champion athlete, a young man committed to deepening the faith of his youth. For several months after college we shared our first bachelor pad, where I observed Jim sowing some wild oats with several girlfriends who spent the night. But less than a year later, after we had moved to opposite coasts, Jim wrote to me in great confusion. A prestigious performing arts school had given him a full scholarship, and within a year of his arrival there a friendship with a male roommate had become sexual. Jim returned to the Midwest for a time to sort things out, and later he wrote to me expressing great appreciation for my letter, but eventually he stopped writing and moved back to the East. That was in 1980. I wonder whether Jim is still alive, and I wonder if we could still be friends.

Another face I see is that of Laura, a deep thinker and committed believer with whom I attended a Christian college. Recently she wrote after a fifteen-year lapse and remarked that she would like to attend one of our class reunions, but she knew she would never find acceptance there with her lesbian lover. Through college she had struggled privately against her desires for intimacy with other women, but afterward she gradually came to the conclusion that her desires are a gift from God and not a temptation. Now she must live with the confusion of having one foot in a gay world that is largely anti-Christian and one foot in a Christian world that is largely antigay. I wonder how Laura experiences the justice of God.

And then I see the face of Frank—a relative whose first sexual experiences came as a boy with a member of the clergy of his own church. Frank found those experiences pleasurable. As an adult he prefers sexual intimacy with men and is an activist for gay causes. His well-meaning Christian family wants to "hate the sin but love the sinner," yet they struggle with the conflict between Frank's values and those they want to instill in their own children. For his part, Frank struggles to maintain loyalty to a family that disapproves of what he perceives as his very identity. I wonder what family means to Frank.

Finally, I see the face of Bill, who is a student at the Christian college where

I teach. Recently he wrote anonymously to the student newspaper about his loneliness. He does not believe it is right for him to engage in homosexual activity, but among his peers he finds little sympathy for his struggle. He notes that when other students speak openly of their heterosexual temptations and failures, their peers view them as models of vulnerability who merit prayers and support. But Bill keeps his own temptations and failures all inside, because he fears that if he were to speak of them, he would become a social leper. I wonder who has the hands of Jesus to touch him.

These are some of the faces I see and some of the things I wonder about when I think of them. I do not mean for these stories to be taken as representative of homosexual experience in general. Nor do I mean for these stories to elicit either a positive or a negative judgment concerning the behavior of these individuals. They are simply people I have known, some of the faces I see when I think about the issues involved. I describe them here for several reasons.

Authority, Experience and Me

One reason I hinted at as I introduced the stories: the issues cannot be addressed apart from human experience. Because our experience is varied, complex and emotionally charged, it is always dangerous to become too general or too abstract. Unfortunately, those on the conservative side of today's controversy often seem not to understand this, with the result that debates regularly pit gay men or lesbians with warm stories of victory over self-doubt and persecution against coldly rational ministers who quote verses about sexual sin and eternal judgment. Those who defend the objective approach fail to understand public debate, which is less a search for truth than a spectator sport. Like it or not, spectators respond to emotional stories and cheer for the underdog. Moreover, since the reigning value of modern culture is not truth but tolerance, anyone who takes a stand disapproving of another's behavior is bound to lose a debate.

Is the answer then to encourage both sides to trade only stories or only arguments and to stop acting like ships passing in the night? No. Life consists of both story and argument, both experience and authority. The two should be in conversation, not opposition. That is, the experiences of real people should temper our abstractions; at the same time, our activities should answer to higher authorities such as reason, family, tradition and Scripture. To err in either direction produces exactly the same proud claim: "I know better than you." The only difference is that those who pit experience against authority stress *I*, whereas those who pit authority against experience stress *know*. Both claim to serve the *cause* of Christ. Both have lost sight of the *way* of Christ.

My Own Story

So who am I to address the issue? Having just explained the importance of a conversation between experience and authority, I would do well to apply that to myself and be as open as I can be about who I am and why I am writing. What can I reveal of my story, my face and any claim I might have to expertise that will help the reader appreciate the perspective of this book?

In professional terms, I am trained to interpret ancient texts pertaining to Christian origins, and I specialize in New Testament ethics. I earned a Ph.D. at Cambridge University, am active in scholarly societies and write for national and international academic journals as well as for publishers (such as the publisher of this book) whose readers are primarily Christians. This book offers some of the latest scholarly research in a form accessible to a general audience. I am also editing a collection of academic essays on homosexuality by experts from a number of different fields.

In terms of sexuality, I represent that class of people responsible for the vast majority of sexual wrongdoing in the world today: male heterosexuals. I have contributed more than my share of wrongdoing, and I need the forgiveness and grace of God every day to become the sexual being God desires. I have never desired sexual intimacy with another male, nor have I ever been propositioned or treated with anything but respect by gay men I have known.

Apart from the natural concern that some extremist might threaten me or my family in retaliation for the public expression of my views, I do not think I have any reason to fear gay and lesbian people. Without exception in my experience, gay men and lesbians have been among the most intelligent, talented and thoughtful people I have known. Their sexual desires and practices differ from mine, but they do not particularly repulse or threaten me. I simply disapprove, as I do of some heterosexual desires and practices.

So I do not feel threatened. What, then, do I feel? To the extent that an emotion led to this book, it is annoyance—but not with gay and lesbian people so much as with their supporters and detractors. My annoyance is two-edged. I began with annoyance at the one-sided discussion in academic circles, which includes a common characterization of the traditional Christian stance on homosexuality as simplistic and fear-based. That led me to investigate some of the issues for myself, and the ensuing academic work led to a lecture series for churches. But there I became annoyed with the unpreparedness of many Christians to deal with this issue. For the most part they have conservative moral instincts, but they know almost nothing of liberal views, they find the possibility of tension between science and Scripture confusing, and they speak of solutions almost exclusively in political terms. As a result they often adopt a siege mentality and a suspicion of conspiracy, which, ironically, creates a mirror image of what they abhor in the homosexual community.

There is frustration on both sides at not being heard, at not having sufficient power to shape public policy, at not winning fast enough. But all too quickly disagreement degenerates into a battle of labels, the culture war between the Religious Right (who are all "homophobic") and the Homosexual Agenda (empowered by "secular humanism"). Despite the partial truth represented by such labels, they actually undermine the efforts of those who employ them. Those who already disagree move even further away, and wise people still making up their minds suspect that where fear-mongering labels lurk, dishonest arguments follow.

Wanting to be helpful in this volatile situation, I first had to ask to whom I should write. My choice of publisher narrows the scope somewhat, since InterVarsity Press serves primarily the moderately to well educated, morally conservative Christian community. That scope implies that I am not writing to persuade the gay and lesbian community or its supporters, but rather to deepen the understanding and sensitivity of those who question or disapprove of homosexual practice.

But even within that scope, I write to many different kinds of people. To a friend who has known a long, lonely struggle to reconcile his faith and his desires for same-sex intimacy. To an older churchgoer who has never been bothered by the issue and who wonders what all the fuss is about, since the Bible seems so clear on the subject. To a health care professional working with AIDS patients. To a concerned woman who wants to encourage a new depth of discussion in her church. To a college student with a deadline who hopes desperately to find all the needed information in one source. To a family member whose loved one has just announced a homosexual orientation. To a physician or a psychologist or a pastor who wants to bridge the communication gap between science and theology. To a believer dying of AIDS.

All of these people look over my shoulder as I write. More faces, more people to whom I am accountable for the truth, for clarity, for fairness. No small order. May the reader extend some grace to me at those points where I fail.

Although I see my primary responsibility to encourage deeper understanding and sensitivity among morally conservative Christians, I hope that I serve another purpose for those who disagree with my conclusions—that is, to demonstrate the possibility of disagreement without stupidity, without hatred, without slogans. Argue with me, but do not put me in a box, do not make a caricature of me in order to dismiss my conclusions. Allow me a face.

An Evangelical Focus

My face is an *evangelical* face, and that can be a difficult face to bring into focus, especially for those who like their opponents extreme and predictable. Evangelicals will often threaten people's assumptions concerning the so-called Religious Right and its presumed stances on the issues of our day. Some evangelicals are active in the international leadership of traditionally "liberal" causes like prison reform, health care reform, hunger relief and Third World development. Many evangelicals dissent from evangelical majority positions concerning abortion, violence, the morality of war, women in ministry, evolution, biblical criticism and political affiliation. It happens that I hold minority views in most of these areas myself, and I am free to do so without having to attend a special church for the doctrinally disabled. On the issue of homosexuality I happen to hold the majority view, but even then I would never call my position "*the* Christian position," or even "*the* evangelical position."

If my views on this and other topics cannot *disqualify* me as an evangelical, what *qualifies* me as one? If there is no party line on such issues, how does one get invited to the party in the first place? Difficult questions to answer. Scholars cannot seem to agree on a definition of the word *evangelical*. Like *Bible Belt* and *Midwestern,* terms that are only loosely related to geography, *evangelical* defies religious mapmakers. The phenomenon spans a bewildering diversity of opinions, denominations and social groups, and any attempt to explain or to give examples leaves some insiders feeling poorly represented.

Since there is no governing body distinguishing insiders from outsiders, evangelicalism cannot be described as a system with clearly defined borders but must be understood in terms of central principles. In other words, it is not so much about what is *excluded* as what is *affirmed*. (Some who have tired of the label would prefer to call themselves "mere Christians," taking their cue from the title of the influential book by C. S. Lewis.)

My outline of some central evangelical affirmations will attempt to clarify the perspective of this book, especially in distinction from fundamentalism of both the right and the left. I also want to make it clear at the outset that this is not an attempt to be comprehensive, but to describe those affirmations that I believe have a particular bearing on this topic.

The Center of All Things

First, evangelicalism affirms the centrality of Jesus. More specifically, Jesus is the only Son of God who willingly suffered death and then triumphed over it in order to set every person free from the consequences of human rebellion against God. Jesus is also, to some, dispenser of folk wisdom, capitalist, feminist, leadership instructor, symbol for human community and exemplar of social justice. But these titles represent at most additions—never substitutions—to what the Bible itself describes, and Jesus himself affirms, as his primary role.

While some work to clothe Jesus in the silk suit of a televangelist or the khaki fatigues of a revolutionary, the harder and humbler task is to hold ourselves accountable to the truth given two thousand years ago. To be sure, part of that task is to guard against cultural blind spots and empty religious clichés. But the central affirmation about Jesus will remain relevant as long as suffering, death and sin remain relevant; it will remain life-changing as long as faith, hope and love abide.

Scripture and Other Voices
The second affirmation of evangelicalism, wrapped up with the first, is the primacy and finality of the Bible's authority for faith and practice. I choose the words *primacy* and *finality* carefully. They mean that Scripture is the first place to look and the last place of appeal for guidance. They also allow for other voices to be heard in the process of interpretation and application.

A few examples can demonstrate the positive input of three other important voices. *Human experience* is an important teacher, as we observe in the case of race relations—a subject about which the Bible says almost nothing. *Human traditions* produce a rich tapestry of patterns for worship, devotion and church governance, few of which Scripture expressly commands. The Bible tells us to care for the sick and the needy, and *human reason* produces medicines and machines and programs to implement our care.

Of course experience, tradition and reason all have destructive uses, but the point here is that they also have the potential to contribute to our love for God and neighbor. Experience, tradition and reason are essential participants in a conversation intended to apply Scripture to our lives. To say that they have no place, that the Bible speaks alone, is simplistic and perhaps deceptive—there is always some interpretation going on. On the other hand, to suggest that experience, tradition and reason should or inevitably do overrule Scripture is to lose accountability. In either extreme—and both are well represented in the current debate about homosexuality—the desire to wield power overcomes the desire to find truth. Battles may be won, but the winner ends up far removed from the gospel preached and lived out by Jesus, which demands the renunciation of power in the interest of love.

Affirming the primacy and finality of biblical authority helps keep Scripture from becoming a tool in a manipulative hand, be it the right hand or the left. We will always struggle against our tendency to manipulate the Bible, and today we struggle with the absence of a universally agreeable method to find truth. We can only try, weighing opposing voices and attempting first and last to attune those voices to God's Word.

Context in Interpretation

A third affirmation, which helps to make the second affirmation more specific, is that the primary task of Bible study is to seek the intended meaning of its authors. While it is true that every reader brings a certain amount of baggage to complicate the task of reading—a different language, cultural conditioning, personal bias—it is also true that the original writers meant something by their words. In order to give the writers' ideas a fair hearing, especially on a complex or controversial issue, we must take responsibility to learn what we can about their languages, history and thought world. Only when we have attempted to understand their words can we begin to assess the ongoing relevance of those words.

It is lazy or self-serving, or both, simply to create our own meaning. Again, both kinds of fundamentalists indulge in this behavior. Those on the right often ignore ambiguities or historical context in a rush to find contemporary applications; those on the left often pounce on those same ambiguities or differences in historical context to justify making up their own applications.

Biblical Morality in Our World

Fourth, evangelicalism affirms the ongoing relevance of biblical morality—what some call its *normativity*. Certainly the world changes, and we cannot simply re-create biblical codes of conduct in all respects. At the same time, each new generation is not free to produce a new code of behavior, no matter how enlightened it thinks itself. The inspiration of Scripture and the righteousness stimulated by centuries of its influence suggest that biblical values are lasting values. We should resist tampering with the morality of the Bible unless a compelling case is made.

On rare occasions it is. For example, the repeated biblical prohibition against usury (taking money at interest) was normative until fairly recent times, because in a simple economy, money taken as interest, often at crippling rates, only enriched private lenders. In a complex economy, however, money taken as interest works in the system to benefit people other than the lender, and the lender is most often an institution whose rates are controlled by regulation and competition. The changing situation led gradually to new thinking about the biblical prohibition. In such cases experience, tradition and reason may all contribute to a reassessment of a particular biblical command, but the evaluation must proceed with extreme caution.

The Unity of the Bible

A fifth evangelical affirmation is that the Bible is a unity, in that it is inspired by God's Spirit. This does not mean that its words somehow dropped from heaven—they are fully human words. Nor do the words always say the same thing about the same subject. Some ideas about right and wrong behaviors change over time within Scripture (what some call "progressive revelation"), and on some subjects there are different answers.

On the subject of wealth and possessions, for example, we move from God's material support of the Old Testament patriarchs and the business advice of the Proverbs, to the critique of wealthy landowners in the Prophets, to the radical renunciation demanded by Jesus, to the community of possessions in Acts, to the missionary support requested by Paul, and finally to James and Revelation with more social critique—and, at last, streets of gold. Where is unity in this? The fundamentalist of the right may select Old Testament passages about material blessing and tithing and spiritualize the more threatening material. The fundamentalist of the left may transform the prophets and Jesus into protosocialists and dismiss other material as culturally conditioned.

But to view disagreeable material through the lens of agreeable material is too simple and too obviously self-serving. When the Bible presents diversity,

we should consider the alternatives of development and of different responses appropriate in different situations or for different individuals. In
some cases, unifying principles (in the case just cited, justice and dependence
on God) may be more important for us to understand than any particular
situation described in the Bible. The search for unity is sometimes difficult,
but it flows from the conviction that the same unchanging God inspires the
whole and invites us to see something of his character in every part.

God's Care and God's Judgment

Sixth, evangelicals affirm that the world is both under God's care and under
God's judgment. This implies that contemporary culture, the world order or
whatever designation we use for "what's going on out there" may present
opportunities for us to learn as well as opportunities for us to confront.

We should not assume that all change is degenerate and pull into a circle
of wagons; neither should we assume that all change is progressive and jump
on bandwagons. Moral issues presented by changing times are difficult to evaluate without the benefit of hindsight. Have Christians learned in the last few
decades that divorce and remarriage are acceptable avenues of growth for
some, or have we rationalized our own participation in the decline of the
family? Have new opportunities for women's leadership in churches resulted
from the movement of the Spirit of God or the pressure of the spirit of the age?

I offer these examples not to imply an answer but to demonstrate the
ambivalence and confusion that evangelicals often feel as they attempt to look
critically in two directions at once. One cynic suggested that fundamentalists
are those who talk like they hate the world and act like they hate the world,
liberals are those who talk like they love the world and act like they love the
world, and evangelicals are those who talk like they hate the world and act
like they love the world. It is an ugly shoe if it fits, but the challenge remains
to walk, however poorly shod, in a world that God both labors to redeem and
promises to destroy.

The Image of God

A seventh affirmation of evangelicalism is that people matter, one at a time, as beings who are both spiritual and physical. Evangelicals share with fundamentalists of the right an interest in world evangelization and political influence. They share with fundamentalists of the left an interest in social responsibility and sensitivity to diverse cultures and traditions. But ultimately an evangelical is not one who merely approves of Billy Graham but one who might invite a neighbor to attend a Billy Graham crusade with a view toward that person's conversion. Ultimately an evangelical is not one who merely approves of Mother Teresa but one who might join a medical mission team to a developing country.

The gospel is about individuals with eternal souls and a God who will hold each of us accountable for the way we treat them, one at a time. Social systems and political structures are important, but secondary. The particular labels we use to identify a person—black, educated, gay, female, Republican—are important, but secondary. What is primary is that each person is an everlasting creature for whom Jesus died and for whom God's desire is "that you may lead lives worthy of the Lord, fully pleasing to him, as you bear fruit in every good work and as you grow in the knowledge of God" (Col 1:10).

Because this is true, Christians are commanded by the Bible to be people of both gentleness and conviction, to hold each other accountable, to love toughly. When evangelicals take a stand on a moral issue, people on the left may accuse them of insufficient love; when they take that stand with humility and respect, people on the right may accuse them of insufficient toughness.

Perhaps there is some comfort in the fact that Jesus was crucified when the people who were let down by his refusal to be a king turned him over to the Romans on the charge that he claimed to be one. Neither group understood that their mockery, their robe and thorn crown, their labeling transformed the cross into a throne. Here is a God of high comedy, a God of paradox. The contemporary culture of victimization, where fundamentalists of the right and left whine in harmony, can hardly comprehend a God who embraces victimization in order to redeem people, one at a time.

The Book's Organization
Again, the foregoing outline of evangelical affirmations does not define evan-

gelicalism. There are other affirmations perhaps more distinctive and no less central than these. I intend here merely to sketch features that will introduce the perspective of this book.

That perspective dictates the sequence. I will proceed from a detailed treatment of relevant biblical passages to a consideration of their application, then to the implications of medical and psychological findings, then to a personal letter to a fictional friend (who is actually a composite of several nonfictional friends). Endnotes will allow interested readers to follow up for themselves on recent scholarship.

Choosing Terms

I have devoted a great deal of space to the identity of the reader and the identity of the writer, but I must lay a final piece of groundwork regarding the *subject*. The reader may have noted an alternation up to this point between the terms *homosexual, gay men and lesbians,* and *same-sex intimacy.* Justifying a choice between these terms might in itself require another book.

One problem is that some gay men and lesbians regard the term *homosexual* as a clinical term used originally by German psychologists for a sickness, in distinction from "normal" or "healthy" heterosexuality. On the other hand, some who disapprove of same-sex intimacy dislike this word because it appears to lend legitimacy to the practice or to the orientation by giving it a "respectable" label—after all, we don't dignify promiscuous people as "polysexuals." Others regard the word as simplistic, because together with *heterosexual* it implies two options rather than a range of options.

Still others (including both defenders and detractors of same-sex intimacy) deny that "orientation" is a meaningful concept or that same-sex intimacy in ancient times meant anything like what it does to us—so why use a term like *homosexual* that implies both orientation and historical continuity? Or should we coin a new term, like *homosex,* to denote activity without reference to orientation? Or would it only confuse the matter to add one more term to the list of options?

Gay men and lesbians is the terminology currently preferred by those who practice same-sex intimacy, but that may not last. The most militant activists now prefer to call themselves *queer,* reasoning that their own use of traditional terms of derision deprives their persecutors of power. The term *gay,* incidentally, was coined in the middle of the twentieth century by insiders who wanted to combat the stereotype of the depressed, lonely homosexual. The terms *gay men and lesbians* and *same-sex intimacy* share two disadvantages: they are syntactically cumbersome for a writer and, more seriously, they create the converse of the problem posed by the term *homosexual* by denoting nothing about orientation. Do we ask whether a person was *same-sex intimacious* from birth?

No solution will satisfy all parties, and the best I can do is to exercise care that my choice of terms in any given context does not in itself weight the argument in one direction. For the most part I will employ the familiar and syntactically convenient *homosexual/homosexuality,* with this advance acknowledgment that the term is controversial for some.

2

WHAT ALL THE
FUSS IS ABOUT

*A*n *acquaintance at the office, or a neighbor, approaches you and says,* "You're a religious person—tell me, what do you think of all this homosexuality stuff?"

You reply, "Well, I think the Bible is pretty clear that such activity is inappropriate."

You think you have made a simple statement expressing your belief in the authority of Scripture. But what the other person hears may be altogether different. To many people today, it is as though you had said, "Well, I think that the Bible makes it pretty clear that light-skinned people are superior to dark-skinned people."

Why? Because for increasing numbers of people, sexuality is no longer a moral issue but a civil rights issue.

The Culture of Tolerance
How did the shift occur from morality to rights, and why has it proven persuasive? In the broadest terms, we might consider developments in Western

and especially American culture. Begin with the affirmation that all people are created equal, and continue with the principle that the state should not rule in matters of personal conscience. Implication: the state should protect privacy. But then—and here's the rub—gradually remove the notion of a universal standard by which to evaluate behavior (the Judeo-Christian tradition), and people are left to evaluate their own behavior, which is all equally moral because it is all equally legal. The flip side of this is that it becomes immoral—and it could actually become illegal—to express intolerance, and the definition of intolerance could extend to any challenge to a legally protected behavior or opinion.

The confusion between what is legal and what is moral, and the emergence of tolerance as the supreme virtue, stands behind most of the important issues being debated today. The best short critique of the current situation I have seen is the 1978 Harvard commencement address of Aleksandr Solzhenitsyn.[1] But the problem of losing a balance between rights and obligations is not new. Plato predicted that democracy would crumble and pave the way to dictatorship because a foolish majority would turn liberty into license (*Republic* 562-65). Even further back, the biblical book of Judges laments a period of chaos in which "all the people did what was right in their own eyes" (Judg 21:25) rather than "what is right in God's eyes" (Ex 15:26; Deut 13:18). So the particulars change, but the underlying problem does not. God is dead, but long live God, because God is now us.

Minorities, Women . . . and Homosexuals?

Within this cultural climate of confusion, in the past few decades there has been considerable civil rights legislation for minorities and women. Almost no one would argue today that one's skin color or sex is relevant to where one lives, where one works or how much one is paid. Isn't one's choice of sexual partner also irrelevant to economic concerns? To the argument that homosexuals are economically better off than the general population, the response is that they might be even more so if treated fairly, and that there are other kinds of mistreatment than economic discrimination.

But the key issue in the link with civil rights is the issue of choice. Is homosexuality something that you *are,* like being black or elderly or handicapped or female, or is it something you *do,* like adultery or polygamy or incest? Those who practice these latter behaviors have certainly been discriminated against, economically and otherwise, but they are not linked to the civil rights movement.

The difference in the case of homosexuality has to do with public perceptions of the inevitability of the behavior. On what basis do we decide what is or is not inevitable when it comes to sex? When a man makes a rude comment or commits adultery, some shrug it off with the remark, "Well, men are just like that." Others think that masturbation and petting simply come with the turf of adolescence. But when an adult solicits sex with a minor, we don't say, "Let him be—that's just the way he is." Is the homosexual "just that way," and does this imply that we should extend the same civil rights, even affirmative action, to homosexuals that we extend to minorities and women?

Enter the nature-nurture debate, which I will treat at length in chapter seven. For now it is important only to understand that public tolerance dramatically increases when people are convinced that a desire for same-sex intimacy is biologically driven. Even though most scientists dispute the accuracy or the relevance of the research to date, even though very few experts on homosexuality limit causation to biological factors, even though the homosexual community itself is divided over causation—still the mass media persistently portrays, and the public increasingly adopts, a view that homosexuals do not *do* but *are.* If they *are,* and they experience oppression similar to that of minorities and women, then we must accept them—even celebrate them—to the same degree.

It is simplistic, and counterproductive in the moral debate, to blame the portrayal of homosexuality as biologically determined on a conspiracy between homosexual activists and the social liberals who dominate the media. What is more important is to understand how this portrayal changes public opinion. There are at least two factors at work. One is the popular myth that science deals only in absolute, objective truths, real things that grow in little dishes after being warmed up over little burners. By contrast, theologians and ethicists are pathetic characters endlessly arguing over vague abstractions. We may bring them into the discussion for color or comic relief, but everyone knows where *truth* comes from. The priestly garment of our age has become the white lab coat.

The second factor at work in changing public opinion is the simplification of issues for mass consumption, especially in television. It isn't easy to get "around the world in thirty minutes" (as one network puts it), including sports and Hollywood. Few people have the patience for a thorough presentation of a complex issue, even if such a presentation is offered. Instead, news programs sustain interest by giving the extreme positions on an issue, and statements are measured for their value as sound bites.

Thus when a new study appears suggesting that, say, twins are likely to have the same sexual orientation, the televised result is predictable. A ten-second, unqualified summary of the research is followed by the image of a scientist who tells us that "we are excited at the possibilities presented by this new finding." Back to the news room, where the anchor informs us that "the gay community reacted enthusiastically to the news" and presents the leader of a political action group who proclaims that "this confirms what we have always known about ourselves, that our sexuality is a part of who we are." Finally, we see an angry fundamentalist who asserts that "these are lies perpetuated by the sinful servants of Sodom." All of this in approximately thirty seconds, and then we are swept away to Bosnia or Michael Jackson or an ad for a little car that says "Hi."

Whether or not it is calculated, such reporting has a powerful cumulative effect. It creates the impression that science is serving the cause of civil rights against the bigotry of traditional religion.

So it is that the neighbor or the coworker is unimpressed, even offended, by the Christian who claims that disapproval of homosexuality is based on the Bible. But that is only one problem. What may come as a surprise to many readers, and what is in fact the focus of this book, is not the debate between Christians and secularists about homosexuality, but the debate between Christians and Christians about homosexuality.

The Invisible Rabbi
As a college professor, I recognize that students are captive audiences, sus-

ceptible to manipulation by insecure and unscrupulous teachers who set up opposing views only to shoot them down with shallow arguments and ridicule. I cannot completely escape bias, but I can openly state my opinions, and I can attempt fairness toward those with whom I disagree and who are not in my classroom to defend their views. When, for example, I lecture on the Pharisees, those notorious opponents of Jesus in the Gospels, I explain their passion for the study of Scripture, their zeal for God's holiness and their desire to make God's ways practical and applicable to all. Then, and only then, I describe points of conflict with the teaching of Jesus. I like to imagine that sitting in the back of the room is an Orthodox Jewish rabbi, a religious descendant of the Pharisees, with his hand on the power switch to my microphone. During one such lecture the invisible rabbi was nodding (I hope not from boredom) when a student interrupted, "Hey, it sounds like you're on the Pharisees' side." He meant it as a criticism; I took it as high praise.

Pharisees no longer exist, and I do not know an Orthodox rabbi, so I must do my best with imagination. But I do know some homosexual people, people with faces, and out of respect for them I want to do justice to the arguments in favor of homosexual practice. Beginning in the next paragraph and continuing to the end of this chapter, therefore, I will take my classroom principle a step further. I will write from the viewpoint with which I disagree, attempting to convince the reader that from a Christian perspective, homosexual practice is acceptable.

The arguments I use are taken entirely from recent books and articles written by Christian scholars. I will not clutter up the text with names and book titles, but the reader can follow up on sources through the notes. In subsequent chapters of this book, where I will review and then respond to the arguments I present here, I will refer to these as "revisionist" arguments and to their authors as "revisionists"—that is, they advocate that we *revise* the traditional Christian stance in order to affirm homosexual practice.[2]

Argument 1: The Bible Does Not Condemn Homosexuality
Homosexuality is the desire for and the phenomenon of sexual behavior between members of the same sex.[3] The words *desire* and *between* imply that

the behavior involves mutual adult consent. The Bible undoubtedly affirms heterosexuality, but does it condemn homosexuality as we know it today? On close inspection, argue revisionists, it turns out that the handful of passages that supposedly condemn homosexuality actually describe activities that modern homosexuals would condemn.

Genesis 19:1-8 and Judges 19:16-30. The first of these passages is the famous story of Sodom; the second is a less familiar parallel passage. In the Sodom story, Lot gives shelter to two angels for the night:

> But before they lay down, the men of the city, the men of Sodom, both young and old, all the people to the last man, surrounded the house; and they called to Lot, "Where are the men who came to you tonight? Bring them out to us, so that we may know them." Lot went out of the door to the men, shut the door after him, and said, "I beg you, my brothers, do not act so wickedly. Look, I have two daughters who have not known a man; let me bring them out to you, and do to them as you please; only do nothing to these men, for they have come under the shelter of my roof." (vv. 4-8)

In Judges, a man takes in a stranger for the night in the city of Gibeah:

> While they were enjoying themselves, the men of the city, a perverse lot, surrounded the house, and started pounding on the door. They said to the old man, the master of the house, "Bring out the man who came into your house, so that we may have intercourse with him." And the man, the master of the house, went out to them and said to them, "No, my brothers, do not act so wickedly. Since this man is my guest, do not do this vile thing. Here are my virgin daughter and his concubine; let me bring them out now. Ravish them and do whatever you want to them; but against this man do not do such a vile thing." (vv. 22-24)

The Sodom story in particular gradually took on a life of its own in Jewish and Christian history, and the English word *sodomy* has been applied to a variety of sexual practices among both heterosexuals and homosexuals, especially anal and oral sex. But the original event did not involve any kind of male-to-male sex.[4] The Hebrew word *yāḏa‘*, translated in Genesis 19:5 as "know" and in Judges 19:22 as "have intercourse with," is used in a coital sense only ten times out of hundreds of instances in the Old Testament.

In order to understand its significance here, we must appreciate the fact that Lot was an alien in this city (as was the "old man" in the story of Gibeah—Judg 19:16) and was under suspicion of harboring spies. When we are told that the men of the city wanted to "know" the visitors, we should understand that they wanted to *interrogate* them. Because this would have been a terrible breach of hospitality, the host in each story offers women to protect his visitors. Modern readers find this appalling behavior, but that is because they value hospitality less, or women more, than did people of the ancient Near East.[5] Thus the sin of Sodom in this instance was *inhospitality*.

The surrounding context affirms this, as do later biblical references until about the second century B.C., when in reaction to the prevalent homosexuality of Greek culture, some Jews began to reinterpret the story of Sodom in terms of sexual and specifically homosexual behavior. Old Testament passages condemn Sodom only for its general wickedness.[6] Ezekiel 16:49 is more specific: "This was the guilt of your sister Sodom: she and her daughters had pride, excess of food, and prosperous ease, but did not aid the poor and needy."[7] Even in the New Testament, Hebrews 13:2 enjoins hospitality on the ground that some "have entertained angels without knowing it," and Jesus himself associates the destruction of Sodom only with inhospitality (Mt 10:14-15; Lk 10:10-12).[8] Whatever distortions later interpreters have added, the Sodom and Gibeah stories fundamentally address proper treatment of strangers, not sexual morals. Indeed, if they are taken as object lessons about sex, we have to wonder what lessons we should take from the treatment of women as sexual bribes in these passages.

But even if the Sodom story is about male-to-male sex, it is not about homosexuality as defined above. On the contrary, it describes male rape, and that is not necessarily motivated by homosexual desire. Rather, it expresses the habit in many ancient cultures of humiliating an enemy by forcing him to "play the woman."[9] This kind of sex certainly does not involve mutual consent, and it is probably not pleasurable to either party. Modern gays and lesbians condemn such behavior just as vigorously as heterosexuals do. How terribly unfair, then, to apply the (just) condemnation of Sodom to private same-sex activity between consenting adults today.

Leviticus 18:22 and 20:13. These two verses appear at first glance to describe homosexuality:

You shall not lie with a male as with a woman; it is an abomination.

If a man lies with a male as with a woman, both of them have committed an abomination; they shall be put to death; their blood is upon them.

The revisionists remind us, however, that these verses lie within what is commonly called the Holiness Code of Leviticus 17—26, which exhorts the people of Israel to separate themselves from the practices of the surrounding nations. There are in similar contexts a number of references to the cult prostitute, the female *qᵉdēšâh* and the male *qādēš*.[10] Since only men were involved in temple rituals, the *qādēš* was presumably available for penetration by visitors to the temple. The Holiness Code, therefore, has in view prostitution in association with idolatry (hence "abomination"), not homosexual behavior between consenting equals.[11] The King James translation of *qādēš* as "sodomite" typifies the imprecise treatment that has been given to the Old Testament tradition.[12]

In the New Testament, it is noteworthy that Jesus himself never condemns homosexuality. The only sexual sin he mentions is adultery (Mt 5:27-30; Jn 8:1-11), and even then his primary concern is to condemn the hypocrisy of lust and judgmental attitudes. It was certainly not his style at any time to list biblical passages that condemn behaviors.

Romans 1:26-27. Paul, however, certainly appears to condemn homosexuality. In the context of a general pronouncement of judgment on the Gentile world for its idolatry, he writes,

For this reason [idolatry] God gave them up to degrading passions. Their women exchanged natural intercourse for unnatural, and in the same way also the men, giving up natural intercourse with women, were consumed with passion for one another. Men committed shameless acts with men and received in their own persons the due penalty for their error.

There are several ways revisionists interpret this passage as other than a condemnation of homosexuality. One is to set Paul's writing in the context of his time, where the forms of same-sex intimacy commonly practiced were pederasty (sex between men and boys) and prostitution.[13] These practices are degrading (v. 26) because they are unjust, as most modern homosexuals would agree. Another possibility here is that Paul is condemning homosexual acts committed by apparently heterosexual people—that is, those whose occasional actions contradicted their true nature.[14] In either interpretation, it is clear that Paul did not have in mind homosexuality in the modern sense. In either interpretation, what Paul does condemn modern homosexuals would likewise condemn.

Another possibility is to take Romans 1:18-32 as a unit, not intended to convey Paul's own morality but to convey Jewish Hellenistic (Greek-styled) thought about the Gentiles in order to set up Paul's attack on Jewish hypocrisy in the next chapter.[15] If the passage functions in this way, we must exercise caution in assuming that Paul fully agrees with its content.

1 Corinthians 6:9-10 and 1 Timothy 1:10. These lists of immoral behaviors include words that, according to revisionists, have been mistakenly translated as references to homosexuality:

Do you not know that wrongdoers will not inherit the kingdom of God? Do not be deceived! Fornicators, idolaters, adulterers, *malakoi, arsenokoitai,* thieves, the greedy, drunkards, revilers, robbers—none of these will inherit the kingdom of God.

... fornicators, *arsenokoitais,* slave traders, liars, perjurers, and whatever else is contrary to the sound teaching ...

The constituents of *arsenokoitai* are *arseno* (= male) and *koitē* (= coitus or intercourse), but a compound word does not denote the sum of its parts (for example, *understand* does not mean "stand under"); rather, it denotes what people use it to denote. The trouble is, we know of no occurrence of the word prior to 1 Corinthians 6:9, and antihomosexual human traditions may influence later explanations or translations.[16] Accordingly, it makes sense to interpret the passages in light of practices common at the time. *Arsenokoitai* in conjunction with *malakoi* (literally, "soft") may denote solicitors of prostitutes and the prostitutes themselves, or more specifically adult pederasts and their prepubescent companions.[17] Alternately, *malakoi* may have nothing whatever to do with same-sex intimacy but may instead denote "masturbators."[18] *Arsen-*

okoitai alone may denote simply "male prostitute."[19] Once again, Bible translators have often without warrant interpreted these words as references to homosexuality.

2 Peter 2:6-7 and Jude 7. These passages refer to Sodom under the influence of the Jewish reaction against Greek culture, but even then, revisionists maintain, they do not directly describe same-sex practices:

> And if by turning the cities of Sodom and Gomorrah to ashes he condemned them to extinction and made them an example of what is coming to the ungodly; and if he rescued Lot, a righteous man greatly distressed by the licentiousness of the lawless . . .

> Likewise, Sodom and Gomorrah and the surrounding cities, which, in the same manner as they, indulged in sexual immorality and pursued unnatural lust [literally, went after other flesh], serve as an example by undergoing a punishment of eternal fire.

The reasoning here is similar to that applied in the treatment of Genesis 19: the sexual import of these passages involves rape or, in the context of the first century A.D., pederasty and prostitution. It does not apply to homosexuality. The reference in Jude 7 to "other flesh" is in fact probably a reference to the desire to have sex with angels, not men, and is linked to the strange passage in Genesis 6 about giants issuing from sex between humans and angels.[20]

These, then, are the nine biblical passages that supposedly condemn homosexuality.[21] Revisionists argue that when viewed carefully, in the context of the time in which they were written, they turn out to condemn practices that modern homosexuals would condemn as well. We must conclude that biblical judgments against same-sex acts are not relevant to today's debate about homosexuality; the Bible "simply does not address the issues involved."[22]

Argument 2: The Bible's Condemnation of Homosexuality Should Be Qualified

Another approach to affirming homosexuality acknowledges that Scripture prohibits same-sex intimacy or, at the very least, that Scripture assumes heterosexuality is the only acceptable option. Attempts to apply the Bible to the modern day, however, are often "heterosexist" and must be corrected by attention to larger themes in the Bible itself.

There are several different avenues by which homosexuality may be affirmed biblically. We might characterize these in relation to the biblical material by the words *implication, expansion* and *correction.*

The *implication* of the biblical message allows for affirmation of homosexuality by setting aside interests of ritual purity for the gospel values of love and liberation. A development in this direction can be traced chronologically through Scripture. Following the interpretation explained above, the Sodom and Gibeah stories (and by extension, 2 Pet 2:6-7 and Jude 7) are irrelevant. The Levitical passage prohibits same-sex intimacy, but it is important to understand that it does so in the context of the Holiness Code, including elements of ritual purity from which the gospel sets Christians free.[23] In Romans 1:26-27, Paul is careful to use the terminology of ritual impurity rather than immorality when he describes homosexuality.[24] His Gentile Christian audience would have known Paul's thought well enough to understand that he does not associate homosexuality with sin—it is merely *impure,* as is eating bacon. Paul wants to expose the hypocrisy of legalists among his audience in the next chapter, so he finds an example of a behavior that distinguishes Jews from Gentiles.[25] His real message is in Romans 14:14: "nothing is unclean in itself."

The New Testament frees believers from the constraints of ritual purity (Mk 7; Acts 10) and redefines sin as "intent to harm."[26] Paul condemns (male) prostitution (1 Cor 6:9-10; 1 Tim 1:10) because it harms another by depriving him of his personal sexual property. But while the New Testament does not explicitly condone homosexuality, it sows the seeds of liberation from all legalistic restrictions on human sexuality. Paul's famous baptismal formula, Galatians 3:28, serves notice to the rule of law, the constraints of purity: "In Christ there is no longer male and female, slave nor free, Jew nor Greek . . . [gay nor straight]."[27]

The *expansion* of the biblical message allows for affirmation of homosexuality by removing human sexuality from illogical traditions connecting it to reproduction and male-female complementarity.[28] Sex involves much more than procreation, sexual pleasure is not limited to coitus, and other differences between the sexes are artificial. Without these bases for prohibitions of same-sex acts, we must consider carefully the life-enhancing experience of many contemporary homosexuals,[29] which is essentially no different from that of heterosexuals.[30] In light of their experience, we must expand our traditional categories for loving relationships and ask simply, "What is a right love, a good love?"[31]

A biblical answer to this question will stress several components, all centering on the quality of relationship as the basis of sexuality.[32] First, love must be autonomous; that is, it must involve mutual consent between equals.[33] Second, it must be constant; that is, it must involve some sort of commitment between partners.[34] Third, it must be fruitful; that is, it must nourish others both inside and outside the relationship.[35] We might add other components to this list, but the point is that humans are essentially beings in fellowship whose relationships, homosexual or heterosexual, are governed by the same biblical principles of love.

Because experience has shown that homosexuals have the same capacity to enjoy fellowship in all important respects, we must expand our definitions of marriage to include them. Celibacy is, biblically speaking, a temporary expedient for a spiritually gifted few, and we should not force homosexuals into that lifestyle, depriving them of sexual release and interpersonal intimacy.[36]

The *correction* of the biblical message allows for affirmation of homosexuality by applying the scriptural message of liberation to the troubling passages themselves. In general, this approach affirms the exodus story as central to the biblical message. Oppressed people, including homosexuals, see their own experience when they read the biblical stories that offer deliverance to social outcasts. This experience allows them to correct unjust (and therefore unchristian) elements in the Bible or in traditional interpretations of the Bible.

One variation of this approach involves a feminist reading of the Scriptures. This perspective begins with the recognition that biblical sexuality is patriarchal (male-dominant), rooted not in human biology but in human culture.[37] If the Bible is not to continue as a tool for oppression, only its nonsexist parts and nonoppressive biblical interpretation can have the theological authority of revelation.[38] The Old Testament passages that condemn homosexuality are all patriarchal, and the attitude carries over into the key New Testament text. When Paul labels same-sex intimacy as "unnatural" in Romans 1:26-27, he mistakenly equates "natural" with a social order that assumes an active, dominant role for men. He condemns lesbian relations because he follows his culture in assuming that the activity involves a grasping after maleness. This "theft" of male superiority corresponds to the disgrace of the loss of maleness when one male is penetrated by another. Experience teaches us, however, that homosexuality defies such stereotypes of cross-gender behavior and instead involves a symmetry of mutual pleasuring. This is "natural" for some people. Therefore we can set aside the Pauline assumption of sexual asymmetry or active-passive roles. We can define sexuality in terms of equality and justice.

Another variation of the liberation approach acknowledges the patriarchalism of Scripture but gives greater stress to the identification between homosexuals and oppressed people in the Bible. It is the children of Israel who suffer in Exodus, rather than those who control and exclude in Leviticus or Romans, who provide the pattern for Christian discipleship.[39] Jesus came to set captives free, and homosexual people experience themselves as such captives.[40]

To act as a disciple of Jesus, to live out the implications of the gospel, is to work for liberation; that is, to grasp power in the interest of justice for those who have been oppressed.[41] Power has too long been in the hands of oppressors who have written rules to serve their own interests. By turning homosexuals into social outcasts, and especially by doing so in the name of God, they have caused the guilt and fear that have led many gay and lesbian people into promiscuity, substance abuse, depression and suicide. Just as in the case of minorities and women, a reversal of pressures must occur and must remain in effect for a long period of time so that kingdom values can take hold. To work for this is to obey the gospel.

Summary
The approaches outlined above overlap in some respects and conflict in

others. I present them merely to give the reader an idea of the range of options being presented within the church to justify rethinking the traditional Christian prohibition of homosexuality. Some denominations (Metropolitan Community Church, United Church of Christ) have already adopted a revisionist position in some form. It appears that other denominations (Episcopal, United Methodist, Presbyterian Church [U.S.A.]) are moving toward change, as many of their leaders and seminary professors attempt to influence rank-and-file church members, who are generally resistant. Still other groups (most Baptist groups, Roman Catholics,[42] Pentecostals) are for various reasons decades from even discussing the matter. But discuss it they will, eventually. The question is, How well?

Whatever the stage of discussion in a given denomination, individual Christians are responsible to think, to evaluate new viewpoints, to discern right from wrong and true from false, to disagree with respect. If you have read this far, you are almost certainly a person who is prepared to take up that challenge. Now that you have been introduced to revisionist approaches, I invite you in the remaining chapters to consider a response interwoven with a Christian perspective on the morality of homosexuality.

3

SEXUALITY FROM
THE BEGINNING

*C*hapter two showed that the pattern in revisionist approaches is to list the apparent biblical prohibitions of same-sex intimacy and question either their relevance to modern homosexuality or their importance in relation to major biblical themes. There are, after all, so few verses. Is the heterosexual majority merely "prooftexting," producing a handful of verses to rationalize a bucket full of fear and prejudice?

I do not think so. The reason is that a biblical view of sexuality does not depend on lists of prohibited activities but on the pervasiveness and reasonableness of an affirmed activity: heterosexual marriage. I will maintain in this chapter that the Bible, reason and tradition combine to tell us what is good and how to understand departures from that good.[1]

Working from Creation

The story of the creation of humanity in Genesis 1—2 offers clues about God's intentions for humanity:

So God created humankind in his image,
  in the image of God he created them;
  male and female he created them.
God blessed them, and God said to them, "Be fruitful and multiply, and
fill the earth and subdue it; and have dominion over the fish of the sea
and over the birds of the air and over every living thing that moves upon
the earth." (1:27-28)

Then the LORD God said, "It is not good that the man should be alone;
I will make him a helper as his partner." (2:18)

Then the man said,
  "This at last is bone of my bones
    and flesh of my flesh;
  this one shall be called Woman,
    for out of Man this one was taken."
Therefore a man leaves his father and his mother and clings to his wife,
and they become one flesh. (2:23-24)

Of course these verses contain descriptions, not commands, so how can we
know that it is appropriate to use them to help define sexuality? Four observations. First, the Bible is full of moral lessons conveyed in story form, so at
least we *cannot rule out* the normativity of these verses. Second, the description
here is given special significance by its *placement* before the rebellion, when
the entire scheme of things is pronounced good by God. Third, the descriptions here are *consistent* with commands about sexuality given elsewhere, including many written at about the same time as Genesis. Fourth, and perhaps
most important from a Christian perspective, we observe the direct *quotation*
of these verses in key statements about sexuality by Jesus and Paul:
  Some Pharisees came to [Jesus], and to test him they asked, "Is it lawful
  for a man to divorce his wife for any cause?" He answered, "Have you not
  read that the one who made them at the beginning 'made them male and
  female,' and said, 'For this reason a man shall leave his father and mother

and be joined to his wife, and the two shall become one flesh'? So they are no longer two, but one flesh. Therefore what God has joined together, let no one separate." They said to him, "Why then did Moses command us to give a certificate of dismissal and to divorce her?" He said to them, "It was because you were so hard-hearted that Moses allowed you to divorce your wives, but from the beginning it was not so." (Mt 19:3-8)

"All things are lawful for me," but not all things are beneficial. "All things are lawful for me," but I will not be dominated by anything. "Food is meant for the stomach and the stomach for food," and God will destroy both one and the other. The body is meant not for fornication but for the Lord, and the Lord for the body. And God raised the Lord and will also raise us by his power. Do you not know that your bodies are members of Christ? Should I therefore take the members of Christ and make them members of a prostitute? Never! Do you not know that whoever is united to a prostitute becomes one body with her? For it is said, "The two shall become one flesh." But anyone united to the Lord becomes one spirit with him. Shun fornication! Every sin that a person commits is outside the body; but the fornicator sins against the body itself. Or do you not know that your body is a temple of the Holy Spirit within you, which you have from God, and that you are not your own? For you were bought with a price; therefore glorify God in your body. (1 Cor 6:12-20)

So while it is true that the Genesis creation story does not provide explicit commands about sexuality, it provides a *basis for biblical commands and for subsequent reflection* on the part of those who wish to construct a sexual ethic to meet changing situations. Applying this principle to our subject, it is fair to say that the human author of Genesis was not consciously prohibiting same-sex relations when he wrote the creation account, but it is appropriate for us to explore the relevance of biblical commands about marriage and to evaluate modern homosexuality in light of Genesis.

Critics may charge that the argument is circular; that is, it takes from Genesis only that which confirms prior conclusions derived from human tradition. It is true that different elements of the argument depend on one another, but this does not make the argument circular. Rather, it involves a conversation—

between Scripture, tradition, reason and experience. But because only Scripture has the place of revelation among these conversation partners, perhaps a better image is a conversation between a teacher and three students. What makes one conversation better than another is the quality of its relation to biblical authority, the teacher. In this case, does the conversation about Genesis honor the original intent of the author and the relation of the material to its use elsewhere in Scripture? Is it consistent with larger biblical themes concerning sexuality, love and justice? Are traditional interpretations of Genesis helpful? Is our reflection on the material reasonable, and is it consistent with well-established scientific findings and with human experience?

Asking these kinds of questions makes for a good conversation. Asking them in this order is also important, because the sequence builds from specific to general and from "teacher" to "student." Since I will address some of these questions in later chapters, my comments about Genesis here depend in part on ideas yet to come. The reader may need to exercise some patience until the whole conversation takes place.

Genesis Affirmations

The story of the creation of humanity in Genesis, its correspondence to general biblical sexual morals, and especially its use by Jesus and Paul generate several affirmations concerning human sexuality. All are crucial to the discussion that follows.

First, *reproduction is good.* Genesis 1:28 commands people to multiply, and the text goes on to proclaim that God looked over "everything that he had made, and indeed, it was very good" (Gen 1:31). From this point, the Bible assumes the goodness of reproduction, perhaps most clearly in the promised blessing to Abraham that God will make him "exceedingly numerous" (Gen 17:2). Especially in the Old Testament, to bear children is to know a blessing from God (Ps 127:3). In fact, it is through reproduction that God begins to provide salvation, centered first on the covenant with Israel, then on the Messiah "come in the flesh" (1 John 4:2) and finally on the perfected community of the New Jerusalem (Rev 21—22). At that point salvation is accomplished, so marriage comes to an end (Mk 12:25) and with it presumably sex and reproduction, not because these things are bad but because they have achieved their purpose.

Second, *sex is good.* The fact that the man rejoices at the gift of the woman with whom he becomes one flesh and the fact that the two are unashamed in their nakedness (Gen 2:23-25) imply that the process by which children are produced is not a shameful necessity but a beautiful experience, expressed here in song. This celebration of sexual love is confirmed in the erotic poetry of the Song of Solomon, which if read at face value will make even modern people blush.[2] In the New Testament, Paul asserts that husband and wife have mutual rights to sexual pleasure and only invite temptation if they abstain for long (1 Cor 7:4-5). The first-century Jewish culture of which Jesus and Paul were a part was modest and strict but hardly inhibited, as numerous graphic discussions in the writings of the rabbis show.

Paul and other New Testament writers worked to combat the notion prevalent in the Greco-Roman world that the body was less important than the soul and therefore irrelevant to one's actions.[3] In the first century, this mindset most often led to licentious behavior. But gradually its effect on Christian history was in the opposite direction, toward ascetic behavior—that is, the notion that people should deny the "dirty" body all its desires. Both manifestations of the mistaken separation of body and soul run counter to the biblical view that each person is an *embodied soul* for whom the good of physical existence, including sexual identity, goes back before the Fall and forward beyond the resurrection.

Third, *marriage is good.* This is implied in Genesis, assumed throughout the Old Testament and radicalized by Jesus in the passage quoted above. The Lord explains that God's original intent is to establish marriage not as a contract but as a union—in chemical terms, a solution rather than a mixture. Interestingly, the disciples recognize in this a threat to male control and remark, "If such is the case of a man with his wife, it is better not to marry" (Mt 19:10). Jesus' response implies that if they cannot handle the responsibility, they should consider celibacy, becoming "eunuchs for the sake of the kingdom of heaven" (19:12).

Paul likewise affirms marriage as an indissoluble union in 1 Corinthians

6—7, although he quotes Genesis to discourage fornication rather than divorce. What is common to the understanding of Genesis in Jesus and Paul is the implication that marriage is lifelong because it involves a profound bond between two people.

Fourth, *male and female are necessary counterparts.* Humanity is created male and female (Gen 1:27). Adam is not given a mirror-image companion, he is given a *her* (Gen 2:18), and he delights in her *correspondence* to him (Gen 2:23), which resides both in her likeness (human) and her difference (female). The pair are, literally and figuratively, made for each other. Because union is the remedy of incompleteness ("for this reason," Gen 2:24), humans possess a drive to "leave and cleave" in marriage.

These statements are not expounded within the Bible, but we may derive reasonable implications from them. What I am *not* confident that we can derive from them is a definition of creation "in God's image" as either sexual differentiation or human fellowship.[4] It seems more natural to understand God's action here as creating a counterpart with whom God can communicate. In relation to creation, humanity acts as steward for God, exercising "dominion" (Gen 1:28). It is necessary that humans "be fruitful and multiply" in order to create enough humans to exercise stewardship; hence sexes are necessary; hence "male and female" (1:27).

But the crucial implication of the passage does not hinge on the precise meaning of *image.* What is crucial is that sexual differentiation is good, and good because the union of the corresponding sexes remedies their incompleteness apart from each other. Furthermore, their correspondence is not limited to the social or spiritual dimension (the woman is "helper" and "partner," 2:18). That is important, but to leave the relationship at that level would create an abstraction utterly foreign to the context and to the Hebrew understanding of a human being as an embodied soul. The fit between the two is in fact described in *physical* terms ("bone of my bones," "become one flesh," 2:23-24). The pair are complete counterparts, including their physical natures.

These affirmations and implications from Genesis 1—2 lead to further questions and challenges. We may grant that all of this is good, but is it good for *everyone*? Might there be situations or conditions that constitute exceptions to the norm? In the following section I will attempt to construct a case for the exclusivity of heterosexual monogamy in relation to homosexuality.

Reproduction, Complementarity and Responsibility

Historically, Christians have focused discussions of sexuality on reproduction. With regard to homosexuality, where the union cannot produce children, the argument is that sex is not being used as it was intended from the beginning and is therefore "unnatural" both in the biological and in the biblical sense. There are, however, several reasonable objections to limiting an argument against homosexual practice to concerns about reproduction. For one thing, sexuality itself is not limited to reproduction. Sexuality is deeper than reproduction, involving everything that makes us male or female. It develops well before, and lasts well beyond, a person's reproductive capacity. Most heterosexual couples enjoy sexual intimacy in many ways prior to or other than the potentially reproductive act of coitus (penetration of the vagina by the penis). Furthermore, Scripture honors celibacy; and childlessness may have been a shame in biblical times, but it was no crime. Indeed, in our overpopulated world we might argue that the creation mandate to reproduce has been fulfilled, and stewardship of creation now requires that we *not* reproduce so much.

The notion of complementarity may pose an additional important objection to homosexuality.[5] The Genesis narrative affirms that male and female are different in correspondence to one another such that their union constitutes a completion. Scholars debate about whether some of the differences between men and women, such as ways of thinking or social roles, are present from birth or are a result of training.[6] Certainly, whatever their cause, the differences in gender are deeply ingrained. And whether or not we regard sexual differences as symbolic of other differences between the sexes, physical complementarity is undoubtedly present. That is, the penis fits inside the vagina, and the fit is pleasurable to both partners. Variations on this activity—manual, oral, anal—whether performed between opposite-sex or same-sex partners, whether performed alone or with other humans or with animals or

sex toys, involve the same essential complementarity: the male is stimulated
by the envelopment of his penis, the female is stimulated by the penetration
of her labia and/or vagina.[7] In homosexual acts, either a penis or a vagina
is missing, so the act can only *simulate* penetration and envelopment. Therefore, at *least* in a physical sense, such an act cannot realize full complementarity.

To the extent that other male-female differences are also lacking, this lack
of complementarity extends beyond the physical. That is, the less that homosexual couples embody the stereotypes of lesbian couples who play consistent
butch-femme roles, or gay male couples who play macho-fairy roles, the more
likely the couple is to present mirror images to one another. In other words,
ironically, the more "like everybody else" homosexual couples appear, the
less like complementary heterosexuals they actually are. They have not found
partners, they have found mirrors. Heterosexual partners are called not merely to fit physically into corresponding body parts, they are to open themselves
in humility to the mystery of the other gender in order to know union.[8]

The argument from complementarity alone, however, has some liabilities.
As I explained above, we may reasonably derive it from the Bible, but the
Bible itself does not make the point in so many words. Critics will argue that
sex roles are too indistinct and changeable to allow for a timeless notion of
complementarity beyond the physical structures involved in sex. And even
that limited definition of complementarity is debatable as a reason to exclude
homosexuality. When heterosexuals freely enjoy sexual pleasure apart from
coitus, we call it foreplay or birth control, not "noncomplementarity." Moreover, homosexuals "fit" well enough to give each other pleasure, so unless
the argument shifts back to the concern about reproduction, why make rules
about what appendage belongs in which orifice? Finally, one might raise the
objection that sexual complementarity is secondary in importance, and that
we should understand complementarity as a fit of two *personalities* whose sex
is coincidental to their partnership and whose sexual activity is merely the
expression of their spiritual union.

The objections to the arguments from reproductive capacity and complementarity are in some measure met by seeing both arguments together. The

notion of complementarity acknowledges that sexuality is deeper than repro-duction, that it extends to the core of who we are as people. On the other hand, the fact of reproductive capacity suggests that we cannot ignore or discount the physical aspect of complementarity, that the way the sexes fit together has consequences that carry implications.

Some will object that this looks like an argument from biology to morality—what ethicists call the "naturalistic fallacy" of shifting from "what is" to "what ought to be."[9] But Scripture does not shift between biology and morality; it views them together, just as it views body and soul together. That is, we humans as embodied souls must serve God with our bodies (Rom 12:1-2; 1 Cor 6:20), and the activities of our bodies must agree with the way we were made. To honor our reproductive capacity and to honor our male-female complementarity is to honor God.

Furthermore, we must understand that neither sex nor anything else is made by God simply for our pleasure. Rather, we are made so that we might love as God loves, and God makes it pleasurable for us to love sexually. Indeed, it is only by God's gift of sexual reproduction that we can share in God's generativity: in and through love, making people to love.[10]

Still one might ask, why should heterosexual monogamy be the only way to honor God in our capacity as sexual beings? Here I introduce a new factor in the equation: the notion of *responsibility*. This notion builds on truths I have already established: that heterosexual union is good because only it can produce children and because only it joins in partnership two fully comple-mentary people. Children are of course a consequence of heterosexual un-ion; and the production of children is good because it involves parents in another level of love, that is, the gift and nurture of a new and dependent life. The nurture of children by their parents is good because it allows chil-dren to learn from both sexes and especially to find a model in the same-sex parent for the development of their own sexuality.

In the Bible, there are two alternatives to reproductive sexuality: child-lessness and celibacy (long-term or permanent abstinence). In the biblical world, childlessness was involuntary and considered unfortunate but not sinful.[11] Adoption as a remedy was an acceptable option from earliest times

(Gen 16) to the adoption of Jesus by Joseph (Mt 1:24-25). Celibacy is affirmed in the New Testament for believers who are not yet married (1 Thess 4:3-8), who were formerly married (1 Cor 7:8, 39-40; compare 1 Tim 5:9-16) or who choose to focus their energies on ministry (Mt 19:10-12; 1 Cor 7:25-38).

What distinguishes these alternatives from homosexual practice is that they operate within the framework of heterosexual monogamy. Those who practice these alternatives affirm that heterosexual monogamy is good for them now, or it will be later, or it was formerly, or it would be if they were not able to focus on ministry. Homosexual practice, on the other hand, lifts sexuality out of the context of time and place and constitutes a living declaration that another *expression* of sexuality is good.

Why not? So what if the majority go along merrily making babies, or hoping to, within the traditional confines of marriage? What harm is there if a few people, privately and consensually, express their sexuality in another way altogether?

At this point the notion of responsibility applies not only to the individual in relation to a sexual counterpart, and not only to the couple in relation to the reproductive consequence of sex, but also to the *community* of which the couple is a part. In other words, there is more to sexuality than "what's in it for me" or "what's in it for the two of us." We must also consider "what's in it for everyone." Homosexual practice constitutes a denial in practice of the good instituted by God from the beginning. That is not to say that the homosexual consciously intends to deny the good, but that the result is a declaration in practice that something else is good.

On what basis is homosexual practice good? The most sophisticated rationale written to date maintains that in the last analysis, an individual discovers that it simply feels good.[12] This will not do. It is unaccountable to the implications of creation for the body and for the partner; and perhaps most important, it is unaccountable to the human community. As a variant expression of sexuality, homosexual acts do not advance the good of heterosexual union, nor do they remain neutral. Instead, they undermine heterosexual union and the family.

Homosexuality Versus the Family

The more outspoken advocates of liberation are perfectly straightforward about the demise of the family unit in their own popular literature, and their claims have serious philosophical underpinnings. Consider the words of French philosopher Michel Foucault, a self-proclaimed pedophile who died of AIDS in 1984, who has been a major contributor to the contemporary "postmodern" relativization of knowledge and morality, especially in the area of sex:

> Rules are empty in themselves, violent and unfinalized; they are impersonal and can be bent to any purpose. The successes of history belong to those who are capable of seizing these rules, to replace those who have used them, to disguise themselves so as to pervert them, invert their meaning, and redirect them against those who had initially imposed them; controlling this complex mechanism, they will make it function so as to overcome the rulers through their own rules.[13]

Such a revolution cannot take place in a vacuum but must revolt *against* something, against "the rules," which according to Foucault and other ideological leaders of the movement means the family unit.[14] This is clear by implication, but readers of the more sophisticated advocates of homosexual liberation do not need to take my word for it. A more extreme and explicit example is Michael Swift, who proclaims that "the family unit—spawning ground of lies, betrayals, mediocrity, hypocrisy and violence, will be abolished. The family unit, which only dampens imagination and curbs free will, must be eliminated."[15]

I draw attention to advocates of change like Foucault and Swift only to make the point that my analysis is not imaginary—but what I consider an indictment, others consider a manifesto. Activists who write for the wider public, as well as most religious revisionist publications, present a toned-down version of advocacy couched in civil rights language in the attempt to bring homosexuality into the cultural mainstream. Apart from some fundamentalists who alienate most people with their fiery rhetoric, few outsiders read advocacy literature written by and for homosexuals. As a result, most people—including many homosexuals—are surprised that the movement would consciously or unconsciously oppose heterosexual marriage and the family. It is more comforting to suppose that only a few extremists in the movement think in these terms and that most homosexuals simply want to be left to themselves.

The point, of course, is not how many people think what, but whether the underlying principle of opposition between heterosexuality and homosexuality is an accurate representation. Without clarity on this point there is apt to be confusion about responsibility.

One interesting example of this confusion is the 1993 film *Philadelphia*, the moving story of a homosexual man dying of AIDS whose employer unjustly fires him when his condition is discovered. In one of the key scenes the hero and his lover visit the hero's big family home in the country, where his half-dozen married siblings and his parents sit in a circle and without exception express support for the hero's lawsuit and (indirectly) his homosexuality. The mother even says, "I didn't raise my kids to sit in the back of the bus," drawing an obvious parallel between her son's case and the civil rights movement. The rather heavy-handed moral here is that families should offer this kind of unanimous and unqualified support to their homosexual members.

But it strikes me as odd that this kind of support must come from the hero's biological family (and such an *Ozzie and Harriet* collection at that!) rather than from the homosexual community. If the message of homosexual liberation is that heterosexual fidelity, childbearing and family nurture are not necessary to human fulfillment, why does the hero need to go *there* of all places to find strength for the coming crisis? Everything about the scene screams tradition—except the explicit message. One comes away with the suspicion that this family is being used by a person whose lifestyle symbolizes its negation.

Finally, without ever attempting to answer enormous plot questions (did the hero neglect his job? was there an obligation for him to inform his employer that he was dying? did his boss know he was gay?), the film resorts to the heart-tweaking gimmick of an enormously favorable jury verdict just after the hero collapses, dying, on the courtroom floor. Is this only Hollywood, or has sympathy become the measure of justice?

Whatever my abilities as a film reviewer (I did like the opera scene), my point remains that there are fundamental problems involved in the existence side by side of heterosexual monogamy and homosexual practice. Philosophically, as I have argued, they probably undermine one another; the least we can say is that they do not support one another. We cannot understand homosexuality, then, simply as a variant of sexuality along the lines of childlessness or celibacy. It is an expression of sexuality contrary to heterosexuality, involving opposing views of the interdependent values of reproduction, complementarity and responsibility.

These opposing views center on the principle of self-fulfillment as a rule of life. That is, each person owns an inalienable right to "life, liberty and the pursuit of happiness." Sexually, as in all areas of life, each person has the right to chart an individual course toward personal satisfaction. Otherwise that person will be "repressed" or "oppressed."

Reproduction, in this view, is an incidental or optional side-effect of heterosexual pleasure. The main thing about sex is pleasure, and homosexual practice is the ultimate expression of this, because it allows a full range of pleasures without the possibility of confusion by connection to children.

Complementarity, in the revisionist view, is a myth devised to support an outmoded tradition that men and women are essentially different and that their physical differences are significant. Homosexual practice opposes this myth, demonstrating that physical differences are irrelevant to sexual pleasure. Thus it offers symmetry as an alternative to the imbalance and inequality of traditional relationships.

Responsibility is redefined in terms of the self, and perhaps the primary partnership insofar as it serves the self. Personal fulfillment involves no necessary obligation to the wider human community and its procreative family model. Homosexual practice proclaims the independence rather than the interdependence of each relationship or individual. Self-actualized persons or couples are free to love and serve biological family members or the wider human family, but they do so by choice and not by connection.

In all of these particulars, homosexual practice sets up a disconnection between the person involved and the body, both individual and corporate.

But any attempt to disembody sex is a contradiction in terms. It is also unworkable: the homosexual population continues to rely on the procreative population for familial support, patterns of relationship and of course the production of more homosexuals. It is as if someone's spleen had declared its independence, departed through an incision in the abdomen, and then periodically returned, leechlike, to draw nourishment from the same body. Are the critics spleenophobic, or is this misplaced organ living in a dream world?

Homosexuality in Relation to Sexual Sin

I noted at the beginning of this chapter that the proper starting point for a consideration of homosexuality is not a list of prohibition texts but an understanding of what the Bible affirms in heterosexual monogamy. It is important now to understand the place of homosexuality among the departures from this norm. We observed in the previous chapter, for example, that some revisionists recognize a biblical prohibition of homosexual acts but consign that prohibition to the vestiges of a legalistic system based on ritual purity. In the next two chapters I will treat the prohibition texts in detail, but in the following paragraphs I will argue more generally that the New Testament prohibits same-sex relations not on the ground of their impurity but on the ground of a creation-based morality. In other words, the New Testament presents homosexual practice as a violation of *marriage*, as an activity akin to adultery.

In order to understand the connection between homosexual practice and adultery, we must look carefully at Paul's lists of sinful behaviors in 1 Corinthians and Romans. It is clear, first, that the list of prohibited behaviors in 1 Corinthians 6:9-10 is not random. It follows the sequence and content of the Decalogue (Ex 20:1-17),[16] with the addition of *malakoi* (literally, "the soft") and *arsenokoitai* (literally, "those who lie with males") just after adultery (Ex 20:13) and just before theft (Ex 20:14). Paul moves directly on to prohibit sexual relations with prostitutes on the ground that it violates the notion of marital union established in Genesis (1 Cor 6:12-20). The sins mentioned in Romans 1:26-30 also correspond to Exodus 20, but in this instance homosexuality replaces adultery. Both passages begin with reference to idolatry, which, as a violation of the first commandment (Ex 20:3), was considered the root cause of immorality.

Why the similarity in most respects to the Decalogue, with this specific departure? The answer has nothing to do with concerns for ritual purity. Rather, it has to do with the specific purpose of the author in each case. In Romans 1 Paul wishes to offer an example of a peculiarly Gentile sexual sin, so he mentions only that sin and then proceeds to a list of nonsexual sins. In his letter to the Corinthians he wishes to remind his audience of their deliverance from the various sexual sins of their corporate or individual past, so he offers a more comprehensive and specific list. Same-sex relations are mentioned not because they are particularly repulsive or impure but because they are relevant to the particular situation.[17]

In both instances the reference to same-sex relations is closely tied to adultery, which is a concern of unchanging moral law, not a mere peculiarity of Jewish purity regulations (Rom 7:7-25). With explicit reliance on the creation narrative (Gen 2:24), the New Testament strictly prohibits violation of the marriage bond (Mt 19:1-12; 1 Cor 6:12-20)—even by thought (Mt 5:27-28)—and exalts marriage (again quoting Gen 2:24) by comparing it to Christ's relationship with the church (Eph 5:21-33).[18]

Every sexual act that the Bible calls sin is essentially a violation of marriage, whether existing or potential.[19] So it is that Paul makes reference to same-sex relations as a supplement to, or a substitution for, adultery. And so it is that Paul never makes direct reference to procreation in reference to sexual morality, because he is less concerned about reproduction than about union— a troublesome point to those who mistakenly suppose that Paul's sexual ethic is driven by outmoded Jewish ideas about the importance of "the male seed."

And so it is, incidentally, that childlessness, celibacy and periodic abstinence or noncoital sex within marriage do not constitute sins—they do not involve liaisons extraneous to marriage. The focus of New Testament sexual morality, then, is on the act, not on its potentially procreative result. Reproductive capacity, complementarity and responsibility to the community are more or less implicit in the notion of marital union, but the notion itself does not require defense in the New Testament beyond an appeal to God's intent as revealed in the Genesis creation narrative.

Romans 2 Comes Next

It is important to note that in the New Testament view of sexuality, all departures from the norm of marital union are equal. Some sexual sins may be worse than others in that they involve more people or do greater damage to individuals, but the New Testament leaves no room for repulsion or hatred based on custom or taste, which would amount to a reinstitution of the Jewish ritual purity code. Those who applaud the message of Romans 1 against Gentile immorality must listen to the message of Romans 2 thundering up from behind:

> Therefore you have no excuse, whoever you are, when you judge others; for in passing judgment on another you condemn yourself, because you, the judge, are doing the very same things. You say, "We know that God's judgment on those who do such things is in accordance with truth." . . . You, then, that teach others, will you not teach yourself? While you preach against stealing, do you steal? You that forbid adultery, do you commit adultery? You that abhor idols, do you rob temples? . . . For, as it is written, "The name of God is blasphemed among the Gentiles because of you." (Rom 2:1-2, 21-24)

This shoe fits every heterosexual who reacts with disgust at a broadcast of a gay rights demonstration and then turns the channel to stare uncritically at adultery in a drama, trivialization of sex in a sitcom, fornication in a music video, and virtual prostitution in advertisements that sell by provoking sexual interest. Are these sins acceptable because they are the sins of the majority? For surely the sins of homosexuals are, in terms of quantity, a speck in the eye next to the log of heterosexual sin. Neither is excusable, but what is most damnable according to Paul here, and according to Jesus in Matthew 7:1-5, is to look for the speck without noticing the log.

Some might object that adulterers and fornicators do not march in the streets demanding rights and blaming others for their venereal diseases. Fair enough. But heterosexual Christians must face the hypocrisy of their misplaced indignation if they hope to convey moral convictions in the power of the gospel.

More to the point, the power of the gospel is not about looking at sexual sin on a television screen but about looking at sexual sin in the mirror. There is no heterosexual who is not troubled by fallenness in the area of sexuality. We sin in different ways. Many of us confuse sexuality with self-fulfillment and seek romance or thrills in new partners, numerous partners or new practices. Others find sex threatening and so withdraw physically and emotionally from spouses. Still others accumulate guilt from secret addictions to private fantasies and practices.

The God who knows all of our thoughts and deeds (Ps 139) knows that we need forgiveness, every one of us, in the area of sexuality. God offers that forgiveness (1 Jn 1:5—2:2), and the power to move each person on to maturity in the area of sexuality (Eph 2:1-20; 1 Pet 4:1-6), and the promise ultimately and eternally to "restore, support, strengthen, and establish you" (1 Pet 5:10; see also Col 1:21-23). This is the hope of the gospel, which "we who have fled for refuge" have "as a sure and steadfast anchor of the soul" (Heb 6:18-19 RSV).

The imagery of fleeing and clinging is appropriate for every person who is honest about sexual temptation. For most of us, moral survival is like crossing a choppy sea in an overturned boat. Get a little sleepy, or get a little reckless in your hold, and suddenly the boat and you are bobbing apart in cold, dark water. So you desperately scramble back, trusting that somehow, eventually, this boat will get you to land.

People who picture themselves as soggy sailors clinging to overturned boats are not apt to treat their fellow flotsam with contempt. Likewise, the proclamation of Christian morality has no place for a righteous majority who scorn those who will not play by the rules. What is needed are unrighteous people who recognize the universal need to receive God's mercy and power for obedience, whatever one's particular distortion of God's intent for sexuality. The log must come out of the eye.

If we Christians express convictions about homosexuality in the context of our general sexual fallenness, and if we openly admit our personal struggles, and if we accompany our exhortation to homosexual sinners with an equal or greater exhortation to heterosexual sinners—then, and only then, will we have something to say. If there are no ears left to hear, we Christians will have to take much of the blame for failing to see ourselves as the modern equivalents of the Jews addressed in Romans 2.

Revision and Response

Up to this point I have attempted to set the discussion in a context of theological affirmations concerning heterosexual monogamy, which in turn carries implications for departures from it and for the manner in which Christians express moral convictions. None of this directly engages the revisionist approaches introduced in chapter two. In the remainder of this chapter I will respond generally to those approaches that set aside the prohibition texts in the interest of larger biblical themes, and in the next two chapters I will consider the prohibition texts themselves in light of approaches that reinterpret them.

Chapter two surveyed several categories of approach that recognize a biblical prohibition of same-sex relations but dismiss the prohibition in favor of the larger biblical themes of love and liberation. The following paragraphs will address these approaches first separately and then collectively.

The *implication* approach, which maintains that the biblical message itself begins to sow the seeds of liberation by replacing a morality of purity with a morality of love, is flawed by mistaken categories.[20] It is true that the New Testament does away with the requirement of ritual purity, especially with respect to Jewish food laws (Mk 7; Acts 10; Rom 12). But sexual morality in the New Testament is not limited to concerns for purity.

Nor does the New Testament redefine sexual sin as "intent to harm."[21] Hardly anyone moved by passion or romance *intends* to harm; that is why we must consider the *result* of an act in relation to a standard of good. The New Testament does just that, but it does not invent a new standard or hint that one is coming. Rather, it carries over the sexual morality of the Old Testament and its standard of the good of marital union. Departures from this model may or may not be impure in Old Testament terms, but they are certainly unjust in the terms of both testaments, because they steal from the gift of marriage, which is the joint property of husband and wife. For this reason the New Testament sets sexual sin alongside greed (Mk 7:22; Eph 5:3; Col 3:5; 2 Pet 2:14) and on occasion even describes sexual sin as "robbery" or "luxury" (1 Thess 4:6; Rev 18:3, 9).

In short, there is an important distinction between the comparative religious superiority of Jew over Gentile, which the New Testament declares obsolete (Gal 3:28), and the moral law governing sexual relations, which the New Testament repeatedly affirms and grounds in the creation story. The Christian faith does not change morality; it offers power for morality, as Paul himself clearly explains:

> Do we then overthrow the law by this faith? By no means! On the contrary, we uphold the law. (Rom 3:31)
>
> Should we sin because we are not under law but under grace? By no means! Do you not know that if you present yourselves to anyone as obedient slaves, you are slaves of the one whom you obey, either of sin, which leads to death, or of obedience, which leads to righteousness? (Rom 6:15-16)
>
> So the law is holy, and the commandment is holy and just and good. Did what is good, then, bring death to me? By no means! It was sin, working death in me through what is good, in order that sin might be shown to be sin. (Rom 7:12-13)

This understanding of law in relation to faith is basic to the New Testament. To sow the seeds of liberation from the moral law is to reap destruction.

The *expansion* approach, which affirms homosexuality by removing human sexuality from connections to reproduction and male-female complementarity, is flawed by an unbiblical notion of personhood. It relies heavily on the debatable notion that we can equate creation in God's image with "being in fellowship." But even granting fellowship as part of the meaning of Genesis, it is still not all of the meaning, and such an abstraction of marriage neglects the fundamental importance of the sexually differentiated body as part of who we are.[22]

This "disembodiment" of marriage leads revisionists to suggest a new standard for loving relationships, but the attempt is disturbingly vague. The requirement of "mutual consent between equals" is unrealistic, because the causes of relational power imbalance are numerous and complex (for example, money, intelligence, age, experience), as are the variables of desire (such as timing, strength, expressiveness); thus "equality" serves only as an after-the-fact justification for any relationship in progress. The requirement of "some sort of commitment," to the extent that it falls short of lifelong fidelity, deprives partners of the security and trust within which they can learn the lengths and depths of love. Furthermore (as chapter six documents), fidelity even in the short term is so foreign to the experience of most male homosexuals that such a requirement by outsiders, however well-meaning, is unrealistic or undesirable. The requirement that the relationship be "fruitful" by "nourishing others" rightly implies that there is more to a union of two people than childbearing, but this truth applies equally to childbearing couples and does not constitute a tradeoff for procreation—it is merely a way of saying "be good" in procreative language. These and other requirements of the "new relationship" are either hopelessly vague or weakly derivative from marriage. Sadly, they produce at best only a shadow of marriage, a disembodied spirit doomed to haunt the tombs of its own victims.

The *correction* approach to the biblical message, which overrules the prohibition of homosexuality by appeal to the scriptural message of liberation, is flawed by lack of accountability to any authority beyond personal experience. The two variations overlap in rejecting biblical sexuality as oppressive, with the feminist variation linking the quality of oppression more directly to male dominance. Both replace biblical sexuality with something like the new definition of relationship described above.

The feminist correction is inconsistent when it dismisses biblical morality while trying to retain biblical theology. The essential salvation story is so full of male imagery and sexual archetypes (God penetrates the sky to bring life, which is his Son, and so on) that attempts to "balance" it with a pittance of scriptural female imagery or to feminize Christ as Christa[23] are feeble. The logical progression of feminist theology is to eliminate this phallic Sky God and his Son altogether and worship the Earth Mother or Goddess.[24] That philosophical move, of course, brings us full circle to sexual ethics, where the attempt is made to eliminate sexual differentiation and to leave us with "symmetry." But as we have seen, symmetry is an illusion, both relationally and sexually, and simulation of complementarity is a hollow substitute for the real thing.

The alternative is not to suggest that God is male (God is spirit and therefore has no sex) or that we must return to the patriarchalism of the ancient Near East. Rather, the alternative is to recognize that the New Testament affirms sexual differentiation but does not imply sexual inequality (1 Cor 11:11-12; Gal 3:28), and married partners have equal rights to sexual gratification (1 Cor 7:4-5). This is, however, not symmetry but *reciprocity* between fully complementary partners. The Song of Solomon witnesses to the equal delight of the man and the woman in the pleasure brought by the other, but they are different pleasures. *His* breasts are not like two fawns; *her* legs are not like alabaster columns. *Viva la différence!*

The more general liberation correction is flawed by its arbitrariness. It claims the right to identify with the entire sweep of Israel's history of oppression and liberation simply because the person who reads the story is also oppressed. The connection is not authenticated by common cause with Israel's righteousness or with the injustice of Israel's oppression, but only by the *experience* of oppression. How then is the experience validated? "The basis and source for knowing myself most intimately are the experiences and desires of my body."[25] Such self-validation prevents any further discussion, but it also removes any accountability to the intent of the biblical text; and ultimately it can offer no reason to invalidate *any* behavior.

Biblical liberation is never so irresponsible. When Jesus encountered a woman caught in adultery (surely a member of an oppressed group), he responded not by saying, "Go and do what your body tells you to do," but "Go and sin no more" (Jn 8:11). The Bible does not liberate people *from* righteousness, it liberates them *to* righteousness.

Liberation and Pedophilia
At some point all of the approaches considered above make experience rath-

er than Scripture the teacher in the conversation; that is, they regard the positive experience of modern homosexuals as decisive for the moral question. One way to point out the weakness of this approach is to apply the same logic to another activity that almost everyone considers morally indefensible. Then we observe that the relativization of biblical morality is a Pandora's box.

Advocates of homosexual liberation rarely discuss incest or prostitution or bestiality (sex with animals), but their moral conclusions vary widely when they do. Why? Because the logic of the revisionist position—that anything is permissible to those who experience it positively—keeps bumping into those pesky moral absolutes that call such acts harmful or perverse.

L. William Countryman, for example, is all over the map with his proposals for a new sexual morality.[26] Adultery is bad, he maintains, because it steals from the spouse's sexual "property." But sex before marriage may be acceptable if a person lacks the gift of celibacy, as well as prostitution if there aren't enough women to go around as wives. Bestiality and pornography are matters of individual judgment. Incest does wrong to the child involved, but its biblical prohibition is based on purity and patriarchy, and Countryman does not address the question of incest by mutual consent between adults within a family. But when it comes to pedophilia (desire for children), Countryman makes the most telling statement, asserting that there is "harm done to the child" and that "the inequality between adult and child . . . means that, in a sexual relationship, the needs of the child will be subordinated to the needs of the adult."[27]

Wait. If Countryman has already defined sexual sin as *intent* to harm,[28] why is he now interested in harm regardless of intent? Might harm accrue even if neither the pedophile nor the child is aware of it? Does it always accrue? And what is the ultimate basis of Countryman's definition of harm? His own experience? The experience of the majority? Even if he has the majority on his side, what gives that majority the right to dictate to the minority? Isn't that exactly what heterosexuals do to homosexuals? The questions fly fast and furious, but there is nothing to say in response, because ultimately *everything but individual experience is disqualified as "prejudice."*

But let us take the case a step further, because the weakness of the revisionist approach is evident apart from the inconsistencies of individual revisionists. Let us consider the approach as applied to pedophilia, or more specifically for our purposes, homosexual pedophilia. Manipulation, or abuse of the inequality of power between man and boy, is the chief charge leveled against the pedophile, the charge that distinguishes his behavior from that of mutually consenting adult homosexuals. In the logic of revisionism, is this charge valid, and is it sufficient to prohibit the activity?

Consider the propedophile argument. *The Journal of Homosexuality* devoted an entire issue in 1990 to "male intergenerational intimacy," otherwise known as pedophilia or man-boy love.[29] Advocates of pedophilia contend that "the gay movement . . . seeks to sanitize the image of homosexuality to facilitate its entrance into the social mainstream,"[30] because gays fear that pedophiles "confirm the bias that homosexuals seduce children."[31] Such suspicions, they say, are groundless. The fact is, "peer gays" (consenting adult homosexuals) are in the majority only because they have succumbed to pressure from the heterosexist culture to define their relationships in terms of marriage between consenting adults. Children are not ready for marriage or even long-term relationships, so we must accept their sexual encounters as predominantly casual.[32]

The common objection to man-boy love is that it cannot be consensual, that the partners are not equals, that children are coerced or manipulated into sex. Of course children should not be forced, the propedophile argument goes, but who is to define "manipulation"? When are sexual encounters between adults fully "equal," involving no seduction techniques or power imbalances that we might define as manipulative? And what of manipulation for the good of another? Don't parents use their power constantly to influence their children's behavior?

The argument continues: the fact that age-of-consent laws vary from state to state, from country to country, proves that age is only a number arbitrarily assigned to limit human freedom. There are thirty-six-year-olds of every sexual orientation whose immaturity precludes meaningful sex; conversely, there are sixteen-year-olds, and perhaps even six-year-olds, who can benefit from sexual experience. What's in a number? Normativity is relative, and human sexual practices are culturally conditioned. Pedophiles are the targets of hatred because parents resist the emancipation of their children, and because the majority are afraid of their own repressed pedophile impulses—which are universal.[33] Our culture suffers from acute pedophilophobia.

Man-boy relationships, advocates argue, can be and often are fully consensual.[34] Such relationships involve great benefits for the child. He is encouraged to be more open about sex, he learns sexual techniques in a nonthreatening, nurturing environment, and he learns about manhood. All of this evokes confidence and helps him to adjust as an adult.[35]

In response to the accusation that such relationships involve harmful dominance on the part of the adult, advocates cite several studies to show that sex can occur between men and boys "without the exercise of any manipulative power on the part of the adult,"[36] and that boys often find it a positive experience.[37] After all, everyone knows that the person in the relationship who most wants sex is at the mercy of the other; so if the man wants it, the boy is in control because he grants permission.[38]

Furthermore, advocates argue, pedophilia is a natural part of the constitution of some individuals,[39] and therapists have been unsuccessful in their attempts at conversion therapy.[40] Its acceptance by the ancient Greeks and by other societies throughout history further demonstrates that it is a natural phenomenon of human experience. Thousands of pedophiles are forced to hide their natural orientation for fear of social disgrace. Thus we must attribute any evidence of psychological maladjustment or occasional behavioral excesses largely to a repressive society that has forced pedophiles to think badly of themselves. In our pedophilophobic society, homosexual pedophiles are a persecuted minority within a persecuted minority, and they are therefore all the more deserving of civil rights (including affirmative action), all the more appropriate as standard-bearers of a theology of liberation.

Convinced? We might apply similar logic to incest, prostitution, bestiality or any sexual activity that some people experience positively. The point here is not to predict that pedophilia represents the next line of dispute in the moral battle (although it may well), but to show that *there is ultimately no argument against pedophilia or any departure from heterosexual monogamy if Scripture is taught by individual experience.*

Summary

This chapter began with the contention that a biblical view of sexuality does not depend on lists of prohibited activities but on the pervasiveness and reasonableness of an affirmed activity: heterosexual marriage. The creation story in Genesis serves as a basis for biblical commands and subsequent reflection on human sexuality. Scripture teaches, and reason and tradition confirm, that heterosexual marriage is not only good but exclusively good. This good involves the production and nurture of children, complementarity between sexually differentiated partners and responsibility to the human community.

Homosexual acts cannot fully realize these aspects of the good of heterosexual marriage and in many ways oppose heterosexual marriage, and so they are rightly prohibited in Scripture as acts akin to adultery. Revisionist attempts to affirm homosexuality by discounting biblical prohibitions in light of larger biblical themes are faulty in many particulars, depending on the approach. But such revisionist approaches all rely finally not on larger biblical themes but on individual experience, which as teacher ends all discussion—and begins all destruction.

4
ROMANS 1:26-27: THE MAIN TEXT IN CONTEXT

*T*he biblical view of marriage developed in chapter three would exclude homosexual acts by implication even if the Bible made no reference to them. But there appear to be several references, and our task now is to examine these to ask, first, if they prohibit same-sex relations, and second, if such prohibitions are applicable to homosexuality as we know it today.

The subject of this chapter is the most important biblical passage, Romans 1:26-27:

> For this reason God gave them up to degrading passions. Their women exchanged natural intercourse for unnatural, and in the same way also the men, giving up natural intercourse with women, were consumed with passion for one another. Men committed shameless acts with men and received in their own persons the due penalty for their error.

According to L. William Countryman, this passage has been mistakenly interpreted (and translated) in Christian tradition to describe same-sex relations as sinful. In fact, Countryman maintains, Paul portrays same-sex relations as impure for the purposes of his argument, but since the gospel releases Gentiles from the purity code, Paul is careful here not to use the vocabulary of sin.[1] While this approach may not have persuaded many, even among revisionists, it provides a word-by-word framework within which to consider this and other revisionist arguments pertaining to the passage.

The Structure of Paul's Argument

According to Countryman, Paul wishes to describe the result of the Gentiles' decision not to worship the true God in such a way that the Jewish segment of his audience will be "set up" for the next chapter.[2] Same-sex intimacy is an appropriate choice as the prime illustration of Gentile "uncleanness," because while it is repulsive to Jews, Gentiles see this repulsion only as a Jewish peculiarity. Homosexuality is simply a fact of Gentile culture, like eating bacon. Gentile Christians know that Paul does not associate impurity with sin, so they will not associate his words here with sin.[3]

Major flaws in Countryman's argument appear even before analysis of the individual words, when we consider Paul's design in the passage. First, it is a colossal mistake to operate under the assumption that Gentiles universally accepted same-sex relations, especially those resembling homosexuality as we know it today. Where sex between males in Greek society found approval, it was heavily qualified by limitation to those who were among the social elite, who had sex with boys between twelve and seventeen years of age, who took only the active role in intercourse and who abandoned the behavior in favor of heterosexual relations as they matured.[4] Some prominent Greek writers, notably Plato, condemned same-sex activity on the ground that it is not directed toward procreation.[5] Earlier Roman society legislated against pederasty and relations between adult males, but gradually under Greek influence Romans accepted pederasty (sex with boys) as an alternate means of sexual gratification for free men.[6]

The Rome of Paul's time operated for the most part by a simple, brutal rule: that a free adult male "may satisfy his sexual desires by subjugating women and boys without distinction."[7] But even Roman same-sex practice had prominent critics like Paul's contemporaries Seneca and Plutarch.[8] Finally—and this is highly important—sex between females was almost always and everywhere strongly condemned.[9] Since Paul's first reference in the passage is to relations between females, and since he then makes a link to relations of mutual desire between males, it would be impossible for any Gentile to limit the application of Paul's words to pederasty, much less find approval or neutrality in those words.

The second problem is chronological. Paul writes from Corinth after settling some major problems there, and he had not visited Rome prior to this letter. How would Christians in Rome know so much about Paul's distinction between impurity and sin? They might have picked up some general knowledge from other missionary travelers, but it is highly unlikely that this knowledge would have extended to specifics about sexual morality. And it is inconceivable that Paul, after the problems he has just had with the Corinthians, would simply assume the Romans had such information. In fact, Paul does not bring up the issue of purity until Romans 14, where his lengthy comments about ritual purity regarding food suggest that he assumes no prior knowledge of his position. Furthermore, since he makes no connection in chapter 14 between food and sex, we can hardly expect his audience to read such a connection back into chapter 1.

The surrounding paragraph supplies further evidence that Paul equally condemns same-sex relations and other behaviors that he mentions in the following verses. Romans 1:18-32 is clearly a unit, introduced by reference to "the wrath of God . . . against all ungodliness and wickedness." Three times Paul writes that as a result of Gentile idolatry, "God gave them up," and this phrase introduces not only verses 26-27 but also the items subsequently characterized as "things that should not be done" in verses 28-32.

A variation on Countryman's suggestion is that Paul employs Romans 1:18-32 as a legalistic condemnation of Gentile behavior in order to lower the boom later on Jewish legalists, but Paul himself is not concerned with legal rectitude.[10] This is a simplistic view of Paul's thought, which does not throw out the baby of righteousness with the bath water of *self*-righteousness. The similarity of the vices described here to the list in 1 Corinthians 6:9-10, which also begins with idolatry, forces the conclusion that Paul must have gone from legalism to enlightenment in the few months between his writing of these two letters. Furthermore, it is impossible to reconcile the supposed secondary or tongue-in-cheek status of Romans 1:18-32 with Paul's later summary remark that "both Jews and Greeks" are under the power of sin (3:9) and the likelihood that a substantial part of Paul's Roman audience, if not the majority, is *Gentile* Christian.[11]

We can account for Paul's argument in the passage without having to resort to such complex and far-fetched explanations. The passage consists of a threefold condemnation of Gentile vice, with each subsection introduced by the words "God gave them up." The first subsection (vv. 24-25) refers generally to idolatry, the second (vv. 26-27) describes a specific sexual vice, and the third (vv. 28-32) gives a list of vices destructive to human relationships. This shows "the inherent connection between idolatry as the lie about one's created status, sexual immorality—especially homosexuality—as the lie about one's relationship with his or her own body, and murder as the lie about one's relationship with the life of another human body."[12]

Same-sex relations are singled out because Paul seeks "a vivid *image* of humanity's primal rejection of the sovereignty of God the Creator."[13] That is, the first evidence of worshiping something other than the true God is that humanity will make of itself something other than true humanity. As we will observe below in numerous examples, Paul writes from the standpoint of Hellenistic (Greek-influenced) Judaism, which regarded same-sex acts as (quite literally) *revolting*, in that they represent a revolt against the created order. Paul does not reject this Jewish rejection but exploits it by maintaining that Jews also stand under God's judgment.

Indeed, there is confirmation of an important point made in the last chapter when we observe that Paul replaces same-sex relations with *adultery* when he confronts the hypocrisy of the Jews in 2:22. Whether stemming from Gentile idolatry or from Jewish hypocrisy, Paul sees sexual sin in relation to the good of marriage, which was from the beginning.

The structure of Paul's argument in Romans 1:18-32, its place in the larger scheme of the letter and the place of verses 26-27 within it are entirely consistent with each other and with Paul's thought elsewhere. Attempts to discount Paul's strong words create so many inconsistencies that we can only see them as weak attempts to save Paul from himself.

Key Terms in Romans 1:24-27

Countryman attempts to distinguish between an Old Testament sexual ethic that condemns same-sex acts on the ground of their ritual impurity and a New Testament sexual ethic that defines sexual sin as "intent to harm," especially in relation to the (sexual) property of another. In order to protect Paul from inconsistency in this regard, Countryman proposes an alternate translation of Romans 1:24-28 that avoids sin language and describes same-sex acts merely as impure. The key words are underlined, with the Greek italicized in brackets.

L. William Countryman's proposed translation:[14]

New Revised Standard Version:

[24]For this reason [idolatry], God surrendered them in the desires *[epithymia]* of their hearts to uncleanness *[akatharsia]* so that they would dishonor *[atimazō]* their bodies among themselves—
[25]these people who exchanged the truth of God for the lie and revered and worshiped the creation instead of the Creator, who is blessed forever, amen.
[26]On account of this [i.e. the sin of idolatry], God surrendered them to passions *[pathos]* of dishonor *[atimia]*, for their females exchanged the natural use for that over against nature *[para physin]*
[27]and in the same way the males, too, having left the natural use of the female, burned with their desire *[orexis]* for one another, males accomplishing shamelessness *[aschēmosynē]* with males and receiving the due recompense *[antimisthia]* of their error *[planē]* among themselves.
[28]And just as they did not agree to keep God in recognition, God surrendered them to a disagreeable mind, to do things that are not proper [kathēkonta]

[24]Therefore [because of idolatry] God gave them up in the lusts *[epithymia]* of their hearts to impurity *[akatharsia]*, to the degrading *[atimazō]* of their bodies among themselves,
[25]because they exchanged the truth about God for a lie and worshiped and served the creature rather than the Creator, who is blessed forever! Amen.
[26]For this reason God gave them up to degrading passions *[pathos atimia]*. Their women exchanged natural intercourse for unnatural *[para physin]*,
[27]and in the same way also the men, giving up natural intercourse with women, were consumed with passion *[orexis]* for one another. Men committed shameless *[aschēmosynē]* acts with men and received in their own persons the due penalty *[antimisthia]* for their error *[planē]*.
[28]And since they did not see fit to acknowledge God, God gave them up to a debased mind and to things that should not be done *[kathēkonta]*.

In the following pages I will examine each key term to demonstrate its association in Paul's mind with sin and not only with impurity. The evidence is more plentiful in some cases than in others. But I can afford to be wrong about several of the words, whereas for Countryman the entire passage must escape the connotation of sin. That is, if *a single term* in Romans 1:24-28 that makes reference to same-sex relations can be linked clearly to sin, Countryman's thesis is refuted.

Excursus: Responsible Biblical Interpretation

Readers trained in the exegesis of texts (discovery of the author's meaning) may want to pass over this section to the subsequent word-by-word analysis. For the rest, the following pages may make more sense after I illustrate and explain a simple principle.

Transport yourself two thousand years into the future, to a time when our language is all but unknown and your Ancient English instructor asks you to write a paper on the meaning of *love* in the opening paragraph of Mother Teresa's Nobel Peace Prize address. All you have to work with is the text of her address, two short books on prayer by her, a book of sermons by Martin Luther King Jr. and the song lyrics of Madonna. Unfortunately, nothing else in English has survived.

Without a dictionary, where do you begin to discover the meaning of *love* in Mother Teresa's opening paragraph? With the paragraph itself. What are the clues in the immediate context—that is, the surrounding sentences? Does Mother Teresa explain here what she means by *love?* Does she give examples? Does she use similar terms like *charity* or *kindness* that might clarify her definition of *love?*

After you explore the immediate context, the next best source of information is the rest of the address, followed by the other books by Mother Teresa; in each of these you look for similar passages, asking the same questions posed above. She is most likely to mean the same things by the same words in the same address. But a degree of caution is in order when considering her other works, because her ideas may change a bit over time, and you may not be sure if the other works were written before or after the Nobel address.

The writings of Martin Luther King Jr. may also help, since he too is a Christian writer, but his use of the word *love* may have political connotations not present in Mother Teresa's writings. As for Madonna, well, she shares the approximate time frame of both Mother Teresa and King, but "love" for her is expressed primarily in terms of erotic self-indulgence.

This illustration is not directly analogous to our analysis of biblical texts, but it clarifies the principles involved. Since the people of Paul's day left behind no dictionaries, people of our day must collect and compare terms to see how they are used in order to determine meanings. The best place to get help for a given biblical passage is the closest place, followed by the next closest place and so on. The surrounding sentences, the same book, another book by the same author (in Paul's case we have several), contemporary Christian authors and contemporary Jewish authors writing in Greek—generally in that order—are likely to help as well.

The further distant from the immediate context we travel in search of meaning, the more variables enter in and the more complicated the process becomes. For example, an Old Testament book might illuminate Paul's meaning, even though it is written in another language and hundreds of years earlier, because we can be confident that Paul knew it and considered it authoritative. On the other hand, a moral philosopher writing in Greek near the time of Paul might use similar words in entirely different ways.

To return to my analogy, a series of instructions in Mother Teresa's own hand requesting medical supplies for the Sisters of Charity might be less helpful in defining her notion of "love" than a medieval Latin treatise on prayer. In other words, to fine-tune the principle of what I call *contextual proximity*, we must consider the kind of writing and the thought world of the writer in question to the writer we are studying.

Applying all of this to Romans 1:24-27, we can begin to evaluate the proposals of Countryman and other revisionists regarding the words of Paul. The best evidence is Paul himself: his words elsewhere in Romans or in his other writings where the same or similar terminology occurs in discussions of sexual morality. After that, we may get help from Christian or Jewish contemporaries who wrote about sexual morality, especially if we can establish a strong link between their thought and Paul's. If we have to go further afield to pagan writers, we must take care to acknowledge the possibility that their morality—and even their terminology—presents only a surface-level similarity to that of Paul.

Epithymia, Pathos, Orexis: Desire or Lust?

These words occur in verses 24, 26 and 27, respectively. Generally in the case of *epithymia* and specifically in the cases of *pathos* and *orexis*, the words denote the inclination of the will that leads to same-sex acts. Are any of these three words strongly linked to sin in Paul's mind?

Countryman grants that Paul, like Stoic philosophers of his day, employs *epithymia* "for the most part in a negative sense," but argues on the basis of a single reference, 1 Thessalonians 2:17 (Paul's "desire" to visit the addressees), that *epithymia* could have a positive meaning and that we should at least render it "neutral" so as not to decide prematurely the question of Paul's evaluation of same-sex acts.[15] There is, however, no justification for such special pleading. The Pauline letters contain seventeen instances of *epithymia*. In addition to 1 Thessalonians 2:17, only one of these (Phil 1:23, where Paul "desires" to be with Christ) allows for a positive connotation. The other instances of *epithymia*—and the number doubles if we factor in the rest of the New Testament—are not merely "negative" but are connected to sin.[16]

These figures are important, but even more important is the kind of writing in which *epithymia* usually occurs. The two instances just mentioned involve autobiographical narrative, while the other fifteen Pauline references—like Romans 1:24—occur in the context of moral teaching. Moreover, four of these occur in Romans itself, and that is precisely where we should look first for evidence of a connection for Paul between *epithymia* and sin.

The evidence is compelling. In Romans 6:12 Paul commands, "Do not let *sin* exercise dominion in your mortal bodies, to make you obey their *passions [epithymia]*." In 7:7-8 he writes, "I would not have known *sin*. I would not have known what it is to *covet.* . . . But *sin*, seizing an opportunity in the commandment, produced in me all kinds of *covetousness [epithymia]*." In 13:14 Paul commands believers to "make no provision for the flesh, to gratify its *desires [epithymia].*"

Perhaps even more telling than these instances in Romans is the use of *epithymia* in a specific reference to sexual sin that contains echoes of Romans 1 in its comparison to the Gentile world. In 1 Thessalonians 4:5 Paul commands believers to express their sexuality "not with *lustful passion [pathei epithymias],* like the Gentiles who do not know God." The equation between *epithymia* and sexual sin here is undeniable: Paul has just prohibited sexual immorality (*porneia*, v. 3), and he defines *lustful passion* by the command in verse 5 not to *wrong (hyperbainō*[17]) or *exploit (pleonekteō)* another (v. 6).

An even closer connection between *epithymia* as sin and Romans 1 is provided by Philo, a Jewish philosopher who wrote in Greek during the early first century, just prior to the New Testament. It is unlikely that any New Testament authors read Philo, but his voluminous writings add to our knowledge of the way words were used and the kinds of ideas that circulated among Greek-educated (Hellenistic) Jews like Paul. In one place Philo writes that the men of Sodom were undeterred from same-sex relations even when they were sterilized as a consequence, because they were "mastered by *epithymia*" (*De Abrahamo* 135); in another place he refers to their "unnatural and unholy *epithymia*" (*De Fuga et Inventione* 144).

Countryman repeatedly discounts any reference to Hellenistic Jews like Philo on the ground that Paul did not fully adopt their purity ethic.[18] Granted, we cannot consider evidence from Paul's cultural context uncritically. In Philo, however, we observe a contemporary Hellenistic Jew, writing about the same subject, describing sexual relations between men as sinful, impure and revolting—and employing *epithymia* in the same context. If this is not evidence that Paul at least partially adopted the Hellenistic Jewish ethical code, it can hardly be said that he advances a distinct view in Romans 1 when he employs terminology identical to that employed by a contemporary Jewish Hellenist. To claim at this point that Paul uses the word but does not associate it with sin is insupportable in light of Paul's own usage in every other pertinent instance.

On the basis of *epithymia* alone, then, we might dismiss Countryman's entire argument regarding Romans 1:24-27 and move on to other questions. Nevertheless, I will continue a word-by-word analysis, not to beat a dead horse but to build a more precise picture of what Paul condemns and why.

In verses 26-27 Paul uses two other terms for homosexual desire, *pathos* and *orexis*. Once again Countryman maintains that we can understand these words in a positive sense.[19] As in the case of *epithymia*, this statement is technically true but actually quite misleading in light of pertinent occurrences of the word. There are only two other instances of *pathos* in the New Testament.[20] The first of these, 1 Thessalonians 4:5, was quoted above and clearly denotes sinful action. The other instance is a list of vices in Colossians 3:5. Countryman's reference to a "positive" sense for *pathos* must derive either from classical Greek, which has little relevance to Paul, or from the related word *pathēma*, which is often used in the New Testament for sufferings endured by believers or by Christ.[21] On the two occasions when *pathēma* is used in an ethical context, however, the association with sin is unmistakable. Romans 7:5 states that "while we were living in the *flesh,* our *sinful passions [pathēma]* . . . were at work in our members." Galatians 5:24 lauds those who "have crucified the flesh with its *passions* and *desires*" *(pathēma* and *epithymia).* Clearly the evidence, particularly from Paul's writings, constitutes a compelling case for the association of *pathos* with sin in Romans 1:26.

In verse 27 Paul employs *orexis* to refer to the desire of males for one another. This is the only New Testament occurrence of this word, but the related verb *oregomai* is used in an ethical context once (1 Tim 6:10), in a warning about "eagerness" for wealth. Philo employs *orexis* fourteen times, always negatively, and twice in discussions of sexual desire.[22] In the Greek version of the Old Testament[23] three instances are relevant. Sirach 18:30 advises, "Do not follow your base desires *[epithymia],* but restrain your appetites *[orexis]."* Sirach 23:6 contains the plea, "Let neither culinary nor sexual desire *[orexis]* overcome me" (my translation).[24] In 4 Maccabees 1:33, 35, the writer links sensual and sexual desire, advocating reasoned control of "the impulses of the body" and "the emotions of the appetites *[orexis]."*

While relevant references to *orexis* itself are scarce, we should not isolate the word from the verb that it modifies in Romans 1:27, *ekkaiō.* Paul writes that males "were consumed *[ekkaiō]* with passion." This imagery has a sinful connotation that Paul employs similarly in 1 Corinthians 7:9 (by means of a different verb, *pyroō*).[25] The association of fire imagery with self-destruction in the case of sexual sin is perhaps obvious, but a few examples will demonstrate its familiarity in Paul's historical context. Sirach 23:16 refers to the passion of a fornicator that "blazes like a fire" and that "will never cease until the fire burns him up." Philo warns that "all those who are rebellious will continue to be burnt . . . by their inward lusts *[epithymia]*, which like a flame will ravage the whole life of those in whom they dwell" (*De Decalogo* 49). In another place Philo contends that "we must reject with scorn the superfluities which kindle the lusts *[epithymia]* that with a single flameburst consume *[kataphlegō]* every good thing" (*De Gigantibus* 34).

As in the case of *epithymia* and *pathos,* analysis of *orexis* makes it impossible to allow a "neutral" sense. The closer the evidence to Paul's context, the stronger the case that the three words Paul employs in Romans 1:24-27 for the inclination of the will toward same-sex relations are not only negative in their connotations but clearly and consciously linked to sin. There is warrant to support translation by a strong English word like *lust.*[26]

Akatharsia: Greed or Lewdness?

In the case of *akatharsia* (v. 24), Countryman contends that Paul removes from the word its connotation of Levitical impurity and adopts a special use, making it a synonym for *greed.*[27] This is a doubtful understanding of the word,[28] but it does not in any case dissociate the word from sin in the minds of the audience of Romans 1:24.

Indeed, it appears that Countryman is caught in a serious contradiction here. First he maintains that uncleanness equals greed but not impurity—and he virtually defines sin as greed—yet when he encounters the word *akatharsia* in Romans 1:24 he claims that it equals impurity but not sin. The truth is that such fine-tuned distinctions would be lost on Paul and on his audience. Attention to the background and Pauline use of *akatharsia* demonstrates its association with sin.

In Paul's time, Hellenistic Jews commonly employed *akatharsia* in discussions of moral and especially sexual wrongdoing,[29] an association borne out by New Testament usage, especially that of Paul. In fact, the only clear references of *akatharsia* in the New Testament to ritual uncleanness are the critique of the Pharisees by Jesus (Mt 23:27) and Peter's response to a vision of unclean food (Acts 10:14, 28; 11:8). Elsewhere the reference is unmistakably to sinful behavior.

There are several particularly pertinent texts. In Romans 6:19 Paul correlates *akatharsia* and "iniquity" (*anomia*, literally "lawlessness") in contrast to "righteousness for sanctification." In 2 Corinthians 12:21 Paul threatens those "who previously *sinned* and have not *repented* of the *impurity, sexual immorality,* and *licentiousness* that they have practiced." Perhaps most succinct is 1 Thessalonians 4:7, where Paul summarizes his sexual ethic, "For God did not call us to *impurity* but in *holiness.*"[30] In these instances Paul is clearly consistent with the expanded contemporary understanding of *akatharsia* in ethical contexts as "immorality," not just "uncleanness," and an English translation like "lewdness"[31] is appropriate for the word in Romans 1:24, given the specifically sexual context of the verses following.

Atimia, Aschēmosynē: Social Dishonor or Ethical Offense?

Countryman regards *atimia* and *aschēmosynē* as designations of social status, not immorality; each is "a synonym for dishonor, not a term denoting sinful behavior."[32] Once again, the question arises of the legitimacy of this neutralization of Paul's terminology. While it is fair to note that in Paul's context, social disgrace in the realm of sexuality was not always the direct result of sinful behavior (as the case of menstruation shows), we must apply such a distinction carefully. The language of social disgrace may imply sinful behavior. In the present case a survey of relevant occurrences reveals just such a connection.

There are only two other occurrences of *atimia, aschēmosynē* in Pauline ethical contexts,[33] but both are instructive. In 1 Corinthians 15:43 Paul writes of the body being "sown in dishonor" before it is "raised in glory." Surely this implies more than death as social disgrace: death is the penalty for sin. The only other Pauline occurrence of *atimazō* is in the very next chapter of Ro-

mans, where the apostle challenges certain Jews: "Do you dishonor God by
breaking the law?" (2:23).[34] Clearly sin here constitutes an offense against
God, not mere social disgrace.

A similar sense prevails for *aschēmosynē* in ethical contexts, although the
rarity of the word precludes extensive documentation. The only other New
Testament occurrence, however, is significant. In Revelation 16:15 the person
is commended "who stays awake and is clothed, not going about naked and
exposed to *shame.*" The ethical import of this statement is clear from the
context,[35] and it is confirmed by other examples. Sirach 30:13 advises a father,
"Discipline your son . . . so that you may not be offended by his shamelessness." Philo remarks that "examples of shamelessness are all those unseemly
actions *[aschēmosynē]*, when the mind uncovers shameful things *[aischros]*
which it ought to hide from view" (*Legum Allegoriae* 2.66); in another place
he equates "unseemliness of flesh and passion" (*Legum Allegoriae* 3.158).
These occurrences confirm that contemporary usage extended the sense of
aschēmosynē beyond social dishonor to immorality. Together with the evidence
concerning *atimia*, these observations lend additional support to the view that
Paul is applying the vocabulary of sin to same-sex relations in Romans 1.

Ta Mē Kathēkonta: Improper Things or Sinful Things?

I noted above that the phrase "things that should not be done" (*ta mē
kathēkonta*, v. 28) refers primarily to the list of sins in Romans 1:29-31, an
observation based on the structure and language of the passage. All three
statements in the passage that include the words "God gave them over" employ general terms for wrongdoing which appear to be interchangeable. But
this poses a challenge to Countryman's thesis, because he contends that *ta
mē kathēkonta* are merely "improper" things and not sinful things, and if we
can apply such an expression to the list in verses 29-31, his distinction between impurity and sinfulness becomes meaningless. In order to avoid this,
Countryman is forced to argue that *ta mē kathēkonta* refers *back* to same-sex
relations in verses 26-27.[36] This is a very strange way to read the passage, but
if it is true it merely moves Countryman's thesis from the frying pan to the
fire, because the evidence suggests that *kathēkei* is yet another word that Paul

and his audience would associate with sin and not only impurity.

The only other New Testament occurrence of *kathēkei* is inconclusive: some hostile Jews shout that it is not *kathēken* for Paul to live (Acts 22:22). Of course "ritually impure" makes no sense in this context, but "sinful" is not a good fit either, and in any case the dissimilar context precludes close comparison.[37]

While *kathēkei* is extremely rare in Jewish Hellenistic sources, the word group is quite common in contemporary, especially Stoic, literature to denote "duty." One illustrative passage not only constitutes strong evidence that Paul has verses 29-31 in mind when he writes *ta mē kathēkonta* but also demonstrates the moral sense of the expression, even if one applies it only to verses 26-27:

> Befitting acts *(kathēkonta)* are all those which reason prevails with us to do; and this is the case with honoring one's parents, brothers and country, and intercourse with friends. Unbefitting, or contrary to duty, are all acts that reason deprecates, *e.g.* to be indifferent to one's brothers, not to agree with friends, to disregard the interests of one's country, and so forth. . . . To live in accordance with virtue is always a duty.[38]

This common use of the word in the Gentile world and its rarity in Jewish Hellenistic texts is precisely the point behind its appearance in Romans 1:28. Paul employs the expression to indicate "that which is offensive to man even according to the popular moral sense of the Gentiles, i.e., what even natural human judgment regards as vicious and wrong."[39] In other words, far from attempting to set up a fine distinction between impurity and sin, Paul is calling attention to the immorality of the Gentiles *in the Gentiles' own terms.*

This explanation not only honors the common understanding of the word but also serves Paul's point in 2:14-15, that those who do not have the Jewish law nevertheless have an idea of morality to which they do not measure up. By using the very terminology of Gentile morality in chapter 1, Paul makes this point more strongly and in a manner parallel to his quotation of the Old Testament in his indictment of the Jews (3:10-18).

Para Physin: Over Against Nature or Contrary to Nature?

This expression, translated "unnatural" in most modern versions of the Bible, has generated more discussion than any other aspect of Romans 1:26-27. Some revisionists simply disagree with Paul's view of "nature" *(physis),* but others reinterpret the apparently negative expression *para physin.*

John Boswell asserts that the expression *para physin* in Romans 1:26 means "beyond nature" with no connotation of immorality.[40] Countryman, similarly, cites "neutral" uses of *physis* by Paul to support the claim that Gentiles have merely "lost a certain continuity with their remotest past"[41] in practicing same-sex relations. Such acts, in this view, are unnatural in the sense that a handshake (a vestigial exposure of one's sword arm) is unnatural—and similarly harmless.

From this common ground, Boswell and Countryman move in different directions. Boswell maintains that Romans 1:26-27 describes individual heterosexuals who occasionally deny their own "natures" by performing homosexual acts.[42] One major weakness of this interpretation is its assumption that *individual* action is in view; that is, each same-sex act involves an "exchange" (v. 26) of that person's true nature for a false nature. This interpretation not only introduces a debatable modern concept of "nature"[43] but also misses the point of the entire section, verses 18-32. Here Paul is describing not individual actions but the *corporate* rebellion of humanity against God and the kinds of behavior that result.[44] This is clear when we consider the word *exchange,* which appears twice in the passage (vv. 23, 25) to denote the movement from worship of God to worship of images. It is ludicrous to suppose that each Gentile reinvents idolatry; rather, Paul is describing the sweep of history. Then the word *exchange* appears again in v. 26, this time to describe same-sex relations. The point is that same-sex relations are a *specific* falsification of right behavior (immorality), made possible by the *general* falsification of right thinking about God (idolatry). Paul's concern is not with individuals who deny their true selves but with humanity that first generally and now specifically (and sexually) has replaced a truth with a falsehood.

A variation on Boswell's misunderstanding of Paul's corporate indictment is the charge that Paul mistakenly attributes same-sex relations to idolatry, which makes his condemnation irrelevant to modern idol-free homosexuality.[45] But Paul is not suggesting that a person worships an idol and decides therefore to engage in same-sex relations. Rather, he is suggesting that the general rebellion created the environment for the specific rebellion: "For this reason God gave them up to," not "As a result of this they did." A person need not bow before a golden calf to participate in the general human denial of God or to express that denial through specific behaviors.

Countryman grants that Paul is describing what we would call homosexuality, but he insists on a "neutral" meaning for *para physin*. Two thorough studies of the contrast "against nature . . . according to nature" *(para physin . . . kata physin)* in relation to sex, however, have provided overwhelming evidence against a "neutral" translation.[46] That is, although Paul uses *nature* or *natural* elsewhere to denote custom, his language in Romans 1 borrows from both Greek and Jewish sources to evoke a much more substantial rejection of same-sex relations.

A few examples will suffice to demonstrate, first, that Paul's terminology in Romans 1 was consistent with contemporary usage. We cannot call Plato (fourth century B.C.) a contemporary, but his influence was long felt. He writes that "when male unites with female for procreation the pleasure experienced is held to be due to nature, but contrary to nature *[para physin]* when male mates with male or female with female, and that those first guilty of such enormities were impelled by their slavery to pleasure" (*Laws* 636C).[47] Diodorus Siculus (c. 50 B.C.) writes of a case of mistaken same-sex relations as *para physin*, in which the "woman" received "unnatural *[para physin]* embraces" (*History* 32.10.8-11). Dionysius of Halicarnassus (c. 30 B.C.) refers to a coercive homosexual act as "doing violence to the male's natural *[kata physin]* instincts" (*Roman Antiquities* 16.4.2-3). Plutarch (c. A.D. 100) contrasts "natural" *(tē physei)* love between men and women to "union contrary to nature *[para physin]* with males," and a few lines later he repeats that those who "consort with males" do so *para physin* (*Erotikos* 751 C, E). Of course pagan authors do not necessarily or consistently condemn as immoral what they describe as unnatural. The point here is only that they meant something much deeper than "custom" by *para physin*.

The second step toward an understanding of Paul's use of *para physin* is to consider evidence from Hellenistic Jewish writers. Philo remarks that the men of Sodom "threw off from their necks the law of nature *[physeōs nomon]"* (*De Abrahamo* 135) to mount males, "not respecting the common nature *[physin]* with which the active partner acts upon the passive."[48] Elsewhere he characterizes pederasty as a "transformation of the male nature *[physin]"* and several lines later as *para physin* (*De Specialibus Legibus* 3.37-42). The late-first-century Jewish historian Josephus makes reference to the same-sex relations of the people of Elis and Thebes as *para physin,* a few lines later listing such acts with incest as characteristic of the "monstrous and unnatural *[para physin]* pleasures" of the Gentiles (*Against Apion* 2.273-75).[49] In these sources, which are much closer to the context of Romans 1 than Paul's use of *nature* or *natural* in other places, the specific expression *para physin* has an unmistakably negative connotation.

Now we approach the crucial issue regarding this crucial passage: the *basis* of Paul's condemnation of same-sex relations. What precisely does Paul mean by *para physin?* Let us begin by noting that many Jews of Paul's time appear to have joined the *kata physin . . . para physin* distinction to their notions of creation and Fall. This is most clearly the case in Wisdom of Solomon 13—14 (first century B.C.), which is often cited for its similarities to Romans 1:

> For all people who were ignorant of God were foolish by nature; and they were unable from the good things that are seen to know the one who exists, nor did they recognize the artisan while paying heed to his works. . . . Therefore those who lived unrighteously, in a life of folly, you tormented through their own abominations. (13:1; 12:23)

> For the idea of making idols was the beginning of fornication, and the invention of them was the corruption of life. . . . For they . . . no longer keep either their lives or their marriages pure, but they . . . grieve one another by adultery, and all is a raging riot of blood and murder, theft and deceit, corruption, faithlessness, tumult, perjury, confusion over what is good, forgetfulness of favors, defiling of souls, sexual perversion, disorder in marriages, adultery, and debauchery. For the worship of idols not to be named is the beginning and cause and end of every evil. (14:12, 23-27)

Paul may or may not have been familiar with this text. The point is that it demonstrates the idea of many Jews of Paul's time that Gentile sin, including sexual sin, is a result of humanity's corporate rebellion against the Creator.[50]

Still, can we be sure that this kind of thought lies behind Romans 1:18-32? Granted, Paul does not *quote* Genesis, but the passage is filled with allusions to humanity's creation and fall.[51] "Ever since the creation," verse 20 begins, God's power has been evident in "the things he has made." The Fall involved a temptation toward knowledge; hence, "claiming to be wise, they became fools" (v. 22). God is called "Creator" in verse 25. Perhaps most interesting (but lost in English translations) is the fact that verses 26-27 do not use the usual Greek words for "women" and "men" but instead uses *females* and *males*, as in Genesis 1:27, "male and female he created them." Another hint is present in the unusual choice to mention female same-sex relations first: the woman fell first (compare 1 Tim 2:14).

These observations strengthen the connection that we might already suppose for Paul between "natural" and the creation account of sexual differentiation and marriage. What is "unnatural," then, is the active negation of marriage in the form of same-sex relations. Thus, into the mental vacuum left by the Fall, rebellious humanity invents idols, and into the moral vacuum left by such empty worship, rebellious humanity inverts sexuality, then corrupts relationships (vv. 29-31).

Now we come to the heart of the matter. It is essential to understand that what Paul is stating here is unusual—probably unique. Ancient authors did not, as a rule, connect male and female same-sex relations.[52] Some of Paul's contemporaries among the Gentiles appear to have viewed boys, or (rarely) other men, as an alternative to women for gratification of macho impulses. On a theoretical level both Gentiles and Jews displayed an interest in procreation and in active-passive roles, which they distinguished along gender lines. Paul does not follow these patterns. Instead he links female and male same-sex relations and then uses terminology denoting mutual desire: they were "consumed with passion for one another."

When Paul places such a statement in a passage filled with allusions to the creation narrative, we can be sure that his understanding goes deeper than popular "custom" or the protection of male power. Paul understands that "male and female were created for each other with complementary sexualities grounded in the distinctive constitutions of their sexual organs,"[53] and that this arrangement has been legitimized only by marriage since the creation. He understands, further, that the desire of female for female or male for male dishonors this arrangement by substituting an untruth for the truth. He understands, finally, that this untruth may involve two members of either sex acting in consent to satisfy desire. In this Paul has in view a practice that is virtually indistinguishable from homosexuality as we know it today. From this point on, therefore, I will use the word *homosexuality* when referring to Paul's writings.

At least one question remains. If Paul is concerned about the creation order and understands homosexuality more broadly than his contemporaries, why does he use an expression like *para physin,* which carries so much baggage? The most likely explanation is that Paul wants to use terminology familiar to the Gentiles to point out that they are "without excuse" (v. 20), and thus we should not push too hard for precision in Paul's understanding of the term. Paul may have had a "hybrid" view, adapting Greek philosophical notions of an ideal humanity to his creation theology and his observation of human biology. We might find a modern analogy to this imprecision in the advertisement of a beverage with all "natural" ingredients. We do not analyze the ingredients—we simply acknowledge that the manufacturer wants us to think that the drink is good for us. So with the ultimate Manufacturer, who proclaims human sexuality as "the best stuff on earth" (see Gen 1:31)—accept no sugary substitutes.

Whether Paul's understanding is imprecise in this way or precise in a way that we cannot know with certainty, of this we can be sure: the phrase *para physin* would have had negative connotations for Paul's audience, Gentile and Jew, and only the most careless hearer would have failed to perceive the connection to Paul's theology of creation.

This extended treatment of Paul's use of *para physin* has implications for the argument that we should reject Paul's notion of *nature* and *natural* simply because of his ignorance of the social sciences, which have taught us that each person has a "natural" sexual orientation. Of course Paul did not write of "sexual orientation," but if we apply the category to his thought, it is apparent that he does not assume that each person has a heterosexual orientation; rather, he explains that *created humanity* has a heterosexual orientation that has been corrupted by rebellion against God.

The recognition of Paul's corporate view of humanity's corruption also clarifies the role of experience. Because individual homosexuals do not consciously rebel against anything deeper in their view than societal expectations, few if any are troubled by the notion that their behavior involves a fundamental falsehood. Many experience homosexual relationships as fully loving, life-enhancing experiences. And this is of course also true of many pedophiles. But the lie simply goes back beyond their experience, and so experience cannot be the measure of truth or morality.

It is extremely unlikely that Paul would alter his assessment if he knew about modern notions of orientation, which he would merely regard as secular ways to describe the results of the Fall. Indeed, his lack of distinction between male and female homosexuality and his recognition of it as consensual reveals a rather modern understanding relative to that of his contemporaries. In the final analysis, Paul's first concern is not motivation—whether described in modern terms or ancient terms—but practice in accord with the biblical model of marriage. This, and only this, is *kata physin,* according to nature.

Planē: Error or Perversion?

Let us return now to Countryman's thesis and one last important term in the passage. When Paul refers to the "due penalty *[antimisthia]* for their error *[planē],*" the grammar of the passage dictates that the error is idolatry, not homosexuality, and the penalty is homosexuality, not disease or effeminacy that results from homosexuality, as some have supposed.[54] The consistent reference of *planē* and related words to wrong belief rather than immoral desire or action[55] strongly suggests that Paul uses it here to refer to idolatry, the "exchange of the truth about God for a lie."

This understanding, however, hardly renders the sentence neutral, since "due penalty" *(antimisthia)* has a strong negative connotation. This word does not occur prior to the New Testament, and it is used in 2 Corinthians 6:13

neutrally. The translation "penalty" is justified, however, not only by the context but also by the notion of "due wages" *(misthos)* in Romans 4:4 (compare 1 Cor 3:8; 9:17-18; Rev 22:12) and the connection to Paul's thought in Romans 6:23, "the wages *[opsōnion]* of sin is death."

The negative notion of "payback" is present not only in the vocabulary of the sentence[56] but also in the phrase "in their own persons" *(en heautois)*. English translations consistently translate the phrase in this way as over against Countryman's attempted neutralization, "among themselves,"[57] by which he intends to focus on the Gentile world rather than on the homosexual community or individual homosexuals. In other words, Countryman contends, the recompense for the error of idolatry is *something* "among the Gentiles"—namely, homosexuality.

But in light of the evidence already cited from Jewish Hellenistic sources, it is reasonable to suppose that Paul has in mind some sort of punishments in this life as byproducts of homosexual practice. And even if we suppose that Paul is entirely independent of his own background in this regard, it is still far-fetched to suppose that he would use the language of recompense for idolatry with a neutral view of its product. His language here suggests that he views homosexuality as a byproduct of idolatry that is evil (and harmful) in itself.

The "Vocabulary of Sin" and Romans 1

Countryman takes the position that "Paul did not apply the vocabulary of sin to [homosexual acts] at all."[58] We have seen that this is not true. Close scrutiny of vocabulary, especially as it is used in contexts similar to Romans 1:24-27, reveals not just one—that would suffice—but *eight* terms that connote sin, together with additional features of the context that contribute to the sense that homosexuality is sinful. True, Paul does not use the word *sin (hamartia)* itself or some other common word like *unrighteousness* in verses 26-27, but it is misleading to infer as Countryman does that Paul is thereby avoiding the connotation of sin with regard to homosexuality. The word *sin* does not occur *anywhere* in the first two chapters of Romans, but the description of sin is clearly their primary subject.

Furthermore, we should not expect to find the same vocabulary in every treatment of sin—and certainly not in a two-verse statement on a sin not treated by Paul elsewhere. Indeed, expressions like "unnatural," "things that should not be done," "lusts" and "passions" are peculiarly suited to the Gentile world, and Paul's intent here to expose the sinfulness of that world in its own terms. Romans 1:26-27, far from being an exception to Paul's horror of sin, is in fact a prime and specific example.

Summary

The thesis proposed by Boswell and developed more fully by Countryman, that Paul regards homosexuality as impure but not sinful, is unsupportable. Paul's profound analysis of the human condition in Romans 1 finds in homosexuality an example of sexual sin that falsifies our identity as sexual beings, just as idolatry falsifies our identity as created beings. Homosexual behavior is "revolting," not because heterosexuals find it so—they have their own dirt to deal with (2:22)—but because it epitomizes in sexual terms the *revolt* against God. It is sinful because it violates the plan of God, present from creation, for the union of male and female in marriage.

5

FROM SODOM
TO SODOM

*T*he title of this chapter derives from the observation that Genesis 19 and Jude 7, the first and last relevant biblical passages, both refer to the city of Sodom. We must examine these and other possible references in between to see if they refer to same-sex acts and if they are applicable to modern questions about homosexuality.

Inhospitality or Homosexuality?

But before they lay down, the men of the city, the men of Sodom, both young and old, all the people to the last man, surrounded the house; and they called to Lot, "Where are the men who came to you tonight? Bring them out to us, so that we may know them." Lot went out of the door to the men, shut the door after him, and said, "I beg you, my brothers, do not act so wickedly. Look, I have two daughters who have not known a man; let me bring them out to you, and do to them as you please; only do nothing to these men, for they have come under the shelter of my roof." (Gen 19:4-8)

While they were enjoying themselves, the men of the city, a perverse lot, surrounded the house, and started pounding on the door. They said to the old man, the master of the house, "Bring out the man who came into your house, so that we may have intercourse with him." And the man, the master of the house, went out to them and said to them, "No, my brothers, do not act so wickedly. Since this man is my guest, do not do this vile thing. Here are my virgin daughter and his concubine; let me bring them out now. Ravish them and do whatever you want to them; but against this man do not do such a vile thing." (Judg 19:22-24)

The revisionist view of the Sodom story, presented in greater detail in chapter two, is that the men of Sodom were guilty not of homosexuality but of inhospitality in that they demanded to "know" whether or not Lot's visitors were spies; and if the passage does have sexual implications, it condemns rape and not relationships of mutual consent.

There is strong evidence in the immediate context that the Sodomites were guilty of sexual sin. The verb *to know (yāḏaʿ)*, while seldom used in the sexual sense,[1] is used in that sense just three verses later, when Lot offers his daughters "who have not *known* men" (Gen 19:8). The same verb is used in the very similar passage in Judges (19:22, 25), where its meaning is unmistakably sexual. The repeated promise earlier in Genesis to destroy the city (13:10-13; 14:21-24; 18:16-33) is understandable as the reaction to an unusual and characteristic vice; otherwise we must suppose that the Sodomites characteristically did bad things to strangers but only this time, coincidentally, were those offenses sexual in nature. No scholarly interpreter of Genesis has ever suggested a shift in the meaning of *yāḏaʿ* between verses 5 and 8, a fact that adds to the suspicion that the revisionist argument stretches credibility for the sake of a theory.[2]

Why then do subsequent biblical writers often mention inhospitality, and not sexual perversion, as the sin of Sodom? Several observations are helpful here. First, it is a false distinction to separate inhospitality from sexual sin. What the Sodomites and residents of Gibeah attempted sexually was "an active, aggressive form of inhospitality."[3] This may be evident in Job's testimony that no one in his house ever violated hospitality to a guest by saying,

"O that we might be sated with his flesh!" (Job 31:31-32)—an echo of the language of Genesis and Judges.[4] But the point does not hinge on explicit references. When later writers mention Sodom without necessarily naming sexual sin, they may be generalizing from the particular offense. This is especially likely if, as it appears, homosexuality was rare in Israel. That is, biblical writers generalized in order to show the applicability of judgment on Sodom to people who did not do precisely what the Sodomites did. An example of this is Jeremiah 49:18, which compares Jerusalem to Sodom but specifies only adultery as a sexual sin.

Second, we must appreciate that the Jews were a modest people who often used figures of speech or other kinds of code for sexually explicit subject matter.[5] One pertinent example may be the incident recorded in Genesis 9:20-27, when Noah's son Ham "saw the nakedness of his father." This may be a veiled allusion to rape, "an act so abhorrent that the author is unwilling to spell it out."[6] But whether or not this example applies, we cannot dismiss the possibility that general references to the wickedness of Sodom have sexual sin at least partially, if euphemistically, in view.

Third, we must respect the context of the so-called inhospitality passages. One of the most frequently cited, Ezekiel 16:49, is often quoted without continuing to the next verse: "They were haughty, and did abominable things before me." Various things were *abominable*, but since the word is used to describe sexual sin in the same chapter (vv. 22, 58), and since it refers to same-sex acts in Leviticus 18:22 and 20:13, the passage may imply quite the opposite of the revisionist claim.[7]

Finally, it is misleading to cite only part of the evidence. A look at all of the literature shows that some Jews did in fact connect Sodom to sexual sin.[8] The fact that the author of Judges shows evidence of dependence on the Sodom story demonstrates that the tradition began very early.[9] In the Greek period the tradition merely became more specific in its response to Gentile homosexuality. The second-century B.C. *Testament of the Twelve Patriarchs* labels the Sodomites "sexually promiscuous" (*Testament of Benjamin* 9:1) and refers to "Sodom, which departed from the order of nature" (*Testament of Naphthali* 3:4). From the same time period, *Jubilees* specifies that the Sodomites were "polluting themselves and fornicating in their flesh" (16:5; compare 20:5-6).[10] Both Philo[11] and Josephus[12] plainly name same-sex relations as the characteristic vice of Sodom.

I grant that the original offenders in Sodom and Gibeah probably did not have what today we might call a homosexual orientation; rather, they attempted male rape as a means to humiliate the suspected spies. But I do not grant that the stories are therefore irrelevant. The word *Sodom* simply became a kind of code over time for sexual perversion—more specifically, in Paul's time, for the kinds of same-sex relations common in the Gentile world. The fact that people in New Testament times pictured Sodomite activity and motivation differently from the historical event in Genesis does not invalidate their objection to same-sex relations. They objected similarly to the worship of Jupiter and Apollo, quoting Old Testament passages about Canaanite worship, which differed greatly in form and motivation from the practices they observed among the Gentiles. Indeed, today we quote the same passages about idolatry to object to the "worship" of money or leisure. Whether the issue is idolatry or sex, the form is secondary to the act itself.

There are great differences, to be sure, between the sins of Sodom and the sins of San Francisco—so much so that I prefer not to use the ambiguous word *sodomy* in the discussion of modern morality.[13] But when the issue centers, as it should, on the *act* in relation to the biblically affirmed good of marriage, the biblical judgment takes in both the people of Sodom and people today whose activities are associated with them.

Impurity or Immorality?

You shall not lie with a male as with a woman; it is an abomination. (Lev 18:22)

If a man lies with a male as with a woman, both of them have committed an abomination; they shall be put to death; their blood is upon them. (Lev 20:13)

Revisionists commonly argue against the relevance of the prohibitions of same-sex acts in Leviticus 18 and 20—especially as background for Romans 1—on the ground that such acts are ceremonially unclean but not inherently

evil, because the gospel releases Christians from this part of the Jewish law.[14]
Some also propose that the injunction here involves prostitution or rape but
not modern practices. This second objection to the relevance of the passage
rests on the dubious supposition that the prohibition is grounded only in the
violence or nonconsensual nature of such relationships. But as we have seen,
this is a purely modern imposition on the text which fails to take seriously
the connection between body and soul in the biblical concept of marriage.
That is, just as there is more to marriage than mutual consent between adults,
so there is more to a violation of marriage than theft or inequality—and that
something more is the body.

Furthermore, the text of Leviticus says nothing to imply that the prohibited
activity is forced or unequal, but condemns simply the one who "lies with a
male as with a woman." Whatever specific behavior might have been in mind
in ancient Israel or in Paul's world, this prohibition is sufficiently broad to
include a range of possibilities, including some today that may have been
virtually unknown to biblical writers. In fact, the words imply nothing about
force or prostitution (which are addressed elsewhere: Deut 22:22-29; 23:17-
18), but describe only the act itself.[15] Especially in conjunction with the prohibition of sex with animals, which immediately follows, it is evident that the
form of the sexual activity and not its motivation is in view. All of this suggests
that the Leviticus texts *may* remain relevant if they do not reflect concerns of
ritual purity only.

To what extent, then, does Leviticus remain normative for Christians? In
order to answer that question, we need to ask if there existed in Paul's mind
(or among other New Testament authors) a distinction between purity and
morality with regard to sexuality. More specifically, would the first generation
of Christians isolate the prohibition of same-sex acts in Leviticus as part of
a newly obsolete standard of holiness?

A harmony of Leviticus 18 and 20 shows successive treatments of incest
(18:6-18; 20:11-12, 17, 19-21), sex during menstruation (18:19; 20:18), adultery
(18:20; 20:10), child sacrifice (18:21; 20:2-5), same-sex relations (18:22; 20:13)
and bestiality (18:23; 20:15-16). The list ends with a summary warning about
the "abominations" of the Canaanites (18:24-30; 20:22-26). If these parallel

passages are considered in isolation, they appear to support a limitation of the passage to concerns for ritual purity: only child sacrifice and polygamy, which were not issues in the first century, and adultery, which also involves a sin against property ("your neighbor's wife"), are clear exceptions.

Furthermore, we know that Hellenistic Jews perceived incest and homosexuality as characteristic Gentile vices, and bestiality would probably have joined that list if it were known to be common. We also know from the writings of the rabbis of the time that menstruation continued to fascinate the sages. These factors all appear to support a focus in Leviticus 18 and 20 on purity apart from issues of morality. But on closer inspection such a distinction is highly suspect.

Paul was a well-trained rabbi before his call to apostleship, so it is safe to assume that he knew Leviticus intimately—in fact, he could probably recite it from memory in its entirety in Hebrew. But part of the reason a rabbi learned the Scriptures by heart was that written copies were too expensive for common production and use. Very few Christians therefore would have known Leviticus in the detail required to make the kinds of distinctions required in the revisionist view. Paul knew this, of course, and so it is that when he does discuss Christian conduct in relation to the Jewish notions of food purity, he spells out his position carefully (Rom 14). Therefore the supposition that early Christians would discount the references to same-sex acts in Leviticus unless instructed otherwise has no evidence nor precedent nor probability to support it.

Furthermore, the very concept of classes of prohibitions, or classes of reasons for prohibitions, is a modern idea that would have made no sense to Paul or his audience. Finally, and I think decisively, there is no reason to suppose that Paul or the early Christians would connect the prohibition of homosexuality with, say, the prohibition of sex during menstruation and not with the prohibition of adultery. That is, if they did study Leviticus, they would see much of the moral law in the context, including the chapter between the two verses in question, with its prohibitions of idolatry, injustice to the poor, theft, vengeance and so on—some of the very behaviors condemned in Romans 1:29-32.[16]

Clearly the burden of proof lies with those who would argue that Leviticus 18 and 20 does *not* lie behind New Testament prohibitions of same-sex acts. And as we will see later, there may be warrant to draw the Leviticus passages more directly into Paul's argument.

Qāḏēš: Prostitute for Which Sex?

There are six Old Testament references to "male cult prostitute" *(qāḏēš),*[17] which is translated "sodomite" by the King James Version. The most often-quoted passage is Deuteronomy 23:17-18:

> None of the daughters of Israel shall be a temple prostitute; none of the sons of Israel shall be a temple prostitute. You shall not bring the fee of a prostitute [*zōnâh,* "harlot"] or the wages of a male prostitute [*keleḇ,* literally "dog"] into the house of the LORD your God in payment for any vow, for both of these are abhorrent to the LORD your God.

There are differences of opinion about the activity of these prostitutes, and therefore about the relevance of such references to a discussion of homosexuality. The key question is whether the male prostitutes were men who sold their bodies to other men or to female worshipers. In favor of the opposite-sex theory: same-sex prostitution was virtually unknown in the ancient world; few if any men would want to have sex with other men; and it would be nonsense in a fertility cult for males to mate, whereas females might want to mate with males to cure barrenness.[18] In favor of the same-sex theory: Israelite worship did not involve women; Deuteronomy 23:17 makes the *qāḏēš* parallel to the female prostitute (suggesting a parallel function); and fertility rites did not require opposite-sex coupling, since the act was merely symbolic.[19] Furthermore, the label "abhorrent" is used of same-sex practice (Lev 18:22; 20:13) but not of opposite-sex prostitution.

The second part of the text quoted above, Deuteronomy 23:18, lifts the discussion out of the cult context to state that prostitution is sinful in and of itself. The elimination of the cultic aspect of the argument, together with the prohibitions in Leviticus, cause me to lean in the direction of defining the *qᵉḏēšîm* (plural) as same-sex prostitutes. The curious expression "dog" *(keleḇ)* as a parallel to "whore" may evoke the image of a cowering, filthy animal—

just the sort of terminology used for (passive) homosexuals in later sources, both Jewish and Gentile.

The last Old Testament reference to male cult prostitutes may offer additional evidence that *qāḏēš* refers to same-sex activity. According to Job 36:14, godless men are punished by early death: "They die in their youth, and their life ends in shame [literally, among the *qᵉḏēšîm*]." This may represent an early connection between homosexuality and passionate excess, which has always been associated with a short lifespan. In any case, the verse makes sense only if the *qᵉḏēšîm* are providing their services to males. It tips the balance heavily in favor of the association of *qāḏēš* with same-sex prostitution.

Curiously, D. S. Bailey lists the other five occurrences of *qāḏēš* but makes no reference to Job 36:14, the one text that clearly undercuts his opposite-sex thesis. This is inexcusable, whether it be a colossal oversight or a falsification of the data. To compound the matter, influential authors like John Boswell and R. Scroggs follow Bailey's conclusions apparently without checking his research. As a result, most recent writers usually leave the *qᵉḏēšîm* out of the discussion altogether.

This is probably a case of cumulative carelessness, not deception. But regardless of the cause, the situation highlights the need for constant vigilance (on all sides) against conclusions based on secondhand research.

"Causing a Little One to Sin": Code for Pederasty?

A scholarly article in 1990 drew attention to an interesting parallel between Mark 9:42—10:12 (parallel Mt 5:27-32) and a passage in the Babylonian Talmud (*b. Niddah* 13b).[20] The probable points of contact are highlighted with italics:

> R. Eleazar said, "What does Scripture mean in saying, 'Your hands are full of blood' [Isa 1.15]?—These are they who commit *adultery with the hand.*" It was taught in the school of R. Ishmael, " 'You shall not commit adultery' [Exod 20.14] means there shall be in you *no adultery, neither with the hand nor with the foot.*" Our masters taught, "The proselytes and *those who play with children* delay the messiah." Granted, "proselytes," as is the opinion of R. Helbo, for R. Helbo said: "Proselytes are as hard for Israel as a sore";

but "those who play with children," what does it mean? If we say *homo-sexuality*—they were punished by stoning [cf. Lev 20.13]; if we say *sexual activity involving the limbs*—they were punished by the Flood; thus we must say, those who marry young girls who have not yet reached the age of childbearing. . . . "In the case of men *it is to be cut off*" [*m. Niddah* 2:1]. It was asked, "Have we learned here a law or have we learned a curse? Have we learned a law, as when R. Huna *cut off someone's hand,* or have we learned a curse?" . . . R. Tarfon said, "*A hand touching his genitals is to be cut off, his hand upon his stomach.*" . . . "*It is good that his stomach will be split and he will not go down to the pit of destruction.*"[21]

The similarities may suggest that both this passage and the teaching of Jesus stem from a common discussion of deviant sexual activity. The similarity of sequence is remarkable, especially if the phrase "those who play with children" is the equivalent of the Gospel phrase for those who "cause one of these little ones to sin." The sequence is then pederasty (Mk 9:42), lust (Mt 5:27-28), masturbation (Mt 5:29-30; Mk 9:43-48) and divorce (Mt 5:31-32; Mk 10:2-12). The connection establishes pederasty as a sin, which is no surprise, although it may surprise us to find the reference in Mark's Gospel. But there is a more important point here—the sin violates marriage, not purity:

What we may conclude from this, I suggest, is that the purpose of this discussion was to define these acts of sexual misconduct specifically over against marriage—that is, as a violation of marriage, or "adultery." In other words, we have here an attempt by certain Jews and Christians in the first century to understand human sexuality as having meaning and legitimacy solely within the confines of marriage.[22]

This of course is a point made in other parts of this book, but it bears repeating. The sexual morality of the New Testament, and of Jesus in particular, intends to protect and promote nothing more and nothing less than the marriage of husband and wife.

Pederasts, Prostitutes or Homosexuals?

Do you not know that wrongdoers will not inherit the kingdom of God? Do not be deceived! Fornicators, idolaters, adulterers, *malakoi, arsenokoitai,* thieves, the greedy, drunkards, revilers, robbers—none of these will inherit the kingdom of God. (1 Cor 6:9-10)

... fornicators, *arsenokoitais*, slave traders, liars, perjurers, and whatever else is contrary to the sound teaching ... (1 Tim 1:10)

These passages are vice lists that both contain the plural form of the word *arsenokoitēs*. The word does not appear in any literature prior to the New Testament, and it does not occur again for two hundred years.[23] On the basis of the scarcity of evidence, its later use (and English translation) as a designation for homosexuality has been disputed. Several scholars argue that it is intended to refer to specific practices that modern homosexuals would condemn (such as pederasty) and that therefore these verses have no place in the contemporary moral discussion. Scroggs, for example, contends that we must understand the word in light of its connection to the preceding word *malakoi* (1 Cor 6:9 only)—the two words denoting, respectively, the passive and active partners in male intercourse. More particularly, according to Scroggs, Paul has in view pederasts.[24] Boswell offers an even more narrow definition of the term, contending that it denotes male prostitutes.[25] Countryman follows Boswell against Scroggs primarily because in Countryman's view the independent occurrence of *arsenokoitēs* in 1 Timothy 1:10 strains Scroggs's supposition of a complementary pair of terms.[26]

All of this interesting speculation is intended to create a very specific category of sinners whom we can then reject without rejecting homosexuality. Such intentions were dealt a simple and decisive blow by David Wright's demonstration in 1984[27] that *arsenokoitēs* was a term coined by Hellenistic Jews, perhaps by Paul himself, taken directly from the Greek Old Testament text of Leviticus:

meta *arsenos* ou koimēthēsē *koitēn* gynaikos (Lev 18:22)

Literally: with a man do not lie [as one] lies [with a] woman

hos an koimēthē meta *arsenos koitēn* gynaikos (Lev 20:13)

Literally: whoever lies with a man [as one] lies with a woman

The origin of the compound word *arsenokoitēs* is now obvious, and the finding is important in several respects. First, since the Levitical passages make no distinction about particular forms of same-sex behavior, it is unlikely that the coiner or user of the compound word would make such a distinction. This of course is entirely consistent with Paul's extension of the logic of the pro-hibition of same-sex relations to females in Romans 1:26. In addition, the connection to Leviticus draws attention to Paul's reference to the sentence of death in Romans 1:32 as a possible echo of Leviticus 20:13. This connection was certainly made by other Hellenistic Jews: "What are our marriage laws? The Law recognizes no sexual connections, except the natural [*kata physin*] union of man and wife, and that only for the procreation of children. Sodomy [*pros arrenas arrenōn*, literally "male to male"] it abhors, and punishes any guilt of such assault with death" (Josephus *Against Apion* 2.24 §199).[28]

Finally, the compound word *arsenokoitēs* shows that the prohibition of same-sex relations was consciously carried over from Leviticus, perhaps originally by Paul himself, although in his case not on the ground of ritual impurity but on the ground of immorality. This constitutes a further argument that Paul was not drawing a distinction between impurity and sin when describing homosexuality in Romans 1:26-27.

Sodom in 2 Peter 2:6-7 and Jude 7

And if by turning the cities of Sodom and Gomorrah to ashes he con-demned them to extinction and made them an example of what is coming to the ungodly; and if he rescued Lot, a righteous man greatly distressed by the licentiousness of the lawless . . . (2 Pet 2:6-7)

Likewise, Sodom and Gomorrah and the surrounding cities, which, in the same manner as they, indulged in sexual immorality and pursued unnatural lust, serve as an example by undergoing a punishment of eter-nal fire. (Jude 7)

The revisionist approach to these verses is either to dismiss them as homo-phobic misinterpretations of Genesis or to deny that the first refers to sex and that the second refers to sex with men. All of the arguments in response to the revision of the Genesis passage would of course apply to the revision of 2 Peter 2:6-7: we should see it as a generalization of Sodom's wickedness, including but not limited to same-sex relations. In the case of Jude 7 it is possible to read "unnatural lust" (literally, "strange flesh") as the men of

Sodom's desire for the *angels*.[29] While revisionists would on this basis limit the sin to desire for a nonhuman being, such a distinction between the act and the intended victim is too fine-tuned. Are we to suppose that Jude was accusing his contemporaries of consorting with angels? No, and perhaps in order to show that he intends the charge more inclusively, he joins "unnatural lust" with "sexual immorality."

Both of these passages exemplify the early Christian pattern of borrowing to some extent from contemporary Jewish thought in the search for Scripture that might illuminate their confrontation with the world. The first Christians undoubtedly connected the sin of Sodom to the sin of same-sex relations and used the name of the city as a symbol for extreme sexual wrongdoing, including but not limited to same-sex relations. In the same way Babylon became a symbol of general wrongdoing, including but not limited to sexual sin (Rev 17—18).[30]

Addendum: *Polluted* and *Dogs* in Revelation

But as for the cowardly, the faithless, the polluted, the murderers, the fornicators, the sorcerers, the idolaters, and all liars, their place will be in the lake that burns with fire and sulfur, which is the second death. (Rev 21:8)

Outside are the dogs and sorcerers and fornicators and murderers and idolaters, and everyone who loves and practices falsehood. (Rev 22:15)

These are the only two vice lists in Revelation, and they are clearly similar in many respects to 1 Corinthians 6:9-10 and 1 Timothy 1:10. It is interesting that these two lists appear in close proximity in the same book, with the difference that the first includes "the cowardly, the faithless, the polluted" while the second includes "the dogs." Cowardice and faithlessness are clear enough as references to those who did not "conquer" (Rev 2:7, 11, etc.) by persevering through persecution. Does this leave the "polluted" and "dogs" as equivalent in the two lists, and do the words connote homosexuality?

The word translated "the polluted" in 21:8 is *ebdelygmenois,* derived from *bdelygma,* "abomination," which occurs over one hundred times in the Bible, including Leviticus 18:22 and 20:13 (see also Ezek 16:50). The word can of course refer to many things that are objectionable to God, but there are several reasons to give it a more specific meaning here. First, it occurs in a list that is similar to other New Testament lists (Rom 1:26-32; 1 Cor 6:9; 1 Tim 1:10) that include homosexuality. Second, the word *abomination* was commonly associated at this time with sexual promiscuity, including same-sex relations.[31] Third, at this point in Revelation we have just had a detailed depiction of the sexual sins of Babylon, a "whore" who holds in her hand "a cup full of abominations and the impurities of her fornication" (17:4). The connection to Rome and more generally to the Greco-Roman way of life would have been obvious to the original audience.

Thus, while the whore's lasciviousness is symbolic of all kinds of "cheating" on God as husband, including doctrinal deviation, the audience of Revelation would not limit the application to false teachers. If anything, they would assume that false teachers are also likely to practice sexual immorality (1 Tim 3:5; 2 Pet 2:14; Jude 8).

Finally, we must consider the possibility that "dogs" in Revelation 22:15 refers to homosexuals. The word is used elsewhere in the New Testament as a designation for the (impure) Gentiles.[32] This observation is probably enough to establish an equation between "dogs" and "polluted" (that is, impure), but the two terms together might merely denote all those who follow falsehood, without any particular sexual or homosexual connotation. One objection to this generality, in addition to those I mentioned above, is that "the cowardly, the faithless, the polluted" seems an unnecessarily repetitive list of generalities. Furthermore, we have a probable precedent in Deuteronomy 23:18 for an association of "dogs" with same-sex prostitutes.[33]

I find the evidence for inclusion of Revelation 21:8 and 22:15 in the discussion of homosexuality suggestive but not compelling. For that reason, and because of the likely emotional reaction to the label "dog," I think it best to leave these verses off to one side rather than to push a point that, however valid, may be counterproductive.

Summary
This chapter has offered further confirmation of the position advanced in

chapters three and four—namely, that the Bible views same-sex relations as a violation of the created good of marital union between male and female. A variety of practices and motivations for same-sex relations are evident in the biblical texts, including rape, prostitution, pederasty and relationships of mutual consent. Some references are more general and may apply to different practices. Revisionist attempts to isolate each text and show its dissimilarity to modern practice fail both because some texts defy such limitations and because details of practices and motivations miss the point.

The point is simple, and it runs like a red thread through all the passages discussed in the last two chapters. The point is marriage. When any same-sex act—with angels, with prostitutes, with boys, with mutually consenting adults—is evaluated in relation to the marital union of male and female, it falls short of the plan of God present from creation. As revisionists have rightly pointed out, it is inappropriate for Christians to call such an act *impure* or *disgusting*. But as revisionists have failed to recognize, Christians who give the Bible primary and final authority must still call such an act *wrong*.

6
THE PRICE
OF LOVE

*T*his will be a very unpleasant chapter to read—as it was to write. It is one thing to consider abstract notions of human personhood or the uses of Greek words in the ancient world. It is quite another thing to consider—here and now, for real people—the physical and psychological pain associated with homosexuality.

But we cannot leave the discussion in the realm of the abstract, because people are not abstractions. As I explained in chapter three, the biblical view is that we are embodied souls, individuals whose bodies are not incidental but integral to our identity, and therefore to our morality. That chapter focused on the implications for marital union, but here the subject is health.

The body of each individual is a part of the physical world over which humanity has been given dominion. Scripture affirms that it is the responsibility of the individual to "nourish and tenderly care for" the body (Eph 5:29). More specifically in terms of sexual conduct, a person can sin against the body of another or against his or her own body (Rom 6:12; 1 Cor 6:13, 18-19; 2 Cor 7:1). This kind of sin may involve many kinds of harm, including harm to the physical structure of the body. In this chapter I will explore the modern phenomenon of homosexual practice and will contend that in its most common form it represents such serious health risks—even apart from AIDS—that it constitutes sin against the body.

Because my research for this chapter lies outside my field of professional expertise, I have taken special precautions regarding accuracy of information. Four physicians with relevant specialties reviewed the first draft of this chapter in order to correct any factual errors. I avoided all secondary sources of information such as newspapers and popular magazines or books, and I cite no Christian writers. Instead I document every point of fact in this chapter only from scholarly, secular medical and social scientific publications, and from the most recent research available at the time of writing—virtually all of which is either neutral or affirming toward homosexuality. Whatever inferences I draw from the research data are of course my own, and the reader will easily distinguish information from interpretation by the presence or absence of documentation.

Much of the description of homosexual practice that follows paints a very negative picture, and I am concerned that someone might make destructive use of this information, which to my knowledge is here collected and thoroughly documented for the first time. The overwhelming evidence that people who engage in homosexual acts are harming themselves and others should cause great sorrow. No one should make it into a bludgeon for culture-war speeches or public policy debates. The point in bringing it out in this chapter is only to explore the implications of suffering for personal morality. Or, to put it in the form of a question: Does homosexual behavior incur a sufficient risk of harm to the self or others to call it wrong on health grounds alone?

The Prevalence of Same-Sex Practice

How common is same-sex practice? I put the question this way because there is some ambiguity about what people "are" as compared to what they do, and most of that discussion I must leave to the next chapter. The moral question of homosexual practice, especially as it relates to health, involves questions about the same-sex act itself: how many people do it, how often do they do it, how do they do it and so on. The technical term for quantitative concerns is *prevalence*, which I will treat in this section. In the next section I will treat *patterns* that distinguish homosexual from heterosexual sex. Finally I will consider in some detail the health *problems*, mental and physical, that are common among homosexuals.

Early in 1993 the popular press began to report the result of numerous recent surveys that contradicted the long-standing notion that homosexuals constitute approximately 10 percent of the population.[1] The old figure was based on a study by Alfred Kinsey published in 1948[2] which found that 10 percent of those interviewed had been predominantly homosexual for a period of up to three years between the ages of sixteen and sixty-five. From the standpoint of modern evidence-gathering techniques, the Kinsey study was tragically flawed (for example, 25 percent of its subjects were former or current prison inmates).[3] In fact, the 10 percent figure was itself a distortion of Kinsey's findings, which were that the number of men who *maintain* a homosexual preference over the course of a lifetime was a much lower 4 percent, and about half that for females. But few even read enough of the fine print to distinguish between the 10 percent and 4 percent figures; and more to the point, there were no other data available to contradict the Kinsey report. As a result, the 10 percent figure was so often repeated that it gradually gained a life of its own and was until very recently assumed in most discussions of homosexuality. Numbers do not in themselves establish the morality of an activity, but a number as large as 10 percent—the equivalent of twenty-five million Americans—seems to attach a degree of normalcy to homosexuality. Thus out of the moral fog of the last few decades, the notion emerged that 10 percent equals normal, and normal equals natural, and natural equals acceptable.

This notion is much harder to maintain in the light of more than a dozen recent studies that consistently put the incidence of homosexual practice at around 1 percent. Three separate 1990 surveys conducted by the National Center for Health Statistics found that under 3 percent of men had experienced same-sex relations even once in the past fifteen years.[4] Four separate national studies conducted in the United States in 1970, 1988, 1989 and 1990 by the National Opinion Research Center (total 7,408 subjects) came up with an aggregate incidence of 1.8 percent who had had male-to-male sex during the previous year, with 3.3 percent reporting that they experienced male-to-male sexual contact "occasionally" or "fairly often" as adults, and 5-7 percent estimated as having had such contact ever.[5] Another recent study, which incorporates the results of the NORC studies and three additional post-1988 U.S. surveys, gives a mean of 5.5 percent male, 2.5 percent female, for lifetime same-sex contact.[6] The latest major survey of more than three thousand subjects gives slightly higher numbers: among sexually active women, 1.3 percent reported at least one female partner in the previous year (3.8 percent lifetime since puberty); among sexually active men, 2.8 percent reported at least one male partner in the previous year (7.1 percent lifetime since puberty).[7]

These numbers of course cover a broad range of sexual activities, and we should understand that some homosexuals do not experience same-sex relations in a given year, while some who do experience same-sex relations in a given year are not homosexuals.[8] Furthermore, the term *bisexual* is a misnomer applied to the approximately 5 percent who have experience with both sexes during adulthood. Less than half of 1 percent of the population "go both ways" in a given year,[9] and there are no data available to gauge the relation between occasional experiences, often years apart, and the kind of desire that motivates them.[10] It is not at all clear that bisexuality is an *orientation* as we use the term to describe heterosexual or homosexual desire. Rather, the term denotes a *category* of people who vacillate in their practices— the vast majority of them only occasionally or for periods of time, not constantly.[11]

What is the percentage of the population, then, that consistently desires or practices same-sex relations? The NORC data provide an estimate that of the approximately 6 percent who experience same-sex relations ever, the number of currently active homosexuals is 0.6-0.7 percent of the U.S. adult population.[12]

A 1986-1987 study of 36,741 American adolescents found that 1 percent had had homosexual experience in the previous year (1.6 percent boys, 0.9 per-

cent girls), and the number reporting a homosexual orientation was 0.7 percent for boys (plus 0.8 percent bisexual) and 0.2 percent for girls (plus 0.9
percent bisexual).[13] A 1988 study of 1,880 fifteen- to nineteen-year-old males
found that 0.3 percent had homosexual intercourse in the past year (1.4
percent ever), and 0.5 percent reported a homosexual orientation (plus 1
percent bisexual).[14]

Interestingly, these numbers are consistent with data from other Western
countries. A British survey conducted in 1990-1991 (among 19,000 men) found
that 1.1 percent had homosexual partners in the previous year (3.6 percent
ever).[15] In the Netherlands, widely regarded as socially more liberal than most
Western countries, a 1989 study (1,000 subjects) revealed 3.3 percent of men
and 0.4 percent of women who declared a predominantly homosexual *preference* during the previous year (12 percent men/4 percent women ever).[16] A
1992 French study reported 1.1 percent of men and 0.3 percent of women
having had same-sex relations in the previous year, 1.4 percent/0.4 percent
in the previous five years, and 4.1 percent/2.6 percent ever.[17]

These recent studies contain controls for bias in evidence gathering and
reporting. Researchers work to ensure random samples, neutral questions
and interview techniques, and anonymity for participants. They adjust results
to take into account occasional refusals to answer questions or to answer
truthfully.[18] This degree of care, coupled with the remarkable uniformity of
the resulting numbers, brings a fair degree of certainty to the question of
prevalence.

We may understand the variety of statistics reviewed above more simply in
terms of numbers rather than percentages. What the research tells us is that
in a random collection of three hundred adults, two of the men and one of
the women have had a same-sex encounter during the past year. As many as
four additional men and two additional women have the inclination, at least
occasionally, but in the past year either they were not able to act on it or they
chose not to act on it. An additional six of the men and three of the women
tried same-sex relations at some point in the past but decided that the experience was not what they wanted to do on a regular basis. The rest of the
crowd—282 of the three hundred—practice heterosexuality if they practice

anything. In terms of exclusive same-sex desire coupled with predominantly same-sex practice, as few as *two* of the three hundred are *homosexual.*[19]

If we translate these numbers into national proportions, we begin with the 1990 U.S. Census adult population figure of about 180 million people. Of that number, approximately two million men and one million women engaged in at least one homosexual act during the previous year. The homosexual population—that is, those adults who practice same-sex relations exclusively—is about 1.5 million. If we add those who "go both ways" on a regular basis and assume that many of them have at least partial homosexual desires, we might stretch that number to two million.

These numbers are of course very far from the eighteen million adults suggested by the still popular 10 percent figure. Nevertheless, it is still a large number of people. And of course statistics do not matter much when you or someone you love is included in the number. The point here is simply to survey recent research in order to present the facts. Whether the dramatic downward revision of the numbers affects the popular notion of what is "normal" remains to be seen.

Patterns of Practice

As homosexuality enters the media mainstream, homosexual activities are carefully portrayed as parallel in every respect to heterosexual sex except for the incidental difference of the sex of the partners. From the popular film *Philadelphia* to the children's story *Daddy's Roommate,* homosexual couples are portrayed as highly attractive people who enjoy stable relationships. But the camera always cuts away, or the page turns, before any display of affection goes beyond a brief kiss or caress. Defenders will argue that such portrayals are justified in order to combat stereotypes and "homophobia," the definition of which has expanded to include *disapproval.* On closer inspection, though, what we observe in homosexual practice is altogether different than heterosexual practice in at least three respects.

1. Frequency of sex outside of long-term relationships. The most thorough study of homosexual relationships to date is reported by A. P. Bell and M. S. Weinberg in their book *Homosexualities.*[20] The authors classify as "close-coupled" the nearest approximation to marriage among homosexuals, which involves cohabitors in a "quasi-marriage" where the "amount of cruising [sexual encounters extraneous to the primary relationship] also had to be low."[21] Only 10 percent of the male subjects and 28 percent of the female subjects were found to fit into this category.[22] This is consistent with the results of the 1990 U.S. Census, which found only 145,130 same-sex couples who described their cohabitor as "unmarried partner."[23] Approximately 95 percent of these same-sex couples were concentrated in metropolitan or urban areas—33 percent in just twelve cities—and 25 percent in one state.[24] The number of such couples in San Francisco was an amazingly low 5,669 male, 1,461 female.[25] These numbers appear to verify Bell and Weinberg's earlier finding that the vast majority of homosexual activity, particularly among males, occurs outside the context of quasi-marital partnerships.

We can quantify the phenomenon of homosexual promiscuity, especially among males, more specifically. The numbers are astounding. Bell and Weinberg found that 74 percent of male homosexuals reported having more than one hundred partners during their lifetime, 41 percent more than five hundred partners, 28 percent more than one thousand partners.[26] Seventy-five percent reported that more than half their partners were strangers, and 65 percent reported that they had sex with more than half their partners only once.[27] For the previous year, 55 percent reported twenty or more partners, 30 percent fifty or more partners.[28] The numbers for homosexual women were considerably lower: 60 percent reported fewer than ten partners lifetime, and only 2 percent reported more than one hundred partners; for the previous year, only 3 percent reported twenty or more partners, 1 percent fifty or more partners.[29]

The study of M. T. Saghir and E. Robins found that 50 percent of homosexual men over the age of thirty, and 75 percent of homosexual men over the age of forty, experienced *no* relationships that lasted more than one year.[30] Even during the peak periods of sexual involvement (ages twenty to forty), for those few who had relationships lasting more than one year, only 37 percent of homosexual men and 20 percent of homosexual women had affairs that involved cohabitation for more than three years.[31] Although more homosexual women experienced relationships of at least a year, the duration of those relationships on average was slightly less than that of homosexual men.[32] And overall, only 8 percent of the homosexual men and 7 percent of the homosexual women *ever* had relationships that lasted more than three years.[33]

Another large survey conducted by K. Jay and A. Young found that only 7 percent of male homosexuals had been in a relationship that had lasted more than ten years; 38 percent had never been in a relationship that lasted more than one year; 55 percent had never been in a relationship that lasted more than two years.[34] A study of several hundred male couples in Chicago reported a rate of "nonexclusivity" of 87 percent among those who had been together less than a year, 78 percent among those who had been together one to five years and 91 percent among those who had been together more than five years.[35]

Some might object that these data are all from the late 1970s and that AIDS has markedly changed sexual practices. But more recent research provides fairly consistent confirmation of the numbers. A Los Angeles study conducted in the late 1980s, for example, found that male homosexuals averaged over twenty partners per year.[36] A three-year study in Boston during the late 1980s found that 77 percent of 481 male subjects had had more than ten partners in the previous five years, 34 percent more than fifty partners in the previous five years.[37] Perhaps most tragically, as I will document below, the most risk-prone segment of the male homosexual population is the most promiscuous, the least likely to take precautions and the least likely to inform partners of their own infection.

It is useful to compare the figures on homosexual promiscuity to those of the general population, since one common response is that heterosexuals are no less promiscuous. A major study of American adult sexual behavior published in 1993 found that 17 percent of men and 10 percent of women had more than one partner in the previous year.[38] Another study compared instances of nonmonogamy in the previous year among different groups and found that among "close-coupled" homosexual males, 79 percent reported at least one instance of nonmonogamy in the previous year, as compared to 19 percent among lesbians, 10 percent among married heterosexuals and 23 percent among cohabiting heterosexuals.[39] If we project these numbers out over several years, the number of homosexual men who experience anything like lifelong fidelity becomes, statistically speaking, almost meaningless.[40]

Promiscuity among homosexual men is not a mere stereotype, and it is not merely the majority experience—it is virtually the *only* experience. And even if we set aside infidelity and allow a generous definition of "long-term relationships" as those that last at least four years, under 8 percent of either male or female homosexual relationships fit the definition. In short, there is practically no comparison possible to heterosexual marriage in terms of either fidelity or longevity. Tragically, lifelong faithfulness is almost nonexistent in the homosexual experience.

2. *Sexual techniques.* Although I am aware that many people are disgusted by homosexual practices, my intent here is not to arouse repulsion but simply to point out that homosexual practice is *different* in ways that are often harmful, both physically and psychologically. The myth of similarity propagated by discreet media portrayals disguises characteristic sexual techniques that vary considerably from those of heterosexuals. The reality, unfortunately, is likely to involve brief, anonymous encounters and physically traumatic, disease-prone activities.

The rest of this chapter will focus on male homosexual practice, for the simple reason that homosexual practice is, quantitatively, almost exclusively male. Since two-thirds of homosexuals are male, and since male homosexuals are considerably more sexually active,[41] a fair estimate is that at least 80 percent of homosexual acts occur between men. Since this book focuses primarily on the morality of *practice*, greater attention to male homosexuality seems justified.

Bell and Weinberg[42] found that the most common sexual techniques performed among male homosexuals in the year prior to the survey were, in order of frequency, oral-genital contact (95 percent), mutual masturbation (80 percent), insertive anal intercourse (80 percent) and receptive anal intercourse (70 percent). Mutual masturbation, incidentally, is not limited to genital stimulation but includes a variety of anal stimuli, involving the fingers and various other objects.[43] Among homosexual women, the most common techniques employed were mutual masturbation (80 percent) and oral-genital contact (80 percent). Males named insertive anal intercourse as their favorite sexual activity, with receptive oral-genital contact a close second. Females named receptive oral-genital contact as their favorite sexual activity, with receptive masturbation a distant second.

The survey of Jay and Young reported percentages of 4,329 subjects who during the previous year had "always," "very frequently" or "somewhat frequently" engaged in oral-genital contact (88 percent), mutual masturbation (71 percent), insertive anal intercourse (47 percent) or passive anal intercourse (42 percent).[44] They add or specify additional common practices such as fingering the rectum (38 percent), "rimming," or oral-anal contact (28 percent), "fisting," or insertion of the entire hand into the rectum (5 percent) and sadomasochistic practices including "water sports," or urination on the partner (9 percent).[45] In their chapter on "kinky" sex, they report that 20-40 percent of subjects had engaged in sadomasochistic practices at least once, and that as many as 15 percent expressed a "very positive" or "somewhat positive" attitude toward such practices.[46] They also report that 50 percent had participated at least occasionally in orgies, with 53 percent expressing a very or somewhat positive attitude toward large-group sex.[47]

Saghir and Robins found that 6 percent of their subjects engaged in periodic sadomasochistic behavior.[48] Twenty-nine percent of their subjects had engaged in orgies, and 60 percent of those had done so more than five times.[49] Sexual encounters are also often crowded sequentially, such that some men participate "in a dozen or more sexual transactions in the course of a single day or evening."[50]

Jay and Young confirm the high rate of mutual masturbation and oral-genital contact between subjects among the 952 females they surveyed. Only 9 percent regularly practiced rimming, and only 1 percent regularly engaged in sadomasochism, although 10 percent had a very or somewhat positive attitude toward such practices.[51] The popular assumption that female homosexuals rely on artificial penises or "dildos" for vaginal stimulation is refuted by the finding that only 3 percent use them, although 78 percent value highly and regularly engage in stimulation inside the vagina by manual or oral means.[52]

More recent studies confirm the numbers of Bell and Weinberg for the most common male homosexual practices[53] and the numbers of Jay and Young for the frequency of other practices.[54] From the most recent studies back to those in the pre-AIDS era, the numbers are very consistent for activities regularly practiced by male homosexuals: oral-genital contact (90-98 percent), mutual masturbation of the penis and anus (80-90 percent), anal intercourse (40-70 percent), fingering the rectum (40-60 percent), rimming (30-40 percent), fisting (5 percent) and various sadomasochistic practices (5-10 percent).

The point, once again, is not to encourage repulsion on the part of heterosexual readers, and that is why I limit this description to a survey of the most common practices without extended descriptions and case studies. The reader who has the stomach for sensational details can find them easily enough in the medical and psychiatric literature. My purpose here is simply to lift the media-laid sheets from homosexual practices. After the camera turns away, what often happens is very unlike what happens between heterosexual partners, especially in terms of the susceptibility of participants to physical harm and disease.

3. Alcohol and drug use. Researchers report a significantly higher percentage of alcohol and drug use among both male and female homosexuals. Even apart from substance abuse disorders, which I will treat below, the quantity of substances consumed by homosexuals poses substantial health risks. A Los Angeles study of 823 homosexual men found that during the previous two months 56 percent had consumed at least three alcoholic beverages in one day, 45 percent had smoked at least two cigarettes daily, 50 percent had smoked marijuana, 26 percent had used cocaine, and 32 percent had used "poppers."[55] Poppers are amyl and butyl nitrate inhalants, recreational drugs used almost exclusively by male homosexuals to enhance sexual performance by relaxing smooth tissues, engorging blood vessels, lowering blood pressure, causing dizziness and heightening skin sensitivity.[56]

A 1989 San Francisco study compared results from 1983 and found little change in the history of drug use: 89 percent used marijuana (87 percent in 1983; 25 percent of the heterosexual control group), 50 percent used cocaine (69 percent in 1983; 6 percent of heterosexuals), 72 percent used poppers (73 percent in 1983; 2 percent of heterosexuals), 33 percent used barbiturates (38 percent in 1983; 9 percent of heterosexuals), and 50 percent used LSD (29 percent in 1983; 3 percent of heterosexuals).[57] A Boston study found that for the years 1985-1988, 80 percent of 481 homosexual men had used marijuana, 70 percent poppers, 60 percent cocaine, 30 percent amphetamines and 20 percent LSD.[58] A 1988-1989 Canadian study found that 76.3 percent of 612 male homosexual subjects regularly used alcohol, 32.2 percent tobacco, and 45.6 percent at least one drug.[59] A national study of 1,924 female homosexuals conducted in 1984 found that 83 percent regularly used alcohol (25 percent more than once a week, 6 percent every day), 47 percent smoked marijuana, and 30 percent regularly smoked tobacco.[60]

Whenever these studies consider connections, they show a direct correlation between the number of partners, drug use and the likelihood of unsafe sex.[61] More specifically, another Boston study found that of 262 male subjects, 49 percent used drugs with sex, 9 percent weekly; 57 percent used alcohol with sex, 9 percent weekly.[62] By comparison, in the general population 8.6 percent of men regularly used alcohol, and 1.1 percent any drug, before or during sex.[63]

As will be shown below, recreational drug use is one of several factors that contribute to an epidemic of sexually transmitted diseases among homosexual men, diseases including but not limited to AIDS. Although professional journals rarely include any recommendation beyond "increased education" as a response to patterns of homosexual practice, one brave exception merits quotation:

> Most men in our sample were knowledgeable about the safety of specific sexual acts. Although correct information is important and often a necessary condition for behavioral change, it is often not sufficient. As with cigarette smoking, most smokers know the health risks associated with their behaviors but continue to smoke nevertheless. . . . It appears that many gay and bisexual men may be faced with multiple addiction prob-

lems related to sex, drugs, and alcohol. Further changes in sexual behavior are not likely to occur unless the compulsive nature of their sexual behavior and polydrug use are dealt with more directly.[64]

Mental and Physical Disorders

In this section I will consider three categories of harm associated with homosexual practice: psychopathology, or mental disorders, non-AIDS physical afflictions, and AIDS. While all of these problems are present to some degree in the heterosexual population, the question here is whether there are sufficient problems distinctive to homosexual practice to question the behavior on health grounds.

1. Psychopathology. Bell and Weinberg found that males and females who were "close-coupled" or "functional" (high promiscuity and high self-acceptance) were "no more distressed psychologically than are heterosexual men and women,"[65] a finding generally affirmed by other researchers.[66] It is not appropriate, however, to proceed from this observation to the generalization that homosexuals are psychologically healthy. First, Bell and Weinberg limit their pronouncement of "normal adjustment" to just two of their five categories of relationships, which cover only 25 percent and 38 percent of their male and female samples, respectively.[67] Other researchers recognize that subjects for psychological surveys are often drawn from nonrepresentative samples, including homosexual activist organizations.[68] More specifically in terms of mental disorders, people who partake in such studies are less likely to be suffering currently and are likely to be recruited from supportive therapy groups.[69]

But even if all the samples were random and the results applied to all homosexuals, we could not use the term *adjusted* or *functional* as a measure of psychological health. Such terms are employed by psychologists as measures of *self-satisfaction,* not of therapist approval—much less of appropriate behavior. Sadomasochists, for example, score well on the functional scale in some studies,[70] as do pedophiles in others.[71] To feel good is not necessarily to be good.

Apart from concerns over the misapplication of *functional* to mental health, there is overwhelming evidence that certain mental disorders occur with much higher frequency among homosexuals. The most thoroughly documented problems are alcohol and drug abuse disorders, depression and suicide.

Given the rates of alcohol and drug consumption documented above, it is no surprise that the substance abuse rate among homosexuals is far greater than that of the general population. The combined results of two studies reveal that 47 percent of 405 male homosexual subjects had a history of alcohol abuse (compared to 24 percent of males generally) and 51 percent had a history of drug abuse (compared to 7 percent of males generally).[72] A comparable study of female homosexuals revealed 35 percent with a history of alcohol abuse (compared to 5 percent of females generally).[73] These and other studies tend to confirm that male homosexual substance abuse is likely to occur episodically, or "on and off," whereas female alcohol abuse is more constant.[74] The current consensus of researchers is that about 30 percent of homosexuals (both male and female) are problem drinkers, as compared to 10 percent of the general population.[75]

There is a wide range of explanations for this phenomenon, from the psychoanalytic theory of oral obsession to the assertion that a repressive society drives homosexuals to drink.[76] At the end of this subsection on psychopathology I will consider the implications of intrinsic (from within) as opposed to extrinsic (from without) causation of alcoholism and other psychopathologies. My first aim is to establish the problems apart from their cause.

Depression is another serious mental disorder faced by a disproportionate number of male homosexuals. The two studies cited above for substance abuse combine to show that 40 percent of male homosexual subjects had a history of major depressive disorder (compared to 3 percent of males generally).[77] Bell and Weinberg found high current levels of depression among all groups but the "close-coupled" and "functionals."[78] A study of female homosexuals found that 37 percent had a history of depression but did not compare these numbers to females generally.[79]

The fact that other studies found little significant difference in levels of depression between homosexual and heterosexual women[80] does not of course imply that homosexual women do not have a problem with depression, but that heterosexual women also have a problem—although perhaps for different reasons.

Suicide ideation (serious contemplation) and attempts are another major problem. Bell and Weinberg[81] found that 35 percent of male homosexuals had seriously considered or attempted suicide (compared to 11 percent of male heterosexuals), and 31 percent of female homosexuals had seriously considered or attempted suicide (compared to 24 percent of female heterosexuals). Jay and Young reported the 40 percent of male homosexuals and 39 percent of female homosexuals had either seriously contemplated or attempted suicide.[82] The differences were more pronounced for actual suicide attempts: 18 percent of male homosexuals and 23 percent of female homosexuals had attempted suicide (compared to 3 percent of male heterosexuals and 11 percent of female heterosexuals). Virtually identical numbers for male homosexuals have been obtained by several additional studies.[83] Less work has been done on female homosexuals, but a recent study affirms the Bell and Weinberg figures: 21 percent had suicidal thoughts "sometimes" or "often," and 18 percent had attempted suicide.[84] This amounts to a double suicide attempt rate among female homosexuals and a sixfold rate among male homosexuals. As in the case of depression, the gap between female homosexuals and heterosexuals is narrower not because there is less of a problem among female homosexuals but because there is a greater problem among female heterosexuals.

Substance abuse, depression and suicide are virtually undisputed as epidemic problems, but they are by no means the only problems.[85] One other concern that merits attention is the disproportionate number of male homosexuals who prefer sex with boys. Homosexual men are not necessarily pedophiles. Still, several studies reveal that while no more than 2 percent of male adults are homosexual, approximately 35 percent of pedophiles are homosexual.[86] Further, since homosexual pedophiles victimize far more children than do heterosexual pedophiles (150 to 20),[87] approximately 80 percent of pedophilic victims are boys who are molested by adult males. The number of boys victimized is approximately 3.2 million.[88] It is impossible to determine the number of male pedophiles, but they may constitute as much as 10 percent of male homosexuals.[89]

I repeat, this does not mean that any male homosexual is likely also to be a pedophile, but only that pedophilia is proportionately a far greater problem among homosexuals than among heterosexuals. And as observed in chapter three, the problem is compounded by the fact that many pedophiles deny that it is a problem and demand full inclusion in the homosexual liberation movement.[90]

The revisionist response to problems I have described in this chapter, from promiscuity to pedophilia, is that they originate not in homosexuality but in homophobia.[91] That is, homosexuals "internalize" the negative attitudes of society by engaging in self-destructive behaviors. Although this level of denial may reveal yet another form of psychopathology, I will leave it to the experts to separate politics from reality—if they can agree that there is a difference.

Let us assume, for the sake of argument, that all the problems surveyed above are the fault of heterosexual oppression, whether spoken or simply ingrained in the culture. Unfortunately, while this explanation provides a focus for anger, it provides no real solution. First, it is unrealistic in the extreme to expect that public relations efforts and legal requirements will rewrite the entire human literary and religious heritage, reverse majority attitudes thousands of years in the making, and sustain all of this for the time required to reduce the disdain for homosexual practice to a quaint memory. Human sexuality is not like the flat earth.

We must also acknowledge that recognition of homosexual partnerships as marriages will not make them produce children. Children contribute mightily to the stabilization and health of heterosexual partnerships, not merely as guilt-laced glue for troubled marriages but as vital constituents in the construction of *families*.

Finally, we observe that same-sex partnerships forfeit the complementarity of sex drives that exist in opposite-sex partnerships. In other words, societal repression fails to account for the radically different patterns of sexual behavior between male and female homosexuals, patterns that we may best understand in terms of traditional gender roles. That is, men tend to treat genital sex as a means of self-expression, central to their individual identity, and women tend to treat genital sex as one of several enjoyable options in the expression of affection, which is integrated into their more relational sense of identity. Problems are likely to occur, especially for men, when the balance of the other gender is absent.

These observations are speculative, but I think they are at least plausible in light of the evidence. In any case, the assignment of cause or blame does not in itself eliminate or even reduce psychopathological problems. Until the unlikely goal of societal acceptance of homosexual behavior produces the unlikely result of elimination of homosexual psychopathology, the most sensible course of action is not to engage in behavior that carries with it (or causes) such a high risk of psychological harm.

To abstain is of course likely to produce other problems for the individual. Nevertheless, in the face of overwhelming evidence that the homosexual life is anything but gay, the individual must ask whether more hope, and more integrity, may reside in the difficult choice of self-denial over self-indulgence. It is a choice we all face in important areas of our lives, perhaps nowhere more painfully than in the area of sexuality. The pain we choose may be either redemptive or destructive in the long run, and in making a choice we must take seriously the health of the mind and of the body.

2. *Non-HIV/AIDS health problems.* I will consider HIV/AIDS separately below. It is important to understand that even if a cure for HIV/AIDS were discovered, male homosexuals would continue to pay a terrible physical price for their activities, as they did before the epidemic began. I will categorize these problems in terms of physical trauma, nonviral infections and viral infections.[92] For some of these health problems, homosexual men make up at least 70 percent of the total reported cases. Doctors who work with homosexual men are now trained to look regularly for at least fifteen *common* afflictions apart from HIV/AIDS, and we could double or triple the number by taking into account less common problems.[93]

A brief and simple anatomy lesson is necessary before proceeding. It does not require a medical degree to appreciate the risk of infection by external oral contact with the penis or anus, but few people understand the anus's internal susceptibility to damage. The end of the digestive system, the large intestine, is a long tube consisting mainly of the colon. About six inches from the end the colon takes a sharp turn down and narrows briefly, creating another area called the rectum. The last half-inch of the tube is the anal canal, a nerve-rich area lined with stratified cuboidal epithelial cells and surrounded by the anal sphincter muscle. The rectum is lined with a single layer of columnar epithelial cells designed to absorb liquids.

The vagina, by contrast, is lined with tough cells called stratified squamous epithelium. These cells have a layer of mucus that, along with other secretions and the thicker, more flexible vaginal wall, protects against abrasion and infection. The rectal wall has no surrounding muscular support, and it secretes a small amount of mucus that does not protect well against abrasion. But the key differences between the vagina and the rectum are the cell types and the thickness of the cell layers. The two orifices may feel very much alike to the intruding finger or penis. But one orifice is prone to repel, the other to admit, whatever microorganisms come along for the ride.

In order to appreciate the difference, imagine dipping both hands into a bucket of black ink, then immediately putting one hand in a heavy leather glove and the other in a light silk glove. Your hands would feel much the same, but the gloves would not look the same. A little ink might come through the leather glove, especially at weak points like seams or tears, but the other glove would be a mess.

Before we consider further the "ink" of infection, it is important to understand that physical trauma, or harm to bodily structures, is a common problem among homosexuals. Quite simply, the silk glove of the rectum is not made for the industrial use of insertive homosexual activity. Anal intercourse stretches the opening to the size required for a large bowel movement. The problem, however, is not the size of the opening but the direction and repetition of the movement. The anus is a one-way valve, stimulated to open only by pressure from *inside,* and stimulated to contract by pressure from outside. Sudden or inadequately lubricated penetration can tear the anus itself. But more commonly the cumulative effect of anal intercourse is to cause dysfunction of the anal sphincter muscle, and the result is chronic incontinence or urgency of defecation for about one in three men who regularly engage in the practice.[94]

Nor is that all. Once past the anus, the danger of physical trauma worsens. Irritation of the sensitive rectal mucus layer causes a host of reactions, including diarrhea, cramps, hemorrhoids, prostate damage, and ulcers or fissures which in turn invite infection. The thin cell layer of the rectum is easily perforated, and its insensitivity to pain can lead to serious complications before a person is aware of any harm. Extensive surgical procedures are often required to repair damage caused by the insertion of the penis, the finger or other objects into the rectum.

In addition to traumatic complications, a host of sexually transmitted diseases (STDs) affect the homosexual population. The magnitude of the problem is not shown simply by a tally of people who are currently ill. Some people carry microorganisms (pathogens) and infect others without themselves showing signs of disease. Other people are asymptomatic (show no symptoms), or show symptoms only periodically, or contract the same disease several times. Some afflictions do not seem serious in themselves but lead to, or increase the likelihood of acquiring, more serious diseases. Other illnesses, normally rare, grow to epidemic proportions when they enter the homosexual population. New diseases and new forms of old diseases are even now being discovered in the course of HIV/AIDS research.

All of these factors make it difficult to quantify the disease rate or to know what aspect of the disease rate to estimate. It appears, for example, that at least 75 percent of homosexual men are currently carrying one or more pathogens,[95] but these men are not necessarily feeling sick or infecting others. It appears that at least 75 percent also have a history of at least one sexually transmitted disease,[96] but these men are not necessarily *very* sick or *currently* sick. It appears that at least 40 percent get sick in a given year,[97] but again they are not necessarily *very* sick. On the other hand, to estimate the number who are sick at any one time is to underestimate the general danger of serious illness for any individual homosexual, a danger that is constant and cumulative.

The most common *nonviral infections* among homosexuals are, in order of prevalence, amebiasis, giardiasis, gonorrhea, shigellosis, chlamydia, syphilis and ectoparasites. These diseases are caused by pathogens that are transmitted by oral-genital contact, genital-anal contact and oral-anal contact. They are treatable, if detected early, with antimicrobial agents.

The most common disease is amebiasis, which causes inflammation of the rectum and colon, resulting in severe diarrhea and cramps. It affects 25-40 percent of homosexual men.[98] Amebiasis is linked primarily to oral-anal contact, but this may take place indirectly by transportation of infection from the anus to finger to mouth during finger foreplay or when using saliva as a lubricant for anal intercourse.

Giardiasis, which affects 10-30 percent of homosexual men,[99] is also linked to oral-anal contact. It affects the small intestine and produces diarrhea, bloating, cramps and nausea.

Gonorrhea may cause pain and mucus discharge from either the penis or anus, or the infection may be asymptomatic (especially the oral form), which allows it to spread easily. In the 1970s approximately 40 percent of homosexual men reported a past history of gonorrhea,[100] but after a period of decline the infection rate nearly doubled in the late 1980s.[101]

Shigellosis is the most common of several similar bacterial infections (including *salmonella* and *campylobacter*) that produce fever, abdominal pain, watery or bloody diarrhea and ulcers in the rectum or colon. Like amebiasis and giardiasis, these infections are linked to oral-anal contact. One or more of these pathogens is present in 10-20 percent of homosexual men.[102]

Chlamydia, which affects 5-15 percent of homosexual men,[103] is difficult to detect because it is often asymptomatic or only mildly symptomatic. Like gonorrhea, it produces a mucus discharge from the penis or anus, or a sore throat. In more serious cases it produces severe anorectal pain, bloody discharge, diarrhea and rectal ulcers.

Syphilis occurs in several stages, often beginning with painless ulcers on the genitals or in the rectum. Later it produces fissures, polyps and warts that are easily confused with symptoms of other STDs. In the advanced stage, syphilis may attack the brain and heart and can be fatal. Although syphilis is treatable in the early stages, it may escape detection during a long, quiet period of latency while the symptoms are hidden inside the rectum. As in the case of gonorrhea, control of the disease requires identification of infected persons and partner notification—major problems in a population group where multiple and anonymous partners are common. And as in the case of gonorrhea, the infection rate appears to have increased through the 1980s, with approximately 30 percent of homosexual men now reporting a history of syphilis.[104]

Common ectoparasites among homosexuals create great discomfort but are not dangerous. The most common ectoparasites are pubic lice and scabies.[105] Pubic lice or "crabs," for which 69 percent of male homosexuals report a history,[106] are transmitted primarily by close body contact. They cause itching and inflammation but are easily treatable with insecticide shampoos and lotions. A history of scabies is reported by 22 percent of homosexual men.[107] Scabies are mites that cause itching lesions, nodules and encrustations on parts of the body where skin meets skin. Like pubic lice, they are treatable by various insecticides.

Viral infections that are common among homosexuals include, in order of prevalence, condylomata, herpes, hepatitis B and hepatitis A. Like bacterial infections, these diseases are easily transmitted by oral-genital contact, genital-anal contact and oral-anal contact.

Condylomata, or anal warts, is caused by the human papillomaviruses (HPV) which are transmitted by anal intercourse. They affect 30-40 percent of homosexual men,[108] with the virus present in as many as 65 percent.[109] The warts occur primarily in and around the anus, usually in clusters, often causing itching and burning. Although physicians may remove warts by the usual cutting or freezing procedures, they have a high recurrence rate. Furthermore, a history of genital warts is strongly linked to anal cancer, the incidence of which is rapidly increasing among homosexual men.[110]

Herpes affects 10-20 percent of homosexuals, and as in the case of several other sexually transmitted diseases, the numbers may be increasing.[111] There is at present no cure or vaccine for herpes: a person who contracts it has it for life. Among homosexuals the disease is usually transmitted by anal intercourse, although oral-anal contact with a person who has oral herpes can also transmit the infection. In homosexual men herpes causes severe anorectal pain, headaches and urination/defecation problems. The most serious symptoms are lesions or ulcers in the genital-anal region, sometimes inside the rectum, which remain open for two to three weeks. These ulcers are very painful, and they recur—although less severely—from time to time after the first sores heal. Because these recurring ulcers are often asymptomatic, hidden and painless inside the rectum, they are open doors for the transmission of other viruses—including the most lethal, HIV.

Infectious hepatitis comes in two forms that are epidemic in the homosexual population for different reasons. Outbreaks of hepatitis A (HAV) in several major cities in the early 1990s[112] suggest that the prevalence rate has risen markedly since earlier studies, which showed that the virus is present in approximately 40 percent of homosexual men, of which 5-7 percent will acquire the disease annually—at least three times the rate of the general population.[113] Like many bacterial and viral infections, HAV is present in human feces, and it is linked to oral-anal contact between homosexual partners. The early flulike symptoms of fever, headache and vomiting give way to jaundice as the liver is affected. Fortunately, the disease usually runs its course in a week or two and does not produce chronic liver disease.[114]

Hepatitis B (HBV), which is present in all bodily fluids including saliva, semen and rectal mucus, is transmitted between homosexuals primarily by anal intercourse.[115] At least 65 percent of homosexual men carry the disease or have a history of it, and at least 16 percent contract HBV annually.[116] The symptoms are similar to those of hepatitis A, but are more severe and include the possibility of chronic liver disease and, in rare cases, death. Five to ten percent of those who contract the disease become chronic carriers who may show no symptoms other than fatigue. It is not possible to cure hepatitis B, but a vaccine is available to prevent it.

By comparison to even the most promiscuous segment of the general population, the male homosexual 75 percent lifetime STD incidence rate and 40 percent annual STD incidence rate are remarkable. Among those in the general population who had more than twenty-one partners lifetime, 40 percent report any infection in their lifetime. Six percent of those who had more than five partners report an infection in the previous year. Overall, the general population has a 16.9 percent lifetime STD incidence rate, 1.6 percent for the previous twelve months.[117]

These health problems are rampant in the homosexual population because they are easily spread by promiscuity and by most of the practices favored by homosexuals. It appears that some diseases are on the rise at least in part because the fear of HIV infection has led homosexuals to decrease anal intercourse in favor of oral-anal and oral-genital contact, practices that carry their own risk of debilitating, if not fatal, diseases.

Paul wrote in Romans 1:27 that homosexuals "received in their own persons the due penalty for their error." It is not clear what he meant by "penalty" in his time, but it is hard not to make a connection between his words and the health crisis we observe in our time. Sexual liberation has brought homosexuals out of the closet into a shadow of physical affliction where a score of diseases lurk. And as if this were not gloomy enough, the more deadly specter of HIV infection deepens the shadow, not only for the ever-growing number who die but also for those who are left behind to grieve and to wonder who will die next.

3. HIV/AIDS: cause and prognosis. The origin of human immunodeficiency virus (HIV) is unknown, but it was first recognized in the 1950s.[118] It began to spread rapidly among African heterosexuals in the 1960s and 1970s by means of prostitution, which is extremely common in Africa, and now as many as 10 percent of the population of some African countries—at least six million Africans overall—are seroprevalent (infected). Worldwide, the number of HIV-infected people is over twelve million, a million of them in the United States. HIV may have entered the U.S. homosexual population from Haiti, which was a major resort location for New York homosexuals in the 1960s and 1970s. In 1981 researchers first noticed a pattern of similar deaths among homosexual men, and not long after that the epidemic became public knowledge. The disease had claimed approximately 350,000 lives by the end of 1994 in the United States, with the number of deaths leveling off now at over 50,000 per year.[119] Approximately 250,000 (70 percent) of those who died through 1994 were men who had sex with men, and at least that many more homosexuals are currently HIV-infected. The level of infection among homosexual men is approximately 30 percent, with estimates ranging from 20 percent in a Pittsburgh study to 50 percent in a San Francisco study.[120]

HIV is present in a variety of tissues, but only blood and semen have been implicated with certainty in the spread of the infection between men.[121] Transmission between homosexuals occurs by sexual contact that allows semen or blood to enter the body through cuts, scratches or mucosal surfaces. Anal intercourse is particularly conducive to transmission because of the unique properties of the rectal wall. The risk is compounded by the presence of numerous hidden tears, ulcers and abrasions in the rectum, anus or penis due to trauma or other STDs. There is now considerable evidence to indicate the possibility of transmission by oral-genital contact.[122] This was always a theoretical possibility, since the mouth contains large numbers of small tears that could allow viral transmission, but it was difficult to prove without evidence that subjects engaged *only* in oral-genital sex.

When HIV enters the bloodstream, it attacks cells that are critical parts of the body's immune system.[123] Initially the infection may present no more than mild symptoms, but the virus moves into the lymph system and builds up for nine to ten years. Eventually the virus is strong enough to destroy the body's immune system. At that point the condition is called acquired immunodeficiency syndrome (AIDS), which is simply the end stage or symptomatic form of HIV. At that point of immune-system collapse the body experiences severe impairment of its ability to combat a variety of diseases, which are called opportunistic infections. The median survival time with AIDS is currently about eighteen months.

By far the most common opportunistic infection is *Pneumocystic carinii*, a kind of pneumonia that affects about 85 percent of AIDS patients with chest pain, fever, dry cough and fatigue. Over 50 percent suffer from debilitating bacterial infections that cause chronic diarrhea and from oral candidiasis ("thrush"), which causes lesions in the mouth. Others suffer from various afflictions of the liver, brain and digestive system. Approximately 15 percent contract Kaposi's sarcoma, a cancer that produces red or blue tumors under the skin that gradually enlarge, spread or lead to larger disfiguring tumors. Non-Hodgkins lymphoma is another common cancer that attacks the nervous system or lymphatic system. HIV also appears to work in a mutually reinforcing capacity with other STDs. That is, not only do other STDs increase a person's susceptibility to HIV, but HIV worsens other STDs and contributes to their spread.[124]

In spite of an enormous mobilization of resources, there has been no breakthrough toward a cure or immunization for HIV. The virus presents unusual problems. It occurs in different strains, each of which must be treated separately. Even if researchers can develop a vaccine, testing presents a major ethical dilemma: researchers must study vaccinated humans while they are repeatedly exposed to the virus. For the present doctors can only hope to prolong life by encouraging general health measures and by prevention and treatment of opportunistic infections.

The record of the homosexual population in response to the HIV epidemic is inconsistent. From the mid to late 1980s condom use went up and anal intercourse went down. Unfortunately, the trend did not last, and by the early 1990s dozens of studies showed marked increases in the most dangerous sexual practices.[125] HIV and STDs both went up again, and there was little to show for the enormous effort and expense to promote preventative measures among homosexual men. One report concluded,

> The most striking finding of this study is that HIV infection rates between 1984 and 1988 to 1992 did not vary in this cohort. . . . While it is very encouraging that there have been widespread and significant changes in sexual behaviors, a substantial proportion of gay and bisexual men in this sample still continued to engage in or have relapsed into unsafe behaviors that could lead to HIV infection. This suggests that present levels of change are not sufficient for slowing, much less for ending, the epidemic.[126]

Another study found that only 9 percent of subjects surveyed fit into the "safe" behavior category for the past two months and an additional 10 percent fit in the "possibly safe" category; moreover, those who had engaged in at least one "unsafe" act included 40 percent of those who were already HIV-infected.[127] A Dutch study calculated the probability of infection per partner at 6.1 percent for those who practice anal intercourse without a condom.[128] Although no reasonable person would board an airplane knowing there was one chance in seventeen—or one chance in a hundred—that the plane would crash, tens of thousands of homosexual men board that plane again and again, with tragic consequences.

Why is it that the campaign for "safe sex" turned into a campaign for "safer sex" and now appears to have had so little real success in stemming the tide of HIV and other STDs? This question has spawned another stream of articles that attempt to explain the lack of results to date and to recommend still more education efforts.[129] But it does not require a degree in behavioral research to guess most of the reasons for the failure. Men do not like to wear condoms. It does not take much of an excuse, especially in the heat of the moment, to discourage their use. Moreover, men do not like to hear preachy messages about abstinence and behavior control. Even when their very lives are at stake? Yes, even then, for several reasons. Some feel invulnerable, especially if their primary partner is not known to be HIV-infected. Others feel that attempts to control their sexual behavior are a limitation of their freedom, another form of homophobia. Others feel that regular checkups and general good health are all that is necessary. Many wait for a "magic bullet," a quick technical fix from medical researchers. And others are simply fatalistic, reasoning that the risk of disease is just part of being homosexual.

If condoms were more widely and properly used, they would undoubtedly reduce the epidemic of HIV and STDs, but they are certainly not a fail-safe solution.[130] Studies of the recent general behavioral relapse reveal that those who are most promiscuous are least likely to cooperate with disease-control efforts by using condoms, by informing partners when they are infected or by informing disease controllers who their partners were—if they know. Although condoms seldom break in laboratory conditions, people do not have sex in laboratory conditions. In real life, condoms are often improperly stored, improperly fitted, improperly lubricated, not accompanied by spermicides, used too vigorously and improperly removed. And of course, if HIV is transmitted orally or in some other manner, even complete abstention from anal intercourse is ineffective.

Study after study recommends "more education" as the solution to STDs and HIV in the homosexual population, but few writers are realistic about human behavior in general or the lessons of the recent past in particular. Public heath officials, for example, recommend the location and isolation of all affected sexual partners, who must maintain abstinence during treatment. But even if doctors could secure cooperation, many of the STDs are virtually undetectable in the early stages, and the worst infection, HIV, may remain asymptomatic for up to ten years.

Furthermore, general recommendations about safer sex fail to put together the specific recommendations of the various studies. In other words, one study will consider, say, infectious disease resulting from oral-anal contact and will recommend education about that behavior (that is, people should avoid it). Another study does the same for anal intercourse, another for oral-genital contact, and so on. When all the recommendations of the various educators are taken into account, it turns out that any activity (including kissing) that involves potential exchange of body fluids is unsafe for homosexual men. But that message is as unwelcome and unrealistic as the recommendation of abstinence. Unfortunately, it is only in the dream worlds of film, television and some public health officials that homosexual men limit their activities to hugs and caresses. In the real world, and in the heat of passion, hugs and kisses inevitably give way to practices that are harmful and potentially lethal.

Conclusion

The Centers for Disease Control released a cover story in the November 12, 1993, issue of *Morbidity and Mortality Weekly Report* about the American Cancer Society's sponsorship of the Great American Smokeout, a twenty-four-hour period of abstinence, and an accompanying article about efforts to counsel smokers to stop the behavior that is taking so many lives. The cover story of the very next issue (November 19, 1993) was about World AIDS Day and "the need for action against the pandemic" of HIV/AIDS. The cover story was accompanied by an article on HIV risk-reduction programs involving condom distribution and safer sex education.

Such is the current fashion, that in the one case we attack the behavior (smoking) that produces disease, but in the other case we attack only the disease (HIV). In one case we are interested in prevention, in the other case we are interested only in cure. Condoms do not resolve this inconsistency. They work better than cigarette filters, but they create a similar illusion of safety among those who use them and among those who recommend them. At best they are a partial solution to part of the problem. The crisis of homosexual health involves a wide range of health problems, including but not limited to HIV.

The most poignant way to summarize the barrage of statistics and descriptions in this chapter is to translate them into an illustration. Suppose you were to move into a large house in San Francisco with a group of ten randomly selected homosexual men in their mid-thirties. According to the most recent research from scientific sources, whose authors are without exception either neutral or positive in their assessment of homosexual behavior, and with the use of lower numbers where statistics differ, the relational and physical health of the group would look like this.

Four of the ten men are currently in relationships, but only one of those is faithful to his partner, and he will not be within a year. Four have never had a relationship that lasted more than a year, and only one has had a relationship that lasted more than three years. Six are having sex regularly with strangers, and the group averages almost two partners per person per month. Three of them occasionally take part in orgies. One is a sadomasochist. One prefers boys to men.

Three of the men are currently alcoholics, five have a history of alcohol abuse, and four have a history of drug abuse. Three currently smoke cigarettes, five regularly use at least one illegal drug, and three are multiple drug users. Four have a history of acute depression, three have seriously contemplated suicide, and two have attempted suicide. Eight have a history of sexually transmitted diseases, eight currently carry infectious pathogens, and three currently suffer from digestive or urinary ailments caused by these pathogens. At least three are HIV-infected, and one has AIDS.

This group is not likely to be *gay* as the older dictionaries define the term.

Some may respond that the studies cited are not representative of homosexuality as they observe it or experience it, to which I can only appeal to the evidence: nearly two hundred sources, multiple sources at key points covering different geographic areas, different times, and samples both clinical and nonclinical, random and recruited. Others may suspect that I have padded the numbers or suppressed more positive evidence, hoping that no one will take the time to check up on so many technical sources. Even if I were devious enough to falsify data, it would be a poor strategy, because I assume that skeptics in particular *will* check up on my sources—and pounce on any specific example of bias in order to cast suspicion over the whole book. But even so, I invite the skeptic to assume that all the studies are biased or that I have consistently exaggerated data, and to cut all the disease rates in half. Even then, what is left of the evidence indicates a health crisis of multiple facets and epidemic proportions.

Furthermore, even at half the numbers documented above, the problems are too widespread across the population group to attribute to a small, irresponsible minority within the group. Too many of the problems affect three, four, even eight of ten, and it is extremely unlikely that all of the problems overlap. In other words, it is unlikely that the pedophile in the group is also the sadomasochist, the one with five or six contagious pathogens, the drug abuser, the alcoholic and the one with a constant stream of anonymous partners. No, sadly, these and other problems are distributed throughout the homosexual population, so that the minority—evidently the very small minority—are those who are *not* part of the health crisis.

When I have communicated some of this information in speaking engagements, many people have responded in amazement, "Why isn't anyone telling us all this?" Fundamentalists have been saying some of it for years, but the substance of their message is all too often lost in an abrasive style that makes it seem that they revel in displaying the sinfulness of others. They also tend to undermine the general truth of their claims by focusing on sensational examples rather than thorough research.

The news and entertainment media may have the facts—they certainly have the ability to discover them—but they appear to be more interested in the civil rights issue (as they perceive it) than the public health issue. Only the hopelessly naive doubt that journalism is now a self-consciously political activity.

What of the medical community? Physicians all know what is happening, and they report it fairly, but professional journal policy prevents editorial comment on their findings—and in any case, who but professionals reads professional journals? And those professionals, if they are not already over-worked, are not necessarily gifted as popular speakers or writers. Even if they are, they may not wish to risk reputation, career or safety by taking an un-popular stand. It is enough, many of them feel, to fix what is broken, without investing more time in the seemingly futile effort to keep things from getting broken. Why bother with moral persuasion when it hardly ever works? By the time someone comes into a doctor's office with a disease, it is unlikely that a lecture from a doctor—even if the doctor is willing to offer it—is going to result in major behavioral changes.

One specialist told me that he prefers to discuss his disapproval of homo-sexual practice privately with patients when they bring it up rather than risk having patients avoid his practice because of their prior knowledge of his views. I can see his point. On the other hand, I wonder how many people have gotten terribly sick, or died, because doctors en masse have withheld their considerable clout from the moral debate.

What about moral leaders like pastors and educators? Like doctors, they are usually specialists, and overworked, and hesitant to commit themselves on complex issues. As I well know, it is very time-consuming to track down information from credible sources. Moralists usually have enough to do keep-ing up in their own fields without browsing through *Archives of Internal Med-icine*. Moralists also tend to think abstractly. The best evidence of this is the absence of any treatment of homosexuality, revisionist or traditionalist, that explores the moral dimensions of HIV, other STDs, trauma or psychopath-ology. But those dimensions must be explored, whether one takes the secular position that one's body is part of the environment or the Christian view that care for one's body is a significant part of personal stewardship.

Those who wish to promote a revisionist view of homosexual behavior

would rather that we not imagine anything beyond, in L. William Countryman's words, "an entire class of human beings [who have the] right peaceably
and without harming others to pursue the kind of sexuality that corresponds
to their nature."[131] But no honest look at current scientific research allows us
to view homosexual practice as peaceable and harmless. For the vast majority
of homosexual men, and for a significant number of homosexual women—
even apart from the deadly plague of AIDS—sexual behavior is obsessive,
psychopathological and destructive to the body. If there were no specific
biblical principles to guide sexual behavior, these considerations alone would
constitute a compelling argument against homosexual practice. Our bodies
must not be martyrs to our desires.

7

THE GREAT NATURE-NURTURE DEBATE

*A*t about the age of thirteen I began to notice girls—or should I say, it was then that I began to notice little else. Twenty-five years later the inclination is a bit more refined, a bit more controlled—but only a bit. Wherever I am, I notice women, and I notice particular parts of women. I often entertain fleeting thoughts—at times lingering thoughts—of how I might enjoy having sex with women I have never met. It is, after all, only natural.

Or is it? Was I *born* with an inclination to have sex with several different attractive women each day, an inclination that merely remained dormant for thirteen years? Did my father, whose desires are very similar to mine, train me to think about women in a certain way? Am I the product of lifelong exposure to advertisements, films and popular music? Did the trauma of my parents' divorce when I was three, or my mother's actions during my infancy, create in me particular sexual needs and desires?

All of these questions I find genuinely interesting. They are not, however, *moral* questions. Moral questions have to do with the rightness or wrongness of my actions, regardless of the source or strength of my desires. Whatever

I may attribute to my genes, or to my parents, or to my culture, none of them can force me, at the crucial moment, to turn a glance into a fantasy, or a fantasy into a flirtation, or a flirtation into a sexual act. At that moment my *will* is involved, and precisely such moments define my obedience and growth as a Christian. However good I may feel about my conduct, or however deeply ingrained is my desire to act in a certain way, neither of those factors is the measure of obedience. In fact, more often than not they are measures of self-deception.

This of course is not a fashionable notion today. The overwhelming message of the popular culture, which a thousand films and ten thousand love songs drill into us, is that to find a full life we must seek adventure, drink the cup of passion, follow our heart. "Loving you can't be wrong," the voice croons, "because it feels so right." We want to believe this. We may even get a vicarious thrill from watching it work out happily ever after on the silver screen. But in our better moments, we know otherwise. We know, even without Scripture to tell us, that "the heart is devious above all else" (Jer 17:9), that positive experiences and strong desires can never legitimize immorality. We know it when a pedophile describes his nurturing relationships with children. We know it when an adulterous wife complains of her boring husband. We know it when a pornographer proclaims his rights of free speech. We know it when a stripper rationalizes her exploitation.

Explanations and Justifications

We also know that we cannot justify our behavior by an appeal to our nature. A comic no-good husband in a Woody Allen film says to his wife, "Sure I beat ya—*that's my way*—it don't mean I don't love ya. And I always warn ya first." But there is nothing comic about the growing epidemic of domestic violence, gang bloodshed and interracial strife. Whatever the causes, we cannot excuse violence on the part of a person who claims, "This is just the way I am."

Certainly we want to work at the big picture to reduce the factors that contribute to violence, and certainly we want to work with the individual to encourage self-control. But if in the end the violent person is "just that way," we lock that person up for everyone's good.

This is not an argument to criminalize or imprison homosexuals, but an analogy to the relation between strong inclinations and moral responsibility. We could easily apply the "just that way" defense to a number of social problems that may involve deeply ingrained (even biological) causes—violence, substance abuse, racism, schizophrenia, pedophilia—but we do not, because we recognize that an *explanation* for the behavior is not a *justification* for the behavior.

It is frustrating, almost *unnatural*, for a violent man to seek an outlet for his rage other than harm to another person. If the inclination is deeply ingrained, he cannot gain satisfaction by other outlets available to him, such as talk or exercise. It is similarly *unnatural* for a pedophile to seek meaningful relationships with adults, for a substance abuser to face problems with a clear head, for a racist to look beneath the skin. Likewise, it is *unnatural* for me to be faithful to one woman.

But the word *natural* in the sense that I have just been using it has nothing to do with morality, and it is the moral sense in which Paul uses *natural* in Romans 1. We must make this distinction clear and not allow others to confuse the issue by shifting back and forth between meanings. *Natural* may refer to something that happens repeatedly in nature—that is, in the world—in which case we assign no moral judgment to it. Events occur in nature: for example, spiders kill and eat other spiders, including their mates.

But as a moral category *natural* refers to something that is in accord with God's intention. Actions are good or bad: for example, people sometimes kill and eat other people. But the fact that cannibalism happens in the world—perhaps in satisfaction of deeply held religious beliefs or peculiar culinary tastes—does not make it *natural* in the sense that it conforms to God's will. In summary: that which is *natural* to human experience or human desire is not necessarily *natural* in God's moral design.

The reader should understand that this chapter considers the naturalness of homosexual desire and behavior in the first sense, asking simply why it occurs in human experience. I hope to raise the discussion of causation above the smoke of battle caused by confusion on both sides over the word *natural*, where one side proposes certain theories of causation to justify homosexuality ("see how *natural* it is") and others try to refute those theories in order to preserve their condemnation of homosexuality ("it isn't caused that way, so it is an *unnatural* evil").

Because I separate the explanation of the behavior from the morality of the behavior, I do not feel a need to prove or disprove any single theory of causation. In fact—and it may be helpful to reveal this here—I think there are probably several factors that combine in various strengths to account for any individual's same-sex desires. I will try to show some of the possibilities and limitations of each major theory of causation before proposing what I call a "multiple-variant model." As in chapter six, all of the information about causation comes from recent secular professional literature.

Animals and Humans Elsewhere in Time and Place

My distinction between explanation and justification applies to evidence of homosexual behavior in other species, times or cultures. If the investigation turns up little evidence of homosexual activity, the skeptic might argue that there would be more evidence if the researchers or their sources were not homophobic. If, on the other hand, the evidence is plentiful, such evidence has little or no bearing on the moral question. In either case, I find the subject interesting but far removed from the contemporary moral question. Some mammals eat their own young, and some of history's most advanced cultures practiced human sacrifice, genocide or slavery. The highly civilized Greeks made the abuse of boys a way of life. Not that all these practices compare morally to modern homosexuality, but they are *natural* in the sense that they are observable practices: they occur in nature. The point is that something is not moral merely because animals or people do it.

Numerous studies of the animal kingdom reveal indiscriminate mounting behavior, usually to express roles of dominance and submission, but animals do not engage in long-term homosexual bonding as humans do.[1] Some monkeys and apes mount or fondle each other to the point of sexual arousal, but even this behavior involves numerous qualifications: most important, the behavior does not continue when the individual matures and has a heterosexual option.[2] The consensus of research is that "no evidence has as yet emerged to suggest that any nonhuman primate studied to date would rate a 6 [exclusively homosexual] on the Kinsey scale of heterosexuality/homosexuality."[3]

Throughout the history of human cultures, no society has approved of homosexuality as we know it today: long-term relationships of mutual consent between adults.[4] As we have seen, there was a period of time during which upper-class Greek and Roman males alternated between women and boys for sexual gratification, but approval did not extend to sex between adults, to passive partners or to long-term relationships. Elsewhere, until the modern era, many references to homosexuality in the West are probably standardized attacks on alien peoples and not descriptions of actual behavior. The bulk of the historical evidence for same-sex acts comes from the world of monasticism, where men or women were forced into the company of their own sex with no heterosexual outlet. As in the cases of sailors and prison inmates, it is difficult to discern under such circumstances whether the activity results from homosexual desire or the unavailability of opposite-sex partners.

In John Boswell's book *Same-Sex Unions in Premodern Europe,*[5] he attempts to prove that a kind of quasi-marriage ceremony between men, a vestige of Roman culture, survived in the Eastern Empire until the early Middle Ages. But at every key point Boswell's argument depends on quotations taken out of context, questionable translations and speculation to fill in very wide gaps between very small bits of evidence. What he has "discovered" is a ceremony of ritualized brotherhood that borrows a few elements from marriage ceremonies. Although homosexuality may have been present in some such relationships, there is no evidence that sexual partnership (or even nonsexual marriage) was sanctioned by the ceremony, the church or the culture. Indeed, the ceremony in question typically includes prayers that the two men avoid "offense," "scandal" and "temptation," words that Boswell construes as a promise between two homosexual men to have sex only with each other. But even granting this and other examples of Boswell's highly colored interpretation of the ceremony, the fact remains that he can find no historical data to back up his interpretation, to support the claim that such ceremonies reflected church or societal acceptance of homosexual marriage.

The scarcity of information extends into the Renaissance, in spite of the desperate attempts of some apologists to seize on the slightest possible inference to suggest homosexuality on the part of several creative geniuses (such as Michelangelo, da Vinci, Marlowe and Shakespeare). Increasing evidence of homosexual behavior coincides with the rise of industrial Europe in the seventeenth century, but there is no consensus about the cause. Was it a delayed development of the Renaissance, the popularization of the notion that man is the measure of all things? Was it reaction against the legalistic restrictions of the Puritans (and later the Victorians)? Was it breakdown of the institution of the family due to industrialization and urbanization? All of these are candidates for a historical explanation, but we must qualify all by the impossibility of tracking change in sexual practices. What guesses we make about the past are informed by studies of influences in the present, and these influences may not have worked the same way a hundred—much less a thousand—years ago.

In the present, even those few societies that approve certain forms of same-sex behavior exclude homosexuality as we know it.[6] Some societies approve *transgenerational* homosexuality, where older members of a group engage in social intimacy and sex with younger members as a rite of passage into adulthood; *transgenderal* homosexuality, where people play out the gender role of the opposite sex (as in the *berdache* among Native American groups); and most rarely, *egalitarian* homosexuality, which a few cultures tolerate as a phase primarily between adolescents. Among the major world religions,[7] only Buddhism takes a neutral doctrinal stance toward homosexuality. Hinduism, Islam, Confucianism and Taoism join Judaism and Christianity in prohibiting the behavior. The Japanese have a history of tolerance, due primarily to the Shinto religion, which disdains women as essentially "polluted" (but necessary as vessels of conception). In China and Hindu India, whose people constitute half the world's population, homosexuality is virtually unknown except as a "Western vice."

Of course all of this is not to say that homosexuality does not exist in other times or cultures, nor that human practice always conforms to the official requirements of the prevailing religion. Nevertheless, it does suggest that the extent of practice may vary considerably from place to place and from time to time, and this in turn may imply that culture is one important variable in the formation of a person's sexual identity.

Biological Causation Theories

Much media attention has been given to a number of recent attempts by researchers to associate homosexual behavior with certain brain structures, hormones or genes. Such biological explanations may relate to one another, since brain structures may develop under the influence of hormones, which in turn operate under instructions from the genetic code. The research is only beginning, and the early theories that have garnered much media attention have not yet withstood the crucial test of replication by other researchers. If a Lost Island of Biologic Causation exists out there, separate researchers may have spotted the mountaintops, the jungle or the seacoast, but there is much map work yet to do. For reasons I will describe below, no consensus exists in the scientific community even that the island is discoverable.

In 1991 neurobiologist S. LeVay dissected the brains of thirty-five male cadavers, including those of nineteen known homosexual men who had died of AIDS, and discovered that a part of the hypothalamus in the brains of the homosexual men (INAH3) was on average smaller than that of the other men and the same size as that of women.[8] The study awaits replication, but there are problems with LeVay's finding itself, especially with the notion that it proves prenatal sexual orientation.[9] The sample size was small, and six of the other sixteen males dissected for comparison died of AIDS, which raises questions about their heterosexuality (LeVay had no information on this). It is very possible that AIDS had affected the volume of the INAH3 in the homosexual subjects by reducing testosterone levels during the latter stages of the disease.

If LeVay's result is replicated by another study that includes homosexuals without AIDS, we must still ask if the volume of the INAH3 influences sexual behavior or is influenced by it. We do know that male and female brains develop differently in the crucial early childhood period—as late as four years—and throughout life, with social as well as chemical factors affecting such development.[10] If, on the other hand, the hypothalamus does exert an influence on sexual behavior, we must ask about the strength of that influence. Although the hypothalamus affects the sexual behavior of rodents, the particular region of the hypothalamus in question is not clearly related; and even if researchers can establish a relation, we cannot compare human sexual behavior to that of rodents. I hope it is not insulting to rats—a species I admire greatly in many respects—to suggest that intelligence, culture, training, experience, moral reflection and the operations of God's Spirit make human sexuality far more complex than what we might explain by analogy to the secretions of a rodent's hypothalamus.

A year after the publication of LeVay's study, the research team of L. S. Allen and R. A. Gorski reported that a cluster of nerve fibers between the hemispheres of the brain, the anterior commissure, was on average larger in thirty-four homosexual men.[11] Although this part of the brain has no known connection to sexual behavior, some researchers suspect a connection to the fact that homosexual men are much more likely to be left-handed, dyslexic and stutterers—all factors related to the development of the brain hemispheres.[12] Scientists cannot explore the significance of this finding without replication. The only other study of the size of the anterior commissure in relation to sex got the opposite result.[13] Furthermore, Allen and Gorski's *average* result disguises the tremendous variation *within* their sample, which involved significant overlap with the heterosexual group.[14] Finally, their reliance on subjects with AIDS raises the same questions about the direction of the influence as LeVay's study of the hypothalamus.

Numerous studies of current hormone levels in homosexuals have failed to turn up any difference from heterosexuals.[15] Prenatal hormonal secretions have been found to influence later sexual postures among rodents, but they do not have the same influence in primates, and they are much more difficult to apply to the complexity and diversity of human sexuality.[16] The consensus even among scientists who suspect a prenatal or early postnatal hormonal influence on sexual orientation is that the influence is not clearly defined, and it certainly does not *cause* or *determine* orientation.[17]

Genetic studies of sexuality made the news following the publication of the twin research of J. M. Bailey and J. C. Pillard.[18] Comparing 110 homosexual men who were monozygotic (identical) and dizygotic (fraternal) twins, Bailey and Pillard found that 52 percent of the monozygotic subjects but only 22 percent of the dizygotic subjects had homosexual twins, while the rate of homosexuality among nontwin brothers was 9.2 percent. Comparing 108 women, J. M. Bailey and fellow researchers found that 48 percent of the monozygotic subjects but only 16 percent of the dizygotic subjects had homosexual twins, while the rate of homosexuality among nontwin sisters was 14 percent.[19] Another recent study obtained similar results.[20]

If these rates are accurate, they appear to indicate some kind of genetic association—about half the time, at least—since only monozygotic twins share the same genetic material. Nevertheless, as W. Byne and B. Parsons point out, there are several flaws in these studies. There is some doubt about the representativeness of the samples, since the researchers recruited subjects by solicitation through homosexual organizations and publications. Other twin studies contradict Bailey and Pillard's results, including a recent study that found 25 percent monozygotic and 12.5 percent dizygotic concordance.[21] The double rate of dizygotic twins as compared to nontwin siblings makes no genetic sense, since dizygotic twins share no more genetic material with one another than with other siblings. In fact, this result and the high rate of homosexuality among nontwin siblings as compared to the general population point to shared *environmental* rather than biological factors.[22] And of course, if the cup of concordance is half full, it is also half empty, leaving researchers to wonder why *all* monozygotic twins do not share a sexual orientation.[23]

Less than a year after the Bailey twin studies, a research team led by D. Hamer published a report of their link of male homosexuality to a small stretch of DNA on the X chromosome.[24] The "gay gene," as it became known in the media, was in reality not a gene at all but an observation that thirty-three of forty pairs of homosexual nontwin brothers had homosexual relatives on their maternal sides that were traced to DNA markers in the same chromosome region, called Xq28.

The reactions of the scientific community have ranged from cautious optimism (accompanied by calls for replication and extension of the research) to strong criticism. The first problem is the missing theoretical gene itself: millions of base-pairs reside in the Xq28 region, and as yet no gene has been isolated—if indeed there is only one. The researchers obtained little information from presumably heterosexual relatives,[25] and they provided no control group data,[26] leading to speculation that the gene may occur (how widely?) without being "switched on" (why not?) in the general population.[27] Furthermore, if the determinant of homosexuality is genetic, why did seven pairs of brothers not show it? Was the sample size large enough? Similar theories about depression, schizophrenia and alcoholism have come and gone after further research failed to confirm initial findings.[28]

Finally, correlation between a gene and homosexuality does not equal causation. The gene(s) might, for example, increase the tendency of twin brothers to identify with one another, so that when one becomes homosexual the other is likely to follow suit.[29] Another possibility is a gene that influences novelty seeking, harm avoidance, or dependence—traits that might interact with the child's environment to encourage certain behaviors.[30] Alternately, the gene(s) might give mothers a tendency to smother their sons—a phenomenon traditionally associated with "nurture" rather than "nature" theories.[31]

I review here only the more publicized of a number of interesting biological approaches to sexual orientation. The field of research is in its infancy—even the questions are still in formation—and results carry unprecedented emotional and political baggage. Columbia University psychiatrists Byne and Parsons offer this summary of their review of the present state of the research:

> There is no evidence at present to substantiate a biologic theory, just as there is no compelling evidence to support any singular psychosocial explanation. While all behavior must have an ultimate biologic substrate, the appeal of current biologic explanations may derive more from dissatisfaction with the present status of psychosocial explanations than from a substantiating body of experimental data. Critical review shows the evidence favoring a biologic theory to be lacking.[32]

Nor is it only the scientific community that is slow to jump onto the biologic bandwagon. Homosexuals themselves express concern that isolation of a gene may eventually lead to genetic surgery to "correct" homosexuality, or in the interim, discovery of the genetic trait through amniocentesis and then abortion of the homosexual fetus. It would be an interesting turn of events to see homosexual activists join prolife demonstrators outside family-planning clinics.

But there is another twist already at work that will surprise many readers. That is, a large component of homosexual activists applaud biologic causation theories for their effect on public opinion[33] but are philosophically committed to *personal choice* as opposed to any deterministic theory, biologic or environmental. Consider, for example, the perspective of Darrel Yates Rist, cofounder of the Gay and Lesbian Alliance Against Defamation:

> In the summer of 1991, the journal *Science* reported anatomical differences between the brains of homosexual and heterosexual men. The euphoric media—those great purveyors of cultural myths—drove the story wildly. . . . Reporters seized triumphantly on the renewed presumption that we humans are not responsible for our sexual choices any more than for whatever else we choose to do, that we are chromosomally driven to everything. . . . But [LeVay's work], like all such research, is a futile attempt to convince people who intuitively know better that under no circumstances can their children be lured by queer ideas if the urge is not embedded in their brains from birth. . . .
>
> In the end, science may well discover some way to describe the intricate play of genes and environment that entices any of us to make the subtle choices throughout our lives that lead us to our particular expressions, sexual or otherwise, in a conformity-laden culture. Fine. Ultimately, though, it seems to me cowardly to abnegate our individual responsibility for the construction of sexual desires. Rather, refusing the expedient lie and insisting instead on the right to fulfill ourselves affectionately—in whatever direction our needs compel us, however contrary to the social norm they may be—is both honest and courageous, an act of utter freedom.[34]

Of course Rist would not applaud the assumptions or conclusions of this book, and I want to qualify this quotation carefully. Rist contends, for example, that all of us are essentially bisexual, and that heterosexuals hide behind biologic causation to ward off their own homoerotic fantasies. My point in quoting him is to show that discussion of biologic causation is not a simple matter of Tradition versus Science. In my own case, for example, I argue generally for a traditional moral stance, but I am persuaded (notwithstanding the cautious treatment above) that the biologic theories hold sufficient promise to count as one of several probable influences on an individual's sexual behavior. It is the *exclusive* explanation, sometimes called "biological essentialism," that appears to go much farther than the incomplete and conflicting evidence will allow.

Social Constructionism

In some senses the exact opposite of biological essentialism is the notion that the individual is a vessel waiting for culture and environment to fill it—a social mechanism as opposed to a biological mechanism. I beg the indulgence of specialists as I choose to generalize in this section; others should note that there is diversity in this approach which readers may discover by following up on my sources.[35]

Social constructionism begins with the premise that sexual conduct is social in origin; that is, people learn sexuality as they learn everything else. Sex differences come with birth, gender differences ("masculine" and "feminine") are entirely a matter of training, and sexual conduct is shaped by social forces. Historically, the evidence for this is in the diversity of sexual conduct and attitudes toward it throughout history and across cultures. Constructionists do not necessarily argue from this that sexual rules are so arbitrary that they can change whenever the people in power change,[36] but neither are such rules tied to moral traditions or universal boundaries. Rather, each culture produces its own limits on change by means of the interplay of tradition, religion, politics and other factors. Homosexuality as we know it—that is, long-term relationships of mutual consent between adults—simply did not exist before the nineteenth century, when it was invented by scientists to create a pathological *condition* out of a rarely practiced *behavior* (previously known primarily as "sodomy"). The construction of the condition made it possible for increasing numbers of people to identify with it, and eventually to react against its pathological status.

This brief historical treatment enables us to explain how, generally and sociologically speaking, an individual homosexual identity is formed. There are four stages: sensitization, identity confusion, identity assumption and commitment. First, before puberty, everyone thinks of themselves as heterosexual, but some people are *sensitized* by feelings of marginality (perceptions of being different from others of the same sex, typically "tomboyish" or "sissy"). During adolescence a person may begin to associate this marginality with homosexuality, enduring years of *confusion* and various coping strategies to deal with negative self-perceptions, diverse sexual experiences, social stigma and ignorance about homosexuality. In late adolescence the individual may progress to *identity assumption*, a stage characterized by acceptance of homosexuality and extensive social and sexual association with other homosexuals. Finally the individual may experience *commitment*, a stage that usually continues to develop over a lifetime and involves satisfaction with the homosexual identity, long-term homosexual relationships and free disclosure to nonhomosexuals.

Criticisms of social constructionist theory depend to some extent on the degree to which the particular theorist discounts other factors. Some theorists are quite chauvinistic about the discipline, reducing all truth to sociological terms and reducing people to passive receptacles for cultural influences. As in the case of biological causation theories, then, social constructionism can be deterministic; that is, it can imply that behavior is caused by invisible, impersonal forces over which the individual has no control.

At the individual level, while constructionism might offer a plausible description of the process of homosexual identity formation, the approach seems vague when it comes to the causes behind the process, especially in the early stages. For example, what trips the trigger to cause one person to resolve sexual identity confusion in a certain way? Or to begin further back, why and how does a parent socialize one infant in such a way that gender nonconformity results? Are infants really blank slates on which ideas of masculine and feminine are written by whoever happens to hold the chalk?

Obviously, the sociological answers to such questions often compete directly with biological answers—and both compete with the notion that individual reflection and will are significantly involved at some points.

Early Childhood Environment

The most common "nurture" theories of homosexual causation focus on deep disturbances in the parent-child relationship during the first few years of life.[37] In the classical psychoanalytic explanation, every child moves toward the parent of the opposite sex, and the inevitable frustration of that desire leads the child to resolve the conflict by turning to the same-sex parent (this is called "Oedipal resolution" and usually occurs around age four). But for prehomosexuals something goes wrong with the relationship with the same-sex parent, and the individual remains in sexual immaturity or incompleteness, desiring the same sex and (often unconsciously) hostile toward the opposite sex.

Not all "developmental" theories employ psychoanalytic language, but all benefit from a massive amount of data that associate adult male homosexuality with the presence in childhood of a distant, unavailable and rejecting father and an intensely affectionate, domineering, intimate mother.[38] Alternately, the loss of a parent through death or divorce may disturb the parent-child relationship. Interestingly, in the case of both male and female homosexuals the loss of the *father* by death or divorce occurs at an unusual rate. M. T. Saghir and E. Robins, for example, found that 18 percent of homosexual men and 35 percent of homosexual women had lost their father by death or divorce before the age of ten.[39]

Perhaps as an outgrowth of such early trauma, the child may begin to manifest cross-gender behavior in the preadolescent years. Although few homosexual adults conform to the stereotypical effeminate male or masculine female, the vast majority (up to 70 percent) describe themselves as having been "sissies" or "tomboys" as children.[40] Interestingly, during childhood those who are perceived as tomboys are generally content to be female, while those who are perceived as sissies typically want to be girls. This is almost certainly due to the fact that culture stigmatizes sissies but not tomboys, and it may in turn help to explain the relative numbers of male versus female homosexuals. The male child in this situation may be socialized as a girl by associating with them, and since the girls grow up desiring boys, so does he. Alternately, he may long for love from men, having grown up being rejected by them.

The different statistics about parental loss and acceptance of tomboy status are two indications that development of a homosexual identity in women may not occur as the exact reverse of development for men.[41] Other differences include the high rate of childhood sexual trauma among women who become lesbians[42] and of course the different ways in which women desire and express sexuality (whether these are learned or innate).

The upshot is that in the case of *both* male and female homosexuals, the problem of nurture may involve a difficulty in reconciliation with maleness. Certainly this is the dominant explanation for developmental theorists in the case of homosexual men, whose desire as an adult is not to be a woman but to identify with a man. Sexual desire is an understandable outgrowth of this intense need, but sexual satisfaction does not meet the underlying need. For many homosexual men the cycle of need, temporary fix through sexual gratification, and deeper frustration sets the psychological stage for obsessive and compulsive sexual behavior, most often in the form of promiscuity.

Critics of developmental theory, like critics of biological theories, point to the inconsistency of research results and to the cases that fail to fit the theory. How do we explain the person whose parents were well-adjusted, who experienced no childhood trauma, who exhibited no preadolescent cross-gender behavior and who nevertheless ends up with (and perhaps remembers nothing but) a homosexual preference? Moreover, is the evidence for early childhood trauma really so overwhelming? It is for the most part based on the impressions of therapists or the distant memories of their subjects, and as such it may be manufactured to fit the theory of the moment.[43] With regard to parents themselves, several scholars have recently chosen the egg over the chicken, maintaining that same-sex parents *react* to prehomosexual children by becoming distant and ineffectual.[44] Thus developmental theorists themselves may read the same data in different ways. Others may even reread their own discipline: some psychoanalysts have mutinied, arguing that the discipline must be weaned of negative terminology like "Oedipal failure" and "immaturity" in order to make it clear that "one's positive sense of self and capacity for full relatedness are the salient issues, not the gender of one's attachments."[45] In this brave new world not even Sigmund Freud is sacred.

Moral Environment

While it does not compete for space in the current professional literature on the etiology (causation) of homosexuality, the moral environment merits acknowledgment as an influential factor in the formation of individual sexuality. The human conscience is no less real for being rather ambiguous. To some people it is nothing more than a little voice in the back of the head whispering the rules of childhood training—the last voice heard, perhaps, before one enters the oblivion of passion. To others it is the product of deliberate and mature ethical reflection.

Scripture affirms that the conscience of a Christian is subject to "cleansing" by God's Spirit (Heb 9:14, 22; 1 Pet 3:21), which I understand to mean that God operates in and through experiences to develop a greater facility for moral discernment (see, for example, Col 1:9-10; Heb 5:14).

Some people, through no merit of their own, end up in family or church or educational or marital environments that stimulate and reward moral strength and maturity. Other people recognize their need for such stimuli and choose to place themselves in edifying surroundings, to read good books, to strive prayerfully for growth, to practice goodness. The wise know that righteousness does not develop in a social or spiritual vacuum. They know that conscience is contagious.

It would be a mistake, then, even in the midst of a review of secular etiological theories—*especially* in the midst of such a review—to leave out the influence of conscience in the formation of an individual's sexual identity. If the moral environment of a person sends the message that anything goes, anything just might. Alternately, if the moral environment of a person is shallow and repressive, that person may rebel against rules that seem as empty as the people who try to enforce them. If, on the other hand, the moral environment of a person contains deeply held, lovingly reinforced, reasonably maintained principles to guide sexual behavior, that person is likely to act in accordance with those principles.

Behavioral Reinforcement

Akin in some ways to social constructionist theory, behavioral psychology maintains that we learn about sexuality (and everything else) by reinforcement of experiences.[46] Unlike most psychoanalytic or developmental approaches, behaviorism assigns no values to environment or behavior. It simply observes that people seek to repeat pleasurable experiences and to avoid painful experiences. Whenever reinforcement is immediate, as it often is (either negatively or positively) in the case of sex, it is especially powerful in establishing future patterns of behavior.

Very basic erotic experiences with the same sex may begin in infancy if the child strongly associates the same-sex parent with stimulation of the genitals during bathing or diaper changing. Later, parents may discover a child "playing doctor" and react so harshly that the child associates the opposite sex with pain. Many boys are seduced by men or engage in sex play with other boys and enjoy the experience; some make it the basis of sexual fantasy until they begin to define themselves as homosexual and turn to the behavior as adults. Others of both sexes have negative opposite-sex experiences and turn to members of their own sex for pleasure (this is more common and occurs later in life for women). Others simply lack access to members of the opposite sex.

After some pleasurable experiences with members of the same sex, negative reinforcement in the form of social stigma attached to homosexuality may turn some people back to heterosexuality, or at least to the compromise of bisexuality. But others manage to persist in homosexuality by surrounding themselves with the reinforcements of a long-term companion, a network of supportive friends and a positive self-image.

Behaviorist psychology is subject to the some of the same criticisms as social constructionist theory. More specifically, it fails to account fully for the reasons that one person might experiment in one direction, another in the opposite direction. In addition, it appears to discount will and reflection, reducing human activity to a series of reactions to external stimuli. Partly as a result, behaviorism has developed a notorious reputation, especially among homosexual activists, for its therapy techniques, especially those that accomplish aversion through physical punishment for homoerotic responses.[47]

Excursus: Can Homosexuals Be Recruited?

It is apparent from what we have seen thus far that the formation of a homosexual identity is too complex in most cases to result merely from seduction by a homosexual. Popular fears of recruitment by schoolteachers, for example, may be exaggerated. Still, there is some evidence for concern about recruitment in childhood and early adolescence, and this evidence may be consistent with several of the theories outlined above.

In chapter six I cited data showing that there is a disproportionate problem of sexual molestation of children among male homosexuals. Having been molested in itself does not necessarily have a direct correlation to the sexual identity of a boy. Nevertheless, it is disturbing to find that although under 4 percent of boys are molested by men, a recent major study found that the rate of childhood molestation by men among homosexual or bisexual men was nearly ten times that (35 percent).[48] It is also notable that 75 percent of homosexual men report their first homosexual experience prior to the age of sixteen, as compared to 22 percent of heterosexual men reporting their first heterosexual experience.[49]

A variety of explanations might account for this. From a biologic or developmental perspective, one might argue that prehomosexual children are more likely to be targets for molestation. From a sociological or behaviorist perspective, one might argue that children who have such experiences are more likely to experience confusion over their sexual identity and later to define themselves as homosexuals. From the perspective of the moral environment, one might argue that a society with an increasingly value-neutral view of homosexual behavior will provide fewer and weaker checks on those who associate early homosexual experience with a homosexual identity.

On top of all this, the liberalization of attitudes toward pedophilia and increasing rates of molestation (approved or not) contribute to an ever-larger pool of children who are candidates for influence. Moreover, I have considered only the impact of sexual *experience* on the young. We must also consider the impact of increasingly widespread and intrusive value-neutral or prohomosexual *education*.

As the history and comparison of cultures shows, there is not a constant percentage of homosexual people simply waiting to be born into every society, unaffected by discouraging or encouraging factors. To the extent that childhood and adolescent homosexual experience and education contribute to the formation of a homosexual identity, we must take very seriously the influence of those who, in one way or another, recruit the young.

Individual Choice

Some who object to the deterministic extremes of some biological and sociological theorists take the opposite extreme, arguing that orientation is a self-justifying myth and that homosexuality is a choice, pure and simple. As I noted at the beginning of this chapter, there is in fact a moment when an individual must choose whether or not to have sex with another person. There are also conditions under which a person might engage in same-sex acts without being driven by a long-standing or deeply felt desire for such actions. Prison inmates, for example, commonly engage in same-sex acts without considering themselves homosexuals and without continuing the activity after they leave prison and find opposite-sex partners. Adolescents and counterculture types may choose same-sex acts as a dramatic expression of independence, individuality or freedom from authority. Others may experiment out of curiosity or fascination with the forbidden. Some feminists find that the logical conclusion of their rejection of patriarchal culture is to seek fulfillment in all important areas of life, including the sexual, within the sisterhood.

These are some of the most common circumstances in which a person might choose homosexual activity, at least for a time, without having an inclination influenced by biology, socialization, environment or early reinforcement. The truth is that a person who elects to leave the paved road of heterosexual monogamy may find many paths that lead to sexual gratification. Still, I think that we must make a distinction between those who leave the road thinking to find something better out there and those for whom the road is a strange and objectionable place. That is, there appears to be sufficient evidence that some people do not desire physical intimacy with members of the opposite sex, and they do desire intimacy with members of their own sex. Furthermore, some people have known this desire for as long as they can remember.

I hesitate to call this an *orientation*—a word I have for the most part avoided in this book—because for many people the word has come to imply an inevitable, and therefore justified, behavior. In other words, many think that *orientation* indicates what a person *is*—and of course, the argument goes, we must *act* according to who we *are*. Thus, in two easy steps, it becomes not only morally justifiable but almost morally obligatory for a person with a homosexual orientation to engage in homosexual activity.

The fallacy here lies in the equation of sexual orientation with *being*. Whatever Freud and Foucault and most advertisers may think, the desire for sex is neither central nor necessary to anyone's being.[50] It should not control the person. My truck has a four-wheel drive; however, I should not expect to avoid a citation by explaining to the highway patrol that my vehicle was exploring the freeway embankment because I was being *driven* by my *drive!* Similarly, when I use the term *orientation* I mean only what a person *desires,* not what a person has a right to do, much less what a person is compelled to do as an expression of his or her being.

A Multiple-Variant Model

With tedious repetition, proponents of the various etiological theories call for further research to establish a clear link between the data and their theory. This approach may keep the grant money flowing, but it is highly unlikely that enough evidence will appear to establish any one theory at the expense of all others. To some extent each theory depends on unrecoverable information from the past or from the mysterious workings of the human mind. And to some extent each theory is an apple to the orange of another. For example, does evidence that some people have a genetic disposition rule out the possibility that others may be socialized? Furthermore, if one study shows that fifty of one hundred subjects are genetically disposed and another shows that fifty of one hundred subjects are socialized, does that mean that the two theories account for all cases—or do both theories explain the same fifty? Perhaps it is inevitable that in reaction to so many unanswered or unanswerable questions, some scholars are turning to combined causation theories.[51] It seems to me that this is not merely a concession to confusion but a fair assessment of the complexity of causation. In other words, if it were possible to set aside the emotion and politics associated with various theories, we would probably find several influences at work in various strengths for any one individual.

So rather than to push one explanation or to rule out another, I will propose a model that treats them equally and sequentially. Such a model necessarily oversimplifies, since variables may vary in strength or direction for any one individual. My purpose is simply to show one way in which different theories might work together. In figure 1 (page 152), the underlined terms represent theories of influence or causation in the sequence described above. On either side of each theory are specific variables that allow for (right side) or impede (left side) movement to the next category of influence.

In a simple sequential view, each variable allows for movement to the next. Suppose, for the purpose of illustration, that a boy with a biological disposition to gender nonconforming behavior is born in a confused culture that associates such behavior with homosexuality. The boy has a dysfunctional family in which the mother is overwhelming and the father is ineffectual. The boy grows up with no more moral training than is necessary to keep him out of trouble at home or in school. He experiments with same-sex relations as an adolescent and finds pleasure and companionship. As he enters adulthood, he chooses to move to a large city where he can build a life within the homosexual subculture.

At any point the introduction of a strong contrary variable might stop the succession. If, for example, the boy was born into a traditional culture, or if his dysfunctional family was exchanged for a functional one, or if he experienced a powerful conversion into a mature Christian community as an early

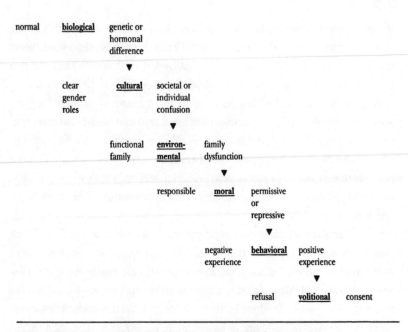

Figure 1. Multiple variable model for homosexual identity formation

adolescent, his adult sexual identity might be heterosexual.

I repeat, however, that the model I outline is too simple to account for every case. Levels might be skipped, or one variable might be present in sufficient strength to overcome the absence of others. Another boy, for example, might have no disposition prior to an adolescent sexual experience that convinces him that he is a homosexual. Another might exhibit such a high level of effeminacy from early childhood that all the input of a functional family and a supportive moral environment fail to protect him from the societal assumption (and eventual self-perception) that he is a sissy and therefore a homosexual. Yet another might experience every influence in the direction of homosexuality but finally, at the level of volition, might say to himself, "No, this is simply too dangerous," and choose against it.[52]

The combinations and relative strengths of the variables make for an almost infinite variety of explanations. To apply any one theory to any one individual, therefore, is almost certainly simplistic. The multiple-variant model itself is intended to aid conceptualization, not to explain particular cases, because faulty memory and guesswork about variable strengths will always cloud the picture. Nevertheless, even an admittedly cloudy picture is better than no picture when we consider the powerful drive to understand and accept one's sexual identity—or to change it.

Therapy and Healing Programs: Trick or Treatment?

Strategies for helping individuals to alter homosexual behavior or orientation differ according to the opinion of the counselor about whether homosexuality is in itself a disorder and, if so, what theory of causation applies. In the past twenty years the official stance of the American Psychiatric Association has changed from the position that homosexuality is a mental disorder, to the position that it is only a disorder when the subject does not want it, to the position that it is never a disorder.[53] Most of the current literature and education focuses on the need to help homosexuals embrace their sexuality and cope with homophobia.[54] Counselors now cooperate with schools and businesses to provide (often compulsory) sensitivity training against heterosexism. Increasing numbers of therapists join homosexual activists to proclaim that homosexuality is immutable, that so-called change is a myth or a temporary and cruel imposition on the lives of a few vulnerable individuals.[55] Some within the American Psychiatric Association are now calling for an official ban on reparative therapy.[56]

Against this pressure, many secular therapists persist in offering help to clients who wish to change. Leadership in this endeavor is supplied by the National Association for Research and Therapy of Homosexuality (NARTH), founded in 1991 by prominent psychiatrists C. W. Socarides and B. Kaufmann. Researchers who have conducted follow-up studies report success rates of 30-50 percent for long-term significant change in behavior or orientation.[57]

For example, W. Masters and V. Johnson conducted a study of fifty-four men and thirteen women who expressed a desire to convert or revert to a heterosexual orientation.[58] Therapists chose candidates for their apparently high degree of motivation and for their accompaniment by an understanding opposite-sex partner who could serve as a support during the transition period. The treatment format consisted of an intensive two-week program followed by periodic follow-up over a five-year period. The client couple worked with a man-woman therapy team who focused on nonjudgmental identification and explanation of the influences that had led to the client's homosexual behavior. The therapists then worked to reduce these influences within the context of the clients' value system and to encourage heterosexual function on the part of the client couple. About 20 percent failed during the initial treatment period, but the five-year follow-up revealed no more than a 30-45 percent total failure rate, much lower than even Masters and Johnson had expected.[59]

Behavioral therapy, consistent with the behaviorist theory of causation, involves immediate negative reinforcement of homosexual responses in the client and positive reinforcement of heterosexual responses. In the early days of behavioral therapy, the former technique, also known as aversion therapy, sometimes involved physical punishment. These methods proved ineffective and were abandoned, although they live on in the graphic accusations of revisionists that compare therapy to Auschwitz.[60] Modern behaviorist techniques involve trained accomplices, visual stimuli, role-playing, assertiveness training and a variety of verbal and nonverbal reinforcement techniques on the part of the therapists themselves.[61]

Another strategy for therapy finds such efforts to replace same-sex function with opposite-sex function misplaced and actually counterproductive, since the essential problem is an arrested development that renders the client unable to relate to the *same* sex in appropriate ways.[62] In this strategy the client must work on identity formation with a same-sex therapist to reestablish the long-detached identification with the same-sex parent and to develop appropriate, nonsexual same-sex friendships.

Client motivation is of course a major factor in all success reports. Other positive variables include youth (under thirty), anxiety over the homosexual condition, recent onset of homosexual activity, some heterosexual experience, lower level of effeminacy in men or masculinity in women, higher education level, loneliness and desire for marriage and children.[63]

Christian therapy programs borrow much from secular therapy techniques (especially psychotherapy) and from recovery programs like Alcoholics Anonymous. An example of this multifaceted approach is the Spring Forth Ministry[64] in Cincinnati, which involves a six-month to two-and-a-half-year program of small group (no one-on-one) counseling, personal history disclosure, personality inventory, twelve-step support groups, and repeatable courses on family systems and Christian thought. After hearing director Hal Scholl's moving story and description of his program at a recent conference, I was quick to ask the obvious question about success rates. He responded candidly that the dropout rate is high. In fifteen years, about twelve hundred have persevered through the program; but for every one who stays for the duration, twenty drift in and out. On the other hand, he noted that the success rates are similar to those for chemical dependency programs.

During the ensuing discussion among conferees, a profound statement on the subject of success rates was made by one conferee, a former homosexual now ten years out of the lifestyle. He explained that "homosexual activists want to convince not only the public but *themselves* that change never occurs, because *if I exist, each of them must be haunted by the possibility that they, too, might find the power to change.*"

Despite the accusations of critics that Christian ministries to homosexuals are led by unprofessional manipulators who make grandiose false claims for the success of their methods, I think the fair-minded observer will conclude otherwise. As numerous books by ministry leaders show, their focus is on changed behavior, they are honest about the probability of ongoing temptations, and they recognize that growth is a lifelong process, not a quick fix. Of course they accentuate the positive and give examples of success (including themselves), because they are trying to offer encouragement to struggling people. They do not provide "scientific" statistics on success rates, but I am not sure that it would mean much if they did. Skeptics might counter any attempt to provide numbers of people who change their *behavior* with the accusation that such people are lying or that they are damaging themselves by repressing their orientation. Similarly, skeptics might counter any attempt to provide numbers of people who change their *orientation* with the accusation that the change is not permanent, not complete or not verifiable by client self-reporting (which is the result of brainwashing) or counselor impression (which is the result of wishful thinking).

These kinds of accusations are also leveled against respected secular therapists, and the accusations allow revisionists to propagate the non sequitur that since reparation has not been empirically verified (according to their impossible standards), reparation is a myth.[65] It is an easy step from that point to call for the marginalization or criminalization of anyone who attempts to perpetuate the myth by effecting change—especially if they do so in an "unprofessional" manner.

It would be interesting to apply the same logic to Alcoholics Anonymous (which, incidentally, refuses to keep statistics). Statistics may be useful to measure observable events, but they are notoriously imprecise in measuring human wills, thoughts and desires. However frustrating this may be, especially to some social scientists, it is not legitimate to conclude from our inability to prove one thing (complete change from homosexual to heterosexual orientation) that we have proved something else (the impossibility of at least substantial change).

The testimonies of real people whose lives have changed suggest that the distinctive of the Christian counseling approach is *power* and the *Person* through whom it is offered. There is a crucial point in therapy where a counselor must attempt to instill strength in the client to take the insights gained in therapy out into the real world. Support groups often help, but there are moments when every person must face temptation and opportunity without other people around to lean on. In the Christian perspective, the ultimate Counselor is always present with the offer of power, forgiveness, hope—and even a healthy model of fatherhood.

I have been greatly impressed by the counseling insights of several Christian writers and the loving spirit in which they communicate their wisdom. They write with the authority of counseling experience—in some cases personal homosexual experience—and as a result their words are alive with hope. The primary purpose of my book is to treat the moral question, and I would do injustice to these other writers by repeating in brief what they communicate more powerfully in detail, especially through real-life stories. I will simply draw attention to the distinctive features of the books I consider the best, with the hope that my brief comments will aid the reader in choosing a more specific direction for further reading.

Leanne Payne's *The Broken Image*[66] stresses the role of specific kinds of prayer to produce forgiveness and relational healing. The book emanates a true healer's loving insight and substantial experience. I had the unforgettable experience of meeting Payne on a park bench in Oxford, England, before I knew the significance of her work. Within minutes I was aware that I was in the presence of an extraordinarily deep channel of God's love. I was prepared by that two-hour conversation to be impressed by her book, and I was not disappointed.

Andrew Comiskey, who acknowledges Payne as a primary influence, wrote one of the most popular books on homosexual healing, *Pursuing Sexual Wholeness.*[67] Comiskey, himself a former homosexual and now a married father of four children, heads the Los Angeles-area Desert Stream Ministry. He offers a refreshingly honest account of his own journey, and he focuses on support and accountability within the Christian community for the person who is making a transition from homosexuality.

Coming Out of Homosexuality,[68] by Bob Davies and Lori Rentzel, is notable not so much for insights beyond those of Payne and Comiskey as for its thoroughness and readability. Davies found help for his struggle with homosexual desires through the San Francisco Love in Action ministry fifteen years ago and is now executive director of Exodus International; Rentzel has worked with Love in Action since 1977. Their book contains a wealth of practical details on coping with temptation, dealing with the past, forming healthy friendships and considering marriage.

I will make brief reference to a few more helpful books. Michael Saia's *Counseling the Homosexual*[69] offers many of the insights of the books described above, with a somewhat more theological flavor. J. R. Cavanaugh's *Counseling the Homosexual*[70] gives a Roman Catholic perspective and stresses the importance of therapy to reduce guilt and to encourage heterosexuality. G. J. M. van den Aardweg's *Homosexuality and Hope*[71] stresses the roles of hope and faith for the person in transition. Finally, I recommend *How Do I Tell My Mother?*[72] the moving autobiography of Jerry Arterburn, written while he was dying of AIDS and supplemented by his brother Steve, who runs the New Life Treatment Center in Laguna Beach, California.

Conclusion

So I end the research portion of this book as I began it, with a survey of recent literature. The contrast between the books just mentioned and the revisionist literature summarized in chapter two is significant, and it leads to a recommendation.

Revisionists repeatedly stress the importance of personal stories over abstract theories. Although I maintained earlier, and I repeat here, that we should not separate story and theory, I will grant the separation for the moment. Compare stories. Consider the most articulate accounts of experience on each side of the moral debate. On one side, read the story of Mel White or Gary Comstock or Robert Williams, along with the prohomosexuality argument of experienced pastor/psychiatrist John McNeill.[73] On the other side, read the story of Andrew Comiskey or Bob Davies or Jerry Arterburn, along with the argument for homosexual healing of experienced pastor/ counselor Leanne Payne. At the very least, linger in a bookstore long enough to read the last two pages of each book.

Here you will have an "apples and apples" comparison—people long out of the closet alongside people long out of the lifestyle. No theorists like me writing from up in the ivory tower, but people who have spent considerable time down in their self-described dungeons, either of homophobia or of homosexuality. I submit that any sensitive reader, regardless of his or her position on the moral issue, will discover by reading these books in close sequence a marked difference not so much in the quality of the *arguments*— leave those to the ivory tower types for the moment—but in the qualities of the *writers*.

I will be more specific. In the first group of writers there is an unmistakable whine of victimization running through the narrative; in the second group there is an equally unmistakable psalm of release. The first group burns with rage; the second group glows with peace. In the first group the writer is invariably the hero; in the second group Jesus is invariably the hero. The first group openly proclaims the will to power, the spirit of self-actualization, the god of this age; the second group openly proclaims the will to serve, the Spirit of Jesus, the God of the age to come.

Can the pain of the writers justify the first set of qualities? To some extent, perhaps. Can deceivers or the self-deceived fake the second set of qualities? To some extent, perhaps. Are there other books out there yet to be written by irenic, humble homosexuals? I expect so: the movement is young. Are there other books out there written by homophobic conservatives with lousy attitudes? I am afraid so: the movement is old. Finally, is it really an "apples and apples" comparison to set the experience of resistance to cultural norms over against the experience of accession to cultural norms? Perhaps not: perhaps these different kinds of experience force us back to abstract and complex questions concerning the relative importance for Christians of the acquisition of justice and the renunciation of power.

And so the words of experience, like the theories of causation, leave us with difficult and perhaps unanswerable questions. In the meantime we are left to consider the best words we can find on both sides of the issue and to discern, with God's help, the spirit within them.

Having reached my own conclusions about the available words on the subject of healing, I end this chapter with what I consider some of the best words, from among the last published words of Jerry Arterburn. These words mark the final transition for one man, but they may apply prophetically to all who facilitate healing among homosexuals:

> Only God knows my future here on earth. I do not concern myself with how many days or months or years are in His plan. I only know I would rather live one day as I am today than for eternity the way I was. . . .
>
> For me, during these difficult times of struggle, as each day grows darker, a new dawn draws closer. That closeness to the God I love gives me a superhuman peace and sensitivity that keeps me filled with hope for a new and better day.[74]

8
STRAIGHT
& NARROW?

*A*s a child I was never satisfied with the parental response *"Because I said so"* when I challenged a command, and when my daughter was born I decided that I would always try to give her reasons that she could understand. I did not foresee that this noble endeavor would produce a forty-pound logician with a heavy arsenal of argumentative techniques, including quotation of contrary authorities, transformation of assertions into facts by sheer repetition, subtle alteration of evidence, selective memory of precedents and remarkably responsive tear ducts. These days her burgeoning powers are employed in causes like the extension of afternoon television beyond *Reading Rainbow*. In time the issues will become more serious and her arguments more persuasive. There will be pride on both sides, and the clashes will grow more intense. Still, I think that our disagreements will occur on the surface of an unshakable foundation of love and a history of *reasoned* authority. I think that parental love should work like that, because God's love works like that.

In my scholarly task, which is to ask "Why?" of biblical affirmations and demands, I am continually amazed at the way biblical morality flows from the wisdom of God and from the person and example of Jesus. This pattern has taught me to trust God's way even in the midst of my questioning, because his way may be narrow, but it is never narrow-minded.

Throughout this book, I have tried to convey the gracious firmness that I have seen in my heavenly Father and that I want to model in my role as an earthly father. The book's title plays on words often associated with conservative morality: in the current cultural climate, to require that people be *straight* rather than gay is to be perceived as *narrow*. I have tried to show that narrow options for sexual activity do not necessarily emanate from a narrow mind. At least, I hope that some of those who disagree with my conclusions will allow that those conclusions are credible—that is, they are reasoned implications from the available evidence.

Certainly my biases show at some points, as do those of revisionists at some points. But we get nowhere in moral debate merely by exposing each other's prejudices. We must evaluate each other's arguments, and we must do so in an atmosphere of respect. I hope that my effort will stimulate others to raise the level of debate to a clash of arguments rather than personalities, to a common concern for people rather than causes.

Summary Statements

After subjecting the reader to a closely packed argument that marches briskly over mounds of documentation, I think it will help to review the main points before discussing some of their implications for Christian practice.

1. Scripture must be the primary and final authority for sexual morality. While tradition, reason, experience and Scripture are all involved in the process of interpretation, only Scripture has the place of revelation among these conversation partners. The Bible, therefore, is not an equal partner but the teacher in the conversation. We cannot overrule its message without great risk of inconsistency and arbitrariness, which are evident in many revisionist proposals concerning homosexuality.

2. Homosexual acts, according to Romans 1:26-27 (and supported by several other biblical passages), depart from the only acceptable avenue for the full expression of sexuality, which is heterosexual marriage. The Genesis creation story provides the primary basis for a biblical perspective on sexuality, and both Jesus and Paul quote Genesis to support their affirmation of marriage as a permanent union between husband and wife. Paul's profound analysis of the human condition in Romans 1 maintains that homosexuality falsifies our identity as sexual beings, just as idolatry falsifies our identity as created beings. For Paul, homosexual behavior epitomizes, in sexual terms, the revolt of humanity against God. It is sinful because it violates the plan of God, present from creation, for the union of male and female in marriage.

A number of other biblical passages prohibit same-sex relations in a variety of forms, including rape, prostitution, pederasty and relationships of mutual consent. Some references are more general, and we may apply them to different practices. Revisionist attempts to isolate each text and show its dissimilarity to modern practice fail both because some texts defy such limitations and because details of practices and motivations miss the point, which is the relation of any sex act to the marital union of male and female.

3. Homosexual acts constitute an active negation of marriage, not merely a variant expression of sexuality. Homosexual acts convey rebellion against sexual differentiation, including its physical aspect, which is fundamental to human personhood. Such acts are, in their essence, untrue or incomplete with respect to the interdependent goods of physical complementarity, procreation and responsibility to the human community. While any of these goods considered alone might provide sufficient reason to prohibit homosexual acts, in combination they justify a distinction between homosexuality and legitimate variants like childlessness and celibacy.

4. Homosexual practice involves a high probability of harmful associated phenomena: promiscuity, substance abuse, depression, suicide and pedophilia. We may attribute some of these phenomena in part to the social stigma placed on homosexuals, but the nature of homosexuality itself is also implicated, especially with respect to promiscuity and pedophilia. In any case, the assignment of blame for these phenomena does not make them go away. They will certainly continue in the near term; and it is extremely unrealistic to expect, in the long term, ideal conditions of tolerance that might be supposed by some to eliminate any negative associated experiences.

5. Male homosexual acts involve practices that are injurious to the body and that involve a high risk of infectious disease. Oral-genital, genital-anal and oral-anal sex are responsible for a multifaceted health crisis of major proportions among homosexual men. More than a dozen common diseases, and a score of other problems, attest the fact that AIDS is only the most publicized and deadly of a variety of afflictions. Safe-sex education has not succeeded in reducing the general health problem or the specific problem of AIDS itself, which claims an ever-increasing number of homosexual men each year. The near certainty of health problems (together with the high probability of associated harms summarized above) requires the conclusion that characteristic homosexual practices involve sin against the body, both of the individual and of his partner.

6. While a homosexual orientation is probably caused for each individual by several factors in combination, at the level of action each person is morally accountable. There is no scholarly consensus about causation. Biological, sociological, developmental, moral, behavioral and volitional variables may all play a part in the formation of a homosexual identity. Several specific factors that may contribute are in themselves pathological or morally suspect: cultural turmoil, a dysfunctional family, alienation in childhood, molestation, permissiveness or repression, aversion to the opposite sex, and contentiousness. Whatever factors, negative or neutral, alone or in combination, may *explain* homosexual desires and actions, they can never *justify* homosexual desires and actions, because causation is not a moral category.

7. Change is possible. Scholars disagree about the degree to which a homosexual orientation might change to a heterosexual orientation. Because these disagreements are often guises for underlying moral arguments, and because there is no agreed-upon standard by which to measure altered desires, it is difficult to quantify change. Nevertheless, many secular therapists and Christian ministries witness to the possibility of substantial change, at least in behavior, for those who wish to change. Christian faith and Christian community in particular offer unique and powerful supports to people in transition.

Orientation and Sin

There are two important questions that I have waited until now to address. The first is the question of responsibility: is a person with homosexual desires condemned for the inclination or orientation? I can respond to this question only by considering the nature of God's judgment.

God wants me to be good, but in assessing my goodness, he is not interested in how I measure up to a universal standard, and he is certainly not interested in how much better I am than my neighbor. Rather, God is interested in how much better I am than I used to be. This truth should make me very cautious in my general assessment of another person, because I do not know that person's starting point with God. Another Christian may be six inches behind me on the yardstick of righteousness, but I have no way of knowing whether that person started two inches ahead of me or eighteen inches behind. It may be a greater act of obedience for a pedophile, calling on the power of God for self-control, to abstain from one act of molestation than for a missionary doctor, acting from a habit of godly obedience, to save the lives of a dozen sick children.

Make no mistake: this perspective does not alter *morality*. Pederasty is always wrong, a movement backward on the yardstick; and charity is always right, a movement forward. Furthermore, I have a responsibility to proclaim morality and to hold fellow believers accountable (1 Cor 5:11-13). This perspective on God's judgment, then, does not alter my ability to assess another person's *actions*, but it does alter my ability to assess another person's *heart*.

Applying this perspective to my inclinations to sexual sin, I understand that God takes me wherever I am and begins to remake me. The raw material with which he works involves a combination of attitudes, inclinations and habits, and each of those may involve a combination of nature, nurture, cooperation and initiation on my part. It is impossible, and probably meaningless, to assign a degree of personal choice to a sexual desire. It is not helpful, therefore, to talk about the sinfulness of an orientation in the same way that we talk about the sinfulness of an action.

That is not to say that our orientations are morally neutral, but only that we do not choose them in the way that we choose actions. A sexual *desire* may involve different levels of responsibility for different people, and in that invisible and complex realm only God is qualified to assign culpability. According to Romans 2:14-16, God judges each person according to the operation of that person's conscience in relation to that person's actions. If we see anything at all, it is only a person's actions, and so it is appropriate that we leave the evaluation of orientation or desire to God and focus on the rightness or wrongness of behavior.

A sexual act may qualify as sinful simply because it occurs outside the context of marriage. This does not mean that all sexual acts inside the context of marriage are good, nor does it mean that all extramarital deeds are equally harmful, but at least it gives us a clear standard from which to begin. As we begin, we may grow in two directions: inwardly, to redirect our desires in appropriate directions, and outwardly, to conform our actions to the will of God.

Celibacy: Gift or Booby Prize?

The focus on action leads to another question that I introduced as a revisionist argument in chapter two and have not yet addressed: Is a person with homosexual desires required to live a celibate life? The revisionist position is this: Celibacy is a special gift of the Spirit, and as such we should not force it on an entire category of people just because they have certain desires. Individual homosexual people may have this gift, but we should not consign the rest to sexual frustration and loneliness. Didn't Paul write in 1 Corinthians 7:9 that it is better to marry than to burn? We should allow a similar compromise for homosexual people: we should recognize their faithful, lifelong unions in a manner analogous to our recognition of heterosexual marriages.

There are several problems with this position. First, it makes a false equation of celibacy and abstinence. Abstinence is not a gift for a few but a responsibility for all who are not married. We do not normally speak of a teenager as "celibate," but we teach abstinence as the appropriate behavior for that person throughout the hot-burning years of late adolescence and early adulthood, until he or she is married. According to the revisionist argument this is not a fair comparison, because young people can hold out in the expectation of an eventual outlet for sexual desire. I submit that those who think expectation fosters self-control have not been teenagers for a long time, and those who think marriage is a sufficient outlet for all sexual desire are mostly still teenagers. The problem for all of us is not holding out for thirty years but holding out for thirty minutes against the popular notion that sexual gratification is essential to personhood. Those who resist, both heterosexual and homosexual, may know unimaginable physical pleasure in that Day when they will remember earthly long-suffering as a blink of the eye. Certainly the beatitudes of Jesus (Mt 5:3-12) promise sufferers that they will receive, precisely and multifold, that which they have given up for the sake of the gospel.

A second problem with the "celibacy is unreasonable" argument is that it appears to give desire priority over righteousness. Celibacy is equally "unreasonable" for the pedophile, but we do not (yet) hear calls within the church to recognize transgenerational unions. The reason, obviously, is that there is no question about the unrighteousness of such unions. So what is really behind the revisionist argument about celibacy is not a belief that frustration is intolerable but a belief that homosexual acts are tolerable. If they are not, no amount of desire will make them so. We cannot, therefore, make homosexual unions analogous to marriage in 1 Corinthians 7. In that context Paul compares a good (marriage) to a greater good (focus on ministry); he does not compromise a good with something he condemns elsewhere.

A third problem is that the proposed solution—recognition of faithful, lifelong unions—may be an unwelcome imposition by well-meaning Christians who want to create a category of union as close as possible to heterosexual marriage. Not only does this category fly in the face of most homosexual practice and much homosexual ideology, but it also manifestly enforces heterosexual standards of union. When children are not an option and where complementarity is not valued, the arguments for lifelong fidelity are considerably weakened. Furthermore, to the extent that homosexual desire involves a need to absorb maleness (or for lesbians, femaleness) from one's partner, the inevitable frustration of that need will lead to a search for another partner, and then another. Other causes or reasons may account for promiscuity. Whatever they may be, there is reason to doubt that major changes will result from the legal recognition of homosexual unions. Why should financial incentives succeed where the probability of disease and death have failed?

Finally, the objection to celibacy rests on a false supposition that the homosexual person is thereby consigned to relational loneliness. This is false on at least three counts. First, intimate relationships need not involve sex, as millions of heterosexuals with opposite-sex friends can attest. Second, relational intimacy need not occur with members of the tempting sex, as millions of heterosexuals with same-sex friends can attest. Third, homosexuals do not have to experience complete conversion to heterosexuality in order to enjoy intimacy, and even marriage, with opposite-sex partners. Minimally, all that is required is the ability to function heterosexually and the ability to control homosexual behavior. If after an honest effort to develop heterosexual desires, a person remains a 6 (exclusively homosexual) on the Kinsey scale—and I freely grant that the desire may be immutable for many people—that person must learn to enjoy intimacy without sex.

I suspect that very few people get unambiguous messages from God that they are "called" as pastors or missionaries—or celibates. Pious language notwithstanding, God rarely speaks today in an audible voice. People find God's will and their special giftedness through prayerful reflection on Scripture, circumstances, abilities and events. Many heterosexual people consider celibacy only after a painful period of failed relationships or neglect by the opposite sex. The cynical view, of course, is that celibacy is God-talk to enable social misfits to make a virtue of a necessity. If celibacy were only a matter of labeling the cup half full rather than half empty, there might be some truth to the charge. But the Christian tradition of celibacy affirms that there is something different in the cup: a rich liquid, closer in some ways to the example of Jesus himself, better able to be poured out on behalf of others.

In this sense the experience or the orientation that prevents a person from enjoyment of heterosexual union may be a gift. Just as many deaf people assert that they would not want to hear at the price of their heightened sense of touch and their solidarity with other deaf people, so single people may develop extraordinary gifts to serve and to understand. The monastic and priestly traditions of Christianity, both Roman and Orthodox, offer vast experience and literature on the gift and discipline of celibacy. This is but one of several possible avenues of wisdom. I do not pretend to understand fully the possibilities presented to the celibate person. But I am confident of this: it is only an aberration of our own sorry generation to equate the absence of sexual gratification with the absence of full personhood, the denial of being or the deprivation of joy.

Relative Morality

The primary concern of this book has been the behavior of the person with homosexual desires. But one of the biggest issues for that person, whether or not he or she is currently practicing homosexuality, is the question of revelation to family members, especially those who are likely to disapprove. Relatives, and especially parents, of people who "come out" as homosexuals often feel guilty about the past and uncertain about the future. Some preventative maintenance on the part of families of known or guessed homosexuals may facilitate relational healing at several levels.

To begin, parents of homosexuals should not torture themselves about the past. Christian parents may be particularly prone to this, both because they are more likely to subscribe to a developmental theory of causation and because they take to heart the biblical mandate to "bring up a child in the way he should go." Whether or not the child's early development answers to the description advanced in chapter seven, parents must remember that there were other factors involved—even from a strictly developmental perspective—over which they had no control. They should also remember that any problems they are blaming on themselves did not fully originate with them, or their parents, or their grandparents. Pass the buck back to its logical starting point, and resentment becomes silly: how angry can you be, really, at Adam and Eve? To be sure, we each bear blame for the trouble of this world, and for the trouble of our families, but we do not bear it alone. And we do not bear it forever—hallelujah!—because it has been borne by Someone else.

That glorious truth frees us from self-torture, but it does not free us from the painful work of self-examination and confession. Parents of those who are comfortable with their homosexuality should normally not confess to the child, because (however well intentioned) doing so would in most cases appear manipulative. Instead, acceptance of a proper measure of guilt should foster humility and sensitivity.

It is those qualities, which are no more and no less than aspects of love, that are needed in the family with a homosexual member. It is difficult under the best of circumstances for most young adults to distinguish unconditional love from unconditional approval. They are trying to make their way as independent individuals in the world, and they inwardly want the yes that only parents can give—even while they outwardly say no to so much that parents represent. It is hard for any parent to offer love without at least a few strings attached. For that reason siblings rather than parents often receive the confidences of other siblings. Brothers and sisters represent the safety of family without the guilt of parental authority.

It is important to appreciate these factors in the "coming out" of a homosexual. As chapter six made disturbingly clear, the homosexual world is anything but safe, either physically or relationally. This truth compounds the already daunting task for any young adult of making an independent start in the world. It is a sustaining thought, whether or not the person takes advantage of the offer, to know that there is a place where rest can be found, where there are familiar foods and surroundings and, most important, where people always offer acceptance and support simply because they are *family*.

Of course no earthly home can be more than a shadow of the Place we truly desire. But this side of heaven, even a glimpse of that home, even the intention of it, even the hope of it, may turn a prodigal's steps. And the way Home may pass through a very normal-looking house.

Notes for a Manifesto

While some readers struggle directly with personal or familial concerns, most come to this book simply to deepen their understanding of the moral issues. But Christians cannot leave moral issues in the study. Each must ask, "What part should I play in the moral drama of our time?" And so I turn at the end of this book to those people who are probably my primary audience: those who want practical suggestions for the translation of moral theory into effective living. I call my suggestions nothing more than "notes for a manifesto," hoping that discussion and the wisdom of the Christian community will refine and add to them.

   1. *We must bring the gospel to individual people.* This statement seems obvious and agreeable to most Christians, but on closer inspection it may invite controversy. When it comes to moral issues, many believers find it difficult to distinguish their responsibility as believers from their responsibility as American citizens. The way I put this in the introductory chapter was to warn against confusing the *cause* of Christ with the *way* of Christ. What I mean in practical terms is that Christians should be wary of public policy debates, which tend to foster issue-oriented rather than people-oriented approaches.

   It does not have to be one or the other; but in my observation, those who get caught up in the political aspect of a moral issue often adopt a simplistic us-them attitude and a set of tactics based on the acquisition of power. They may succeed, but the price may be the loss of humility, tenderness and integrity. There are notable exceptions, but those who are *not* exceptions never seem to notice. Please understand that I do not oppose work through the political process to legislate morality: that is the democratic process. I simply warn that it is a limited and limiting goal. The gospel is ultimately not about changing laws but about changing lives.

   Recently I heard a powerful testimony of Christian service from an elderly woman who had joined her psychiatrist husband in a lifetime of service to his clients by opening their home to them. "The kitchen must be the center of love," she said (and her life proved), "for Jesus is known in the breaking of the bread." True and convicting words for those of us who perceive open homes, unhurried conversation and table fellowship as nostalgic elements of another generation of Christians. True and convicting words for those of us who would march off to fight in the culture war—past Lazarus at our gate.

   The call is clear. If we are to walk in the way of Jesus, it is not the nuclear family that we need to promote but the hospitable family. We do not need people who love family values nearly as much as we need families who value love for people

2. We must understand the relation between morality and truth. Barring an unlikely philosophical reversal or the return of Jesus, our culture will move rapidly away from the notion of absolute truth in the next thirty years, as the last modern generation fades and the first postmodern generation gains power. People will see truth and morality as subject to the changing whims of those in power, and accusations of relativism will fail to sting because people will no longer perceive them as accusations but rather as accurate descriptions of the way truth and morality work.

The clearest indication of this is the observation that already, for many if not most Americans, tolerance is valued more highly than truth. The reason for this is that the only absolute truths are those of religion, and religion is considered a private matter; therefore public morality leaves tolerance as the only virtue. There may come a time when even tolerance is recognized as an arbitrary value, paving the way for rule by the mob or the tyrant.

If Christians disagree, if we find that God has revealed himself and his way in a book, we must place limits on our tolerance in the interest of truth. We should not expect this idea to prevail, or even that our culture will tolerate it much longer. But instead of shaking our heads and lamenting the sorry state of the world, we should recognize that Truth is not meant to be applauded but to be nailed to crosses. And we had better know the Truth well. That means, first of all, knowing Jesus. It also means knowing the Bible, backwards and forwards, and far more deeply than most churches currently require. Finally, and not least, it means knowing well the larger ideas competing for the minds and hearts of people.

The body of Christ got caught with its pants down awhile back when Darwin walked in. Dignity was eventually restored, but the trousers were torn, and sometimes it seems that they are inside out. I wonder if we are ready now for a far more serious intrusion, one that questions not just the words of Scripture in relation to science but the relation of both to truth itself. I am not optimistic that Christians are willing to do the work necessary to prepare themselves. It is all so intimidating, after all—even to college professors. I would rather read a good nineteenth-century novel or go for a walk on the beach and hope that the world leaves me alone. But it won't.

3. *We must express our disapproval of homosexual practice in the context of our own sexual fallenness.* Unless we acknowledge that we are *all* in need of God's grace and healing in our sexuality, we will continue to prevent homosexuals and others from listening to us, because they will hear only our fear and revulsion, not our love and similar need. To be sure, the current hot-topic status of homosexuality justifies special attention, but we should always draw a connection to the inappropriate desires and actions practiced by the heterosexual majority.

This approach kicks the legs out from under the homophobia defense; but more important, it is the right thing to do. Jesus said to the woman caught in adultery. "Go and sin no more" (Jn 8:11 KJV), but first he sent her accusers away by suggesting that they were not without sin themselves. Her accusers were not necessarily adulterers, but they needed to see that there is much more to righteousness than punishing sinners. Only when we show that we have a greater concern about our own sin will we have a right to confront sin in others. This is not tolerance. It is justice.

Our heterosexual sin includes sins of hatred toward homosexuals. I have written almost nothing in this book about the victimization of homosexuals, because I do not think that it is directly relevant to the morality of the homosexual act. But it happens. I do not mean discrimination in a traditional economic sense—homosexuals are generally richer, better employed and better housed than the general population—but in the attitudinal sense. Whenever we initiate or tolerate slang terms, demeaning jokes or derogatory offhand comments, we send a strong message that these people for whom Jesus died are, in civil rights terms, *niggers,* or in biblical terms, *Samaritans.* In so doing we make a lie of the slogan "Hate the sin and love the sinner." That slogan, known and despised by homosexuals, is tired and in need of replacement. We should try something like "Look in the mirror before looking out the window."

My final point on appropriate expression concerns the people who do the expressing. I will be blunt. Christians who cannot yet deal with the issues calmly and compassionately should keep their mouths shut, and they should certainly stay away from the front lines of ministry and public policy debate—not to mention television talk shows. Such people are hard to reach, because they suspect that those who call them to account are "soft on sin." They must be convinced that the way of Jesus is the way of the Wounded Healer, not the Holy Terror.

4. We must work to find avenues of ministry consistent with our moral stance. Churches face an awkward dilemma. The exclusion of practicing homosexuals from worship and ministry may push them away from Christianity; but inclusion in every aspect of church life may send a message of approval of homosexual behavior. The morally ambiguous "don't ask, don't tell" policy, which satisfies neither side in the military, is downright cowardly in a church. The better course is for church leaders periodically to make it clear from the pulpit (and privately in specific cases of concern) that the church represents forgiveness and power to change, and it also exercises redemptive discipline in cases of sexual disobedience, including homosexual acts. If this is done in a humble and inclusive manner along the lines suggested above, it should be well received by all. Hal Scholl, director of Spring Forth Ministry in Cincinnati, traces the radical change in his life back to the moment when a pastor decided to depart from his sermon text and talk about the love of Jesus for the homosexual.

I do not mean to suggest that the only (or even primary) responsibility of the church is to proclaim its stance from the pulpit. The body of Christ is not just a mouth. Individual churches and groups or individuals within them should plan their own specific strategies that take into account differing gifts. I will mention only a few possibilities, from the most indirect to the most direct.

Education within the church is imperative. So few Christians seem to realize that a walk across a nearby college campus or down a city street is every bit as much a mission trip as a boat ride up the Amazon—complete with utterly foreign languages, beliefs and customs. Why train only "foreign" missionaries in crosscultural communication? We need to know what we are up against. And even more critically, we need to know what we stand for. So many capable Christians with at least some college education maintain a pitiably low level of understanding of biblical interpretation and Christian ethics. Classes, seminars, special speakers, discussion groups and reading clubs can cater to a variety of needs and abilities. All Christians need not master the developments in philosophy since the Enlightenment in order to address the moral issues raised by homosexuality. Some might benefit from workshops in effective parenting, while others might serve church-family children by providing release-time moral education to counter some of the ill effects of the "value-neutral" public school system.

Not every Christian is able to engage in moral discourse or to offer counsel, but all should be ready at any time to supply referrals. Churches should make available to their members annotated reading lists, names and contact numbers of local counseling agencies and reputable Christian ministries, and information about the resources of the local church itself, including support groups and counseling opportunities. Such information should be as widely distributed and as readily available as . . . condoms.

Finally, and by no means least important, Christians should be known for the kind of hands-on help that characterized the ministry of our Lord. People with AIDS, in particular, are the lepers of our day. These people lose work, insurance and finally the ability to care for themselves, all before they are sick enough to require hospitalization. They often need errands run, basic housekeeping and home-cooked meals. In areas where no hospice care is available, they may need money or a place to stay. More than anything, they need simple human companionship. As relationships of trust develop, they may open up to spiritual help. But there is no guarantee of this, and we should not make it a condition of service.

We may view many of them as enemies, and the feeling is often mutual. But in a war, would we leave our enemies to die alone on the battlefield, reasoning that they deserve their fate and should not absorb the precious resources of "our side"? I submit that those who applaud these deaths proclaim thereby that their side is not the side of Jesus but the side of Satan, and the words of Jesus himself provide a fitting malediction: "It will be more tolerable for the land of Sodom and Gomorrah on the day of judgment than for those people" (see Lk 10:12).

Words of Hope

For me, this paragraph represents the end of a long search for words to convey strength of conviction in a spirit of compassion. For some I have succeeded, for others I have failed. I end as I began, imagining the faces of homosexual friends looking over my shoulder as I write, wondering whether they have been helped, angered, encouraged, confused or informed. Probably all of these at one point or another.

What final word can I offer to them? Just this. Above and beyond their faces, I envision another Face, infinitely knowing, intimately caring, invincibly loving. I entrust to him all the words of mine that have gone before, and I offer at last these words of his:

Come to me, all you that are weary and are carrying heavy burdens, and I will give you rest. Take my yoke upon you, and learn from me; for I am gentle and humble in heart, and you will find rest for your souls. For my yoke is easy, and my burden is light. (Mt 11:28-30)

Postscript: A Letter to a Friend

Although I have never known anyone named Nick, the following letter is not quite fictional. "Nick" is a composite of several people I have known who are Christians with homosexual desires. Mabel, by the way, was quite real.

Dear Nick,

I don't believe in The Problem of Pain as people discuss it in religion classes. At that level there is no problem, only a debate toy. The problem of pain I believe in is the pain that happens to one person at a time. Pain is a much more serious problem when it is reduced to its proper, personal size. God did not send an earthquake to Guatemala; rather, Pedro, who lives there, lost his wife in an earthquake and seeks the purpose of God in the event.

To me, then, a flood or an earthquake is merely an interesting phenomenon apart from its impact on people, one at a time, who are hurt or who grieve for others who are hurt. Of course the vast majority of pain-causing phenomena are created by a few people acting out of selfish interests to create a world of hurt for others. War, slavery and pornography come to mind. The latter I define very broadly to include any portrayal of people that serves as an inducement to lust. Our society is very inconsistent when, for example, it holds a toy manufacturer negligent for a product that *might* harm children if broken or swallowed, but the greasiest sleaze merchant, whose product is (spiritually) broken to begin with, is accountable only if direct harm can be demonstrated—a virtual legal impossibility. And of course that is only the most obvious case, to say nothing of the legion of film, television and video producers, and especially advertisers, whose products, while legally innocuous, systematically demean women and manipulate the minds of men.

I could go on for some time, waxing eloquent on the subject of societal sexual evil, but it would be too much like complaining about floods and earthquakes. The truth is, I can't get too bothered by the fact that advertisers exercise their diabolical privilege to bombard me with images of gorgeous women who will fall into my arms if I drink the right beer or shave with the right razor. What really bothers me is that I can't seem to stop thinking about those gorgeous women. For me, of course, this is considered "normal." This is the way most guys are, right? And after all, I keep it under better control than most.

So the pain for me is not that people disapprove—and there we differ, you and I. On the other hand, you are not subjected to a constant onslaught of media-idealized images that play to your weakness, so perhaps that evens the playing field of temptation a bit.

In any case, I suspect that the greatest common ground for us is the deeper nature of our pain. The pain, quite simply, is that I can't have what I want. Marriage doesn't provide it, and I don't need a therapist to tell me that all these women wouldn't provide it either if I could have them. Neither do I need a therapist to tell me what I really want or how I came to want it or how it is deeper than sexuality. I know all that. But hunger doesn't go away when you hear a lecture about the physiology of digestion.

I have witnessed, firsthand, great endurance against great temptation, but in a very different form from what I experience day to day. I knew an old woman once who took twenty-eight years to die, blind, deformed by cancerous tumors, bedridden and alone in a state institution. I visited Mabel for three years, amazed at her selfless and thankful spirit, and I learned what sustained her. She prayed and she sang hymns. That was it—virtually nonstop, as far as I could tell.

Once I asked her what she thought about all day. It was almost twenty years ago, but I remember the moment vividly—the stench of the room, the moaning of her vegetable roommate in the background and the long pause before the words came, slowly and garbled—but deliberate—from her twisted mouth: "I think about my Jesus. I think about how good he has been to me." And then she started to sing: "Jesus is all the world to me, my life, my soul, my all; He is my strength from day to day; without Him I would fall." Ten thousand days in a row, Nick. Ten million waking minutes. She didn't fall.

Now, if my only source of information about Mabel was another person, I'd be moved, but I'm not sure I'd believe the story. Largely for that reason I hardly ever talk about her. Another reason is that it almost always makes me cry to talk about her, or even to think about her. I don't cry for Mabel, you understand. I have no Problem of Pain when it comes to her, because I know—I saw with my own eyes, for three years—that she had the answer to pain for each of those ten million minutes. No, I cry for *me*. I don't expect that I'll get many Mabels in my life, and I'll only get so many millions of minutes to apply what I learn. I cry because those minutes pass so quickly, and I use so many of them foolishly. I cry because I fear to pay the price in pain or endurance that will make me more like Mabel.

Do you wonder what I'm getting at? Are you expecting me to draw an analogy between what Mabel endured and what I might ask you to endure, and that I am tossing in some disclosure of my own pain to make sure I convey the proper level of empathy to clinch the argument?

No, Nick. Because there was another person in that state institution I went to see each week before I visited Mabel. Frank was dying of emphysema, and he was moody, sometimes bitter, sometimes self-pitying, usually a difficult conversation partner—more like me than Mabel. He was simply a friend of mine, and I went to see him. It occurred to me at our first meeting that I didn't know what it was like to be eighty years old, left in an institution by an uncaring family while I slowly coughed my lungs out. My answers didn't answer in that situation. They were true enough answers, but it wasn't appropriate for *me* to speak them, even if Frank had asked me to. Mostly we talked about other things.

So why am I writing to you like this, for all the world to see, at the end of such a book? I don't know if you have read up to this point or just scanned the table of contents and jumped ahead to this letter. I'm not even sure I want you to read this book. I wrote it primarily to encourage deeper and better thought on the part of some people on both sides of the moral debate. But a person like you, whose heart is involved, needs more than arguments. You need to know that people care about you, not only that they evaluate your behavior from a coherent ethical framework.

Part of the problem for me, of course, is that once the book goes off to the publisher, I lose control over the timing and context of its individual reception. It may be a bitter pill to swallow alone. And so I pray that for every homosexual person with an ear ready to hear, God will provide people with hearts ready to care.

I can offer that to a few, like you. Know that you are loved and supported in prayer, whatever you do sexually, and whatever you desire to do. Know that I can empathize at least a little—perhaps more than people might guess, given the differences between us on the surface. Pain can be a great equalizer, especially if we apply a little imagination and trust to bring out what we share rather than what divides us.

There is a great example of this in one of Paul's letters. The Christians in Corinth got involved in some heresy and snubbed him, but later they responded to the emissary he sent from the province of Asia and turned back to him. Now, rather than lecturing, rather than patronizing, Paul begins his letter to the Corinthians by likening their pain (shame for wronging him) to his pain (longing for their good). I quote him at length because there is much here that strikes me as relevant:

> Blessed be the God and Father of our Lord Jesus Christ, the Father of mercies and the God of all comfort, who comforts us in all our affliction, so that we may be able to comfort those who are in any affliction, with the comfort with which we ourselves are comforted by God. For as we share abundantly in Christ's sufferings, so through Christ we share abundantly in comfort too. If we are afflicted, it is for your comfort and salvation; and if we are comforted, it is for your comfort, which you experience when

you patiently endure the same sufferings that we suffer. Our hope for you is unshaken; for we know that as you share in our sufferings, you will also share in our comfort.

For we do not want you to be ignorant, brethren, of the affliction we experienced in Asia; for we were so utterly, unbearably crushed that we despaired of life itself. Why, we felt that we had received the sentence of death; but that was to make us rely not on ourselves but on God who raises the dead; he delivered us from so deadly a peril, and he will deliver us; on him we have set our hope that he will deliver us again. You also must help us by prayer, so that many will give thanks on our behalf for the blessing granted us in answer to many prayers. (2 Cor 1:3-11 RSV)

I am always amazed that this man Paul, for all his reputation as a purveyor of creative theology and hard-nosed morality, would have such a capacity to put love for people into action. I can attribute this only to God, who used pain to teach Paul humility, to take off his hard edges without weakening the core of his belief and morality. What strikes me as most profound in this passage is Paul's expression of *dependence* on the Corinthians, the affirmation that his work is supported by their prayers.

You know what I want for you, Nick, and I won't belabor the point here. What you may not know is that along with a message of conviction and power and hope, I also offer you *need*. Nick, it is *we*, not you, who need God's forgiveness and help to transform our sexuality. Can we help each other? "You also must help us by prayer, so that many will give thanks on our behalf for the blessing granted us in answer to many prayers."

Please write. This sort of letter always leaves the writer on edge (in Asia?) until he knows how it has been received.

Love,

Tom

Notes

Chapter 2: What All the Fuss Is About

[1]In *Alexander Solzhenitsyn Speaks to the West* (London: Bodley Head, 1978), pp. 77-99.

[2]Following in chronological order are recent revisionist scholarly treatments. In my view the most important of these are Pronk and Boswell; the most attentive to the biblical material are Countryman, Edwards and Scroggs. D. S. Bailey, *Homosexuality and the Western Christian Tradition* (London: Archon Books, 1975); J. J. McNeill, *The Church and the Homosexual* (Boston: Beacon, 1976; 4th ed. 1993); V. P. Furnish, *The Moral Teaching of Paul* (Nashville: Abingdon, 1979); J. Boswell, *Christianity, Social Tolerance and Homosexuality* (New Haven, Conn.: Yale Unversity Press, 1980); R. R. Ruether, "From Machismo to Mutuality," and W. Norman Pittenger, "The Morality of Homosexual Acts," in *Homosexuality and Ethics*, ed. E. Batchelor Jr. (New York: Pilgrim, 1980); R. Scroggs, *The New Testament and Homosexuality* (Philadelphia: Fortress, 1983); L. S. Cahill, "Moral Methodology: A Case Study," D. Maguire, "The Morality of Homosexual Marriage," M. A. Farley, "An Ethic for Same-Sex Relations," M. D. Guinan, "Homosexuals: A Christian Pastoral Response Now," and M. E. Hunt, "Lovingly Lesbian: Toward a Feminist Theology of Friendship," in *A Challenge to Love: Gay and Lesbian Catholics in the Church*, ed. R. Nugent (New York: Crossroad, 1983); G. A. Edwards, *Gay/Lesbian Liberation: A Biblical Perspective* (New York: Pilgrim, 1984); L. William Countryman, *Dirt, Greed and Sex* (Philadelphia: Fortress, 1988); B. J. Brooten, "Paul's Views on the Nature of Women and Female Homoeroticism," in *Immaculate and Powerful: The Female in Sacred Image and Social Reality*, ed. C. W. Atkinson, C. H. Buchanan and M. R. Miles (Boston: Beacon, 1985), pp. 61-87; R. Williams, "Toward a Theology for Lesbian and Gay Marriage," *Anglical Theological Review* 72 (Spring 1990): 134-57; R. Williams, *Just As I Am: A Practical Guide to Being Out, Proud and Christian* (New York: Crown, 1992); G. D. Comstock, *Gay Theology Without Apology*

(New York: Pilgrim, 1993); R. Goss, *Jesus Acted Up: A Gay and Lesbian Manifesto* (San Francisco: Harper, 1993); P. Pronk, *Against Nature? Types of Moral Argumentation Regarding Homosexuality* (Grand Rapids, Mich.: Eerdmans, 1993); P. B. Jung and R. F. Smith, *Heterosexism: An Ethical Challenge* (Albany: State University of New York Press, 1993). See also the autobiographical book by M. White, *Stranger at the Gate* (New York: Simon & Schuster, 1994).

³Pronk, *Against Nature?* p. 126. Pronk is a gay Dutch ethicist whose treatise will challenge scholars on all sides of the issue for many years. Unfortunately, his sophisticated philosophical arguments are inaccessible to all but the most educated readers, and as Pronk himself might predict, his work is likely to be ignored by liberal theologians who are on the bandwagon of liberation theology. An editor at Eerdmans Publishing Company kindly provided me with page proofs of Pronk's book prior to its appearance in late 1993, and some readers will recognize both debt and response to his work in these pages. I hope that competent ethicists and theologians will give his work a more careful response than I am able to offer in a book written for a general audience.

⁴The following explanation was first advanced in detail by Bailey, *Homosexuality and the Western Christian Tradition,* pp. 1-28, 53-57, and adopted with some modification by nearly every revisionist writer.

⁵On hospitality to strangers, see especially Exodus 22:21 and Deuternomomy 10:18-19.

⁶Genesis 13:13; 18:20; Deuteronomy 29:23; 32:32; Isaiah 1:9-10; 3:9; 13:19; Jeremiah 23:14; 49:18; 50:40; Lamentations 4:6; Amos 4:11; Zephaniah 2:9. This is true in the New Testament as well: see Matthew 10:14-15; Luke 10:10-12. Other possible references that do not explicitly name Sodom are Job 18:15; Psalm 11:6; 140:10; Isaiah 34:9; Jeremiah 20:16; Ezekiel 38:22; Hosea 11:8.

⁷See also the apocryphal Wisdom of Solomon (2nd century B.C.) 19:13-14: "for they justly suffered because of their wicked acts; for they practiced a more bitter hatred of strangers. Others had refused to receive strangers when they came to them, but these made slaves of guests who were their benefactors." Compare Wisdom of Solomon 10:8; Sirach 16:8.

⁸See also Matthew 11:23; Luke 17:29.

⁹See, for example, Edwards, *Gay/Lesbian Liberation,* pp. 42-46; McNeill, *The Church and the Homosexual,* pp. 58-60; Jung and Smith, *Heterosexism,* pp. 68-71. D. Lance ("The Anthropological Context of Genesis 19 and Judges 19," a paper presented at the 1992 annual meeting of the Society of Biblical Literature, San Francisco, California) has accumulated substantial evidence for this interpretation which will probably appear soon in a book.

¹⁰Deuteronomy 23:17; 1 Kings 14:24; 15:12; 22:46; 2 Kings 23:7; Job 36:14.

¹¹Edwards, *Gay/Lesbian Liberation,* pp. 54-69; Goss, *Jesus Acted Up,* p. 92.

¹²Bailey (*Homosexuality and the Western Christian Tradition,* pp. 48-53) argues that the male prostitutes served female worshipers; see also Edwards, *Gay/Lesbian Liberation,* pp. 62-63.

[13]Scroggs, *The New Testament and Homosexuality*, pp. 115-18. On practices in Paul's day, see K. Dover, *Greek Homosexuality*, 2nd ed. (Cambridge, Mass.: Harvard University Press, 1989), and E. Cantarella, *Bisexuality in the Ancient World* (New Haven, Conn.: Yale University Press, 1992).

[14]Boswell, *Christianity, Social Tolerance and Homosexuality*, pp. 108-9.

[15]Edwards, *Gay/Lesbian Liberation*, pp. 85-102. The Hellenistic material primarily in view is chap. 14 of the apocryphal Wisdom of Solomon.

[16]"Abusers of themselves with mankind" (KJV); "homosexuals" (RSV 1946); "sexual perverts" (RSV 1972); "sodomites" (NRSV); "homosexual perverts" (Good News); "homosexuals" (NASB).

[17]Scroggs, *The New Testament and Homosexuality*, pp. 62-5, 101-9, 127.

[18]Boswell, *Christianity, Social Tolerance and Homosexuality*, p. 106.

[19]Ibid., pp. 107, 335-53; Countryman, *Dirt, Greed and Sex*, pp. 117-20; Goss, *Jesus Acted Up*, p. 93.

[20]Bailey, *Homosexuality and the Western Christian Tradition*, pp. 11-18; Edwards, *Gay/Lesbian Liberation*, p. 101.

[21]Revelation 21:8 and 22:15 make reference to "the polluted" and "the dogs," respectively, but the sexual connotations here are tenuous at best: Bailey, *Homosexuality and the Western Christian Tradition*, pp. 41-45.

[22]Scroggs, *The New Testament and Homosexuality*, p. 127; compare McNeill, *The Church and the Homosexual*, pp. 36-42.

[23]Boswell, *Christianity, Social Tolerance and Homosexuality*, pp. 106-7; Countryman, *Dirt, Greed and Sex*, pp. 86, 107-9, 123.

[24]This idea was first advanced by Boswell, *Christianity, Social Tolerance and Homosexuality*, pp. 112-13 n. 73; it is developed in detail by Countryman, *Dirt, Greed and Sex*, pp. 98-123.

[25]Countryman, *Dirt, Greed and Sex*, pp. 122-23. What Paul calls "unnatural" or "against nature" means "beyond nature" (Boswell, *Christianity, Social Tolerance and Homosexuality*, pp. 110-12), not in the sense of wrongdoing but as an observation of social use, that the Gentiles have "lost a certain continuity with their remotest past" (Countryman, *Dirt, Greed and Sex*, p. 114).

[26]Ibid., p. 86; compare p. 140.

[27]Edwards (*Gay/Lesbian Liberation*, p. 76) finds in Galatians 3:28 the correction to Paul's (hetero)sexist interpreters.

[28]Pronk (*Against Nature?* especially pp. 215-63) gives the most thorough argument; see also Jung and Smith, *Heterosexism*, pp. 140-44.

[29]Guinan, "Homosexuals," pp. 71-77; Farley, "Ethic for Same-Sex Relations," pp. 99-100; Goss, *Jesus Acted Up*, p. xvii.

[30]Ibid., pp. 246-63.

[31]Farley, "Ethic for Same-Sex Relations," p. 100.

[32]Edwards, *Gay/Lesbian Liberation*, pp. 103-29; Maguire, "Morality of Homosexual Marriage," pp. 118-19; Goss, *Jesus Acted Up*, p. 116; McNeill, *The Church and the Homosexual*,

pp. 99-108.

[33]Farley, "Ethic for Same-Sex Relations," pp. 101-2; Hunt, "Lovingly Lesbian," p. 148; Comstock, *Gay Theology Without Apology*, p. 130; Williams, "Toward a Theology," pp. 140-44.

[34]Edwards, *Gay/Lesbian Liberation*, pp. 113-23; Farley, "Ethic for Same-Sex Relations," pp. 102-4; Pittenger, "Morality of Homosexual Acts," p. 140; Jung and Smith, *Heterosexism*, pp. 181-86.

[35]Farley, "Ethic for Same-Sex Relations," pp. 104-5; Hunt, "Lovingly Lesbian," p. 149.

[36]Jung and Smith, *Heterosexism*, pp. 28, 110-12.

[37]See especially Goss, *Jesus Acted Up*, pp. 181-90, on the contribution of Michel Foucault to the contemporary understanding of sexuality as a social construct.

[38]E. Schüssler Fiorenza, "Toward a Feminist Biblical Hermeneutics: Biblical Interpretation and Liberation Theology," in *The Challenge of Liberation Theology*, ed. B. Mahan and L. D. Richesin (Maryknoll, N.Y.: Orbis, 1981), p. 108; see also Williams, *Just As I Am*, pp. 37-43. Much of the following explanation of feminist theory as applied to homosexuality relies on an address by Brooten, which I understand will appear in book form soon.

[39]Comstock, *Gay Theology Without Apology*, p. 77; compare p. 38: "Those passages will be brought up and used against us again and again until Christians demand their removal from the biblical canon or, at the very least, formally discredit their authority to prescribe behavior."

[40]Ibid., pp. 100, 112, 128.

[41]Goss, *Jesus Acted Up*, pp. 62, 83-84, 108; Comstock, *Gay Theology Without Apology*, pp. 21, 93.

[42]A large number of American Catholics, as the literature cited here attests, question the Vatican's position, but there is no indication that any change is forthcoming.

Chapter 3: Sexuality from the Beginning

[1]For a more thorough evangelical treatment of sexuality in general, see Stanley Grenz, *Sexual Ethics: A Biblical Perspective* (Dallas: Word, 1990).

[2]I am well aware of the history of allegorical interpretation of this book, turning it into a prophecy about Israel or Christ. While I suspect prudish motivation for such interpretations, even those who take the book primarily as prophecy must admit that the *vehicle* for the prophecy is sexually explicit—downright torchy in places (for example, 2:6; 4:5-6; 5:2-5; 7:7-8; 8:1-3). Nevertheless, and in distinction from contemporary Egyptian parallels, the Song never crosses over into the pornographic. See J. B. White, *A Study of the Language of Love in the Song of Songs and Ancient Egyptian Poetry*, Society of Biblical Literature Dissertation Series 38 (Missoula, Mont.: Scholars Press, 1978).

[3]In addition to 1 Corinthians 6:12-20, quoted above, see 1 Corinthians 15 on the importance of physical resurrection of believers. Dualism may motivate the criticism of licentiousness in 2 Peter 2 and Jude, "faith" without works in James 2:18-26, and disobedience in 1 John 3-5. Conversely, dualism may motivate the criticism of ascet-

icism in Colossians 2:20-23, 1 Timothy 4:3-5 and Hebrews 13:9.

[4]See the discussion in Grenz, *Sexual Ethics*, pp. 31-37, and the major commentaries, especially C. Westermann, *Genesis 1-11* (Minneapolis: Augsburg, 1984), pp. 144-61.

[5]This has been ably argued by several writers, including J. P. Hanigan, *Homosexuality: The Test Case for Christian Sexual Ethics* (Mahwah, N.J.: Paulist, 1988), pp. 100-102. Hanigan's is the best recent conservative Roman Catholic treatment. See also Grenz, *Sexual Ethics*, p. 212; K. Barth, *Church Dogmatics 3/4* (Edinburgh: T & T Clark, 1961), pp. 164-66.

[6]See the discussion and bibliography in Grenz, *Sexual Ethics*, pp. 24-26, and, in this book, the discussion of social constructionism in chapter seven.

[7]Scientific evidence suggests that even stimulation of the anus, which some men find pleasurable whether or not a penis is involved, is still, physiologically speaking, an indirect form of genital stimulation. See J. Agnew, "Some Anatomical and Physiological Aspects of Anal Sexual Practices," *Journal of Homosexuality* 12 (Fall 1985): 77-96.

[8]The argument from complementarity is ably presented from a philosophical perspective (not necessarily Christian) by R. Scruton in *Sexual Desire: A Moral Philosophy of the Erotic* (New York: Free Press, 1986), pp. 253-83, 305-11.

[9]This is the main point of P. Pronk, *Against Nature? Types of Moral Argumentation Regarding Homosexuality* (Grand Rapids, Mich.: Eerdmans, 1993), and he argues it effectively.

[10]This point is well put by D. A. Scott, "The Hermeneutics of Marriage," *Anglican Theological Review* 72 (Spring 1990): 168-71, in response to approaches such as R. Williams's (in the same issue) that reduce God's love to a proprietary vision of what God gives us.

[11]*Voluntary* childlessness by means of birth control (including limitation to noncoital intimacy) presents a new set of questions. Is it now possible for a couple to have their cake and pray over it too—that is, both to enjoy sex and to do ministry without the encumbrance of children or the distraction of desire? Perhaps; but in my observation the motivation for voluntary childlessness is almost always *convenience* (most often related to career), which in my view subjects such a choice to the same charge of irresponsibility as that directed against homosexuality: it accepts the pleasure of sex but rejects its consequence.

[12]Pronk, *Against Nature?* pp. 246-63; compare G. D. Comstock, *Gay Theology Without Apology* (New York: Pilgrim, 1993), pp. 105-26. In the context of Comstock's argument, this must lead to the conclusion that "Jesus loves me, this I know, for my body tells me so."

[13]M. Foucault, *Language, Counter-Memory, Practice* (Ithaca, N.Y.: Cornell University Press, 1977), p. 151, quoted sympathetically in R. Goss, *Jesus Acted Up: A Gay and Lesbian Manifesto* (San Fracisco: Harper, 1993), p. 62. Compare Foucault's *The History of Sexuality*, vol. 1, *An Introduction* (New York: Vintage, 1980), p. 5: "If repression has indeed been the fundamental link between power, knowledge, and sexuality since the classical age, it stands to reason that we will not be able to free ourselves from it except

at considerable cost: nothing less that a transgression of laws, a lifting of prohibitions, an irruption of speech, a reinstating of pleasure within reality, and a whole new economy in the mechanisms of power will be required."

[14]See J. Bethke Elshtein, "Homosexual Politics," *Salmagundi* 58/59 (Fall 1982/Winter 1983): 252-80.

[15]Quoted in the bestseller by M. Kirk and H. Madsen, *After the Ball: How America Will Conquer Its Fear and Hatred of Gays in the 90s* (New York: Plume Books, 1989), p. 361. The authors consider Swift typical of gay media radicals and suggest that homosexuals tone down such rhetoric in order to pursue a "mainstreaming" strategy (pp. 361-66).

[16]For a thorough treatment of this connection, see P. Zaas, "Catalogues and Context: 1 Corinthians 5 and 6," *New Testament Studies* 34 (1988): 628-29.

[17]Note that the very similar list in Mark 7:21-22, which in its original context addressed a Jewish audience (for whom homosexuality was virtually unknown), contains no reference to same-sex relations.

[18]On the importance of marriage, see also Colossians 3:18-19; 1 Timothy 3:2, 11-12; 4:3; 5:14; Titus 2:3-6; Hebrews 13:4; 1 Peter 3:1-7.

[19]The general biblical term for violation of an existing marriage is *adultery*. An even more general term, which applies more specifically to violation of a potential or former bond, is *fornication*. The most common precise manifestations of sexual immorality in biblical times were adultery, use of prostitutes and rape. There is little evidence of other traditionally prohibited activities such as homosexuality, pedophilia, incest, bestiality and premarital sex in the ancient Jewish world. Masturbation may be prohibited by the condemnation in 1 Corinthians 6:9 of *malakoi* (uncertain meaning; "masturbators" according to common contemporary Greek usage) or by the prohibition of lust in Matthew 5:27-28.

[20]This approach involves a special interpretation of Romans 1:26-27, which I will consider in detail in chapter three.

[21]L. William Countryman, *Dirt, Greed and Sex* (Philadelphia: Fortress, 1988), p. 86: "Only intent to harm renders a sexual act impure."

[22]On this point, see O. O'Donovan, "Transsexualism and Christian Marriage," *Journal of Religious Ethics* 11 (Spring 1983): 135-62.

[23]Goss, *Jesus Acted Up*, p. 71.

[24]See, for example, C. P. Christ, "Why Women Need the Goddess: Phenomenological, Psychological and Political Reflections," in *Womanspirit Rising: A Feminist Reader in Religion*, ed. C. P. Christ and J. Plaskow (San Francisco: Harper & Row, 1979), pp. 273-87.

[25]Comstock, *Gay Theology Without Apology*, p. 112. Elsewhere Comstock explains, "We perhaps have regarded Jesus too exclusively as a hero and not permitted him the status of a friend who would value our criticism and contributions" (p. 47). "It is Jesus the master who says, 'Don't look to me for answers; you're on your own. . . . I'm not the boss, simply a friend who's soon dead and gone. Goodbye' " (p. 99). "I have begun to assemble and name as my Scripture a small body of literature in which I find myself

accepted for who I am" (p. 108). "Instead of accepting the oddness of not fitting into and not finding help in the practices and advice handed over to me, I try to step into familiarity and comfort" (p. 110). On the last page of the book, Comstock cites as expressions of self-actualization his desire to "be seized . . . by the spirit of the deer" and to "impersonate the squash blossom" (p. 140). I remind the reader that Comstock is not a New Age shaman but a Protestant chaplain and theology professor at Wesleyan University.

[26]See especially pp. 243-44, 263-64.

[27]Countryman, *Dirt, Greed and Sex,* pp. 257-58.

[28]Ibid., pp. 86, 140.

[29]"Pedophilia" is distinguished from "pseudo-pedophilia," in which adults who generally prefer adults become involved for various reasons with children. The word *pedophilia* is also preferable over something like *pedosexual* or *pederast* because it denotes affection and does not necessarily include sexual contact.

[30]D. Thorstad, "Man/Boy Love and the American Gay Movement," *Journal of Homosexuality* 20, nos. 1/2 (1990): 252. This is confirmed by the recommendations of Kirk and Madsen, *After the Ball,* pp. 306-7, 360: a self-policing social code should include the dictum "If I'm a pederast or a sadomasochist, I'll keep it under wraps, and out of Gay Pride marches."

[31]T. Sandfort, "Pedophilia and the Gay Movement," *Journal of Homosexuality* 13 (Winter 1986/Spring 1987): 96.

[32]E. Brongersma, "Boy-Lovers and Their Influence on Boys: Distorted Research and Anecdotal Observations," *Journal of Homosexuality* 20, nos. 1/2 (1990): 156-57.

[33]Ibid., p. 153.

[34]C. Li, " 'The Main Thing Is Being Wanted': Some Case Studies on Adult Sexual Experiences with Children," *Journal of Homosexuality* 20, nos. 1/2 (1990): 141.

[35]Brongersma, "Boy-Lovers," pp. 159-67; Li, "The Main Thing," p. 137.

[36]G. P. Jones, "The Study of Intergenerational Intimacy in North America: Beyond Politics and Pedophilia," *Journal of Homosexuality* 20, nos. 1/2 (1990): 256-57.

[37]R. Bauserman, "Objectivity and Ideology: Criticism of Theo Sandfort's Research of Man-Boy Sexual Relations," *Journal of Homosexuality* 20, nos. 1/2 (1990): 297-312.

[38]Brongersma, "Boy-Lovers," p. 166.

[39]Li, "The Main Thing," p. 133.

[40]G. van Zessen, "A Model for Group Counseling with Male Pedophiles," *Journal of Homosexuality* 20, nos. 1/2 (1990): 189-98.

Chapter 4: The Main Text in Context

[1]This argument was in fact first advanced by J. Boswell (*Christianity, Social Tolerance and Homosexuality* [New Haven, Conn.: Yale Unversity Press, 1980], pp. 112-13 n. 72). L. William Countryman (*Dirt, Greed and Sex* [Philadelphia: Fortress, 1988]) extends Boswell's thesis with a much more integrative, comprehensive and detailed account of the terminology of the passage.

²Countryman, *Dirt, Greed and Sex*, pp. 98-123. See especially pp. 122-23 on the appropriateness of homosexuality as an example.

³Ibid., p. 123.

⁴E. Cantarella, *Bisexuality in the Ancient World* (New Haven, Conn.: Yale University Press, 1972); K. Dover, *Greek Homosexuality*, 2nd ed. (Cambridge, Mass.: Harvard University Press, 1989).

⁵Plato *Laws* 636c, 838e-839b; see Cantarella, *Bisexuality in the Ancient World*, pp. 58-69. Cantarella notes that Plato's theory did not necessarily match his practice: he was himself probably a pederast.

⁶Cantarella, *Bisexuality in the Ancient World*, pp. 106-54.

⁷Ibid., p. 137.

⁸See Seneca *Moral Epistles* 47.7; Plutarch *Dialogue on Love* 751c-d; compare the later-first-century Dio Chrysostom *Discourse* 77/78.36; 7.151-52.

⁹See B. J. Brooten, "Patristic Interpretations of Romans 1:26," *Studia Patristica* 18, no. 2 (1985): 287-91; B. J. Brooten, "Paul's Views on the Nature of Women and Female Homoeroticism," in *Immaculate and Powerful: The Female in Sacred Image and Social Reality*, ed. C. W. Atkinson, C. H. Buchanan and M. R. Miles (Boston: Beacon, 1985), pp. 61-87; Cantarella, *Bisexuality in the Ancient World*, pp. 91-93, 164-71.

¹⁰G. A. Edwards, *Gay/Lesbian Liberation: A Biblical Perspective* (New York: Pilgrim, 1984), pp. 85-102.

¹¹Virtually all the major commentaries argue for a predominantly Gentile audience; see, for example, J. D. G. Dunn, *Romans 1-8* (Dallas: Word, 1988), pp. xliv-liv; C. E. B. Cranfield, *Romans 1-8* (Edinburgh: T & T Clark, 1975), pp. 18-21.

¹²D. Novak, "Before Revelation: The Rabbis, Paul and Karl Barth," *Journal of Religion* 71 (January 1991): 62. Compare the related passage in the Talmud, *b. Sanhedrin* 58a: "*and he shall cleave*, but not to a male; *to his wife*, but not to his neighbor's wife, *and they shall be as one flesh*, applying to those that can become one flesh, thus excluding cattle and beasts, which cannot become one flesh with man."

¹³R. B. Hays, "Relations Natural and Unnatural: A Response to John Boswell's Exegesis of Romans 1," *Journal of Religious Ethics* 14 (1986): 191.

¹⁴Countryman, *Dirt, Greed and Sex*, pp. 111-12, 116.

¹⁵Ibid, pp. 111-12.

¹⁶In addition to the passages in Romans cited below, see Mark 4:19; John 8:44; Galatians 5:16, 24; Ephesians 2:3; 4:22; Colossians 3:5; 1 Thessalonians 4:5; 1 Timothy 6:9; 2 Timothy 2:22; 3:6; 4:3; Titus 2:12; James 1:14-15; 1 Peter 1:14; 2:11; 4:2-3; 2 Peter 1:4; 2:10; 2:18; 3:3, Jude 16, 18; 1 John 2:16-17; Revelation 18:14. Compare the verb form *epithymeō* in 1 Corinthians 10:6 and Galatians 5:17. The only other positive or neutral occurrence is Luke 22:15, which refers to Jesus's "desire" to eat the Passover meal with his disciples.

¹⁷The word occurs only here in the New Testament, but it is used elsewhere for sin or transgression of law. See Philo *De Posteritate Caini* 180 and *De Praemiis et Poenis* 77; Plato *Republic* 2.366a; Sophocles *Antigone* 449, 481, 663. See also the discussion of the

relation of verse 6 to verses 3-5 in C. A. Wannamaker, *The Epistles to the Thessalonians* (Grand Rapids, Mich.: Eerdmans, 1990), pp. 154-56; and F. F. Bruce, *1 and 2 Thessalonians* (Waco, Tex.: Word, 1982), pp. 84-85.

[18]Countryman, *Dirt, Greed and Sex*, pp. 97-104 and p. 119 n. 31.

[19]Ibid., p. 113. Countryman offers no documentation here, so I am left to speculate that he takes his evidence from classical Greek sources far removed from Paul's context.

[20]The word is employed extensively in the apocryphal 4 Maccabees and in Philo, consistently in a negative sense, to denote the emotions that operate in opposition to reason. Classical lexicons give numerous examples of various positive or neutral meanings in nonethical contexts.

[21]Romans 8:18; 2 Corinthians 1:5-7 (three times); Philippians 3:10; Colossians 1:24; 2 Timothy 3:11; Hebrews 2:9-10; 10:32; 1 Peter 1:11; 4:13; 5:1, 9.

[22]*De Opificio Mundi* 80; *Legum Allegoriae* 3.155, 138; *Quod Deus Sit Immutabilis* 113 (of sexual desire); *De Posteritate Caini* 26, 71, 116; *De Gigantibus* 35; *De Ebrietate* 214, 222; *De Abrahamo* 96; *De Decalogo* 123 (of sexual desire), 149; *De Virtutibus* 136.

[23]Abbreviated "LXX" and including the Apocrypha, this translation was completed by Jews in Alexandria, Egypt, about two hundred years before the New Testament. The LXX, and not the Hebrew version, was the Bible used and quoted almost exclusively by Paul and other New Testament writers. It is therefore important for New Testament language study.

[24]The NRSV reads, "Let neither gluttony nor lust overcome me."

[25]Countryman remarks that 1 Corinthians 7:9 expresses Paul's willingness, "if need be, to accept the legitimacy of sexual desire and its appropriate satisfaction" (*Dirt, Greed and Sex*, p. 113). But Paul hardly legitimates "burning" when he presents marriage as its *antidote*. His references to temptation in the context (vv. 2, 5) imply that burning is linked to sin.

[26]As the NRSV here renders *epithymia;* as the King James Version and the New American Bible render *epithymia* and *orexis;* and as the New International Version renders *pathos* and *orexis.*

[27]Countryman, *Dirt, Greed and Sex*, pp. 105-9.

[28]Countryman's argument weighs heavily on several weak links. The only prior reference in Paul's writings is 1 Thessalonians 4:6, where greed *(pleonekteō)* is used in proximity to *akatharsia* (v. 7). But this is the only metaphorical use of the word group in the recognized letters of Paul, and the only place where it occurs with *akatharsia*. For further corroboration Countryman posits *oral* teaching by Paul which is reflected in but three purportedly non-Pauline passages: Ephesians 4:19; 5:3, 5; and Colossians 3:5-6. Only the first of these supports an integral relation of *akatharsia* and *pleonexia*. In the second, the words are separated by the disjunctive particle *or* (ē). Furthermore, in the second and third passages "idolatry" *(eidolatria)* is equated specifically with *pleonexia* only, not the whole list as Countryman suggests (ibid., pp. 108-9).

[29]So F. Hauck, "ὀργή κτλ." in *Theological Dictionary of the New Testament*, ed. Gerhard Kittel and Gerhard Friedrich, 10 vols. (Grand Rapids, Mich.: Eerdmans, 1967), 5:428;

M. Newton, *The Concept of Purity at Qumran and in the Letters of Paul* (Cambridge: Cambridge University Press, 1985), p. 103. Hauck cites the second-century B.C. *Testament of the Twelve Patriarchs, Testament of Joseph* 4:6 and *Testament of Judah* 14:5, where *akatharsia* is equated with adultery. In Philo for association of *akatharsia/akatharsis* with sexual sin, see *Legum Allegoriae* 2.29; 3.139, 147; *De Migratione Abrahami* 65; *De Specialibus Legibus* 1.150. This Hellenistic Jewish development to include immorality in general and sexual license in particular is an extension of the more narrow connotation of ritual uncleanness in Old Testament texts.

[30]The other New Testament occurrences are Galatians 5:19; Ephesians 4:19; 5:3; Colossians 2:5; and 1 Thessalonians 2:3. For *akathartos*, see 1 Corinthians 7:14; Ephesians 5:5; and especially Revelation 17:4, where the whore of Babylon holds a cup containing "the impurities *[akatharta]* of *her fornication.*" Second Corinthians 6:17 (see 6:17—7:1) includes *akathartos* in an Old Testament quotation and contrasts the actions of unbelievers (characterized by "lawlessness," 6:14, and "defilement of body and of spirit," 7:1) with "holiness" (7:1).

[31]Compare "vileness" (New English Bible); "filthy things" (Good News).

[32]Countryman, *Dirt, Greed and Sex*, p. 113, on *aschēmosynē;* compare his discussion of *atimia* on p. 112.

[33]For occurrences of *atimia, aschēmosynē* in social contexts, see Acts 5:41; 2 Corinthians 6:8; 11:21; and for all instances of *atimos:* Matthew 13:57, Mark 6:4, 1 Corinthians 4:10. For *atimia* in the sense of ritual impurity, see Romans 9:21, 1 Corinthians 11:14 and 2 Timothy 2:20; compare the use of *atimos* in 1 Corinthians 12:23.

[34]The non-Pauline occurrences, which support this sense of *atimazō*, are Mark 12:4, Luke 20:11, John 8:49 and James 2:6.

[35]See Ephesians 4:24-32; 6:14; Colossians 3:12-17; and 1 Peter 5:5 for the association of clothing imagery with righteousness. In Revelation 17, further allusions are made which lend a more particularly sexual cast to the passage: the whore of Babylon is clothed in scarlet and holds a cup full of "the impurities of her fornication" (17:4). Of course the idea of righteousness (including sexual righteousness) as readiness for the end is often present without the clothing imagery: Matthew 24:45-51; Luke 17:22-27; 21:34-36.

[36]Countryman does this (*Dirt, Greed and Sex*, pp. 116-17) by an ingenious translation of the Greek that is technically possible but highly unnatural to the context. One's suspicion that grammatical rules are being forced to fit the theory is increased by the fact that no other commentator or translator has read the passage this way. Greek grammarians will appreciate the peculiarities: Countryman suggests that *peplērōmenous* is the past use of the perfect rather than the more natural intensive, that it is a causal participle rather than the more natural circumstantial and that the antecedent of *toiauta* in verse 32 is strictly limited to verses 29-31 and does not include verses 26-27.

[37]There are two LXX occurrences which are also inconclusive. Second Maccabees 6:4 refers to the desecration of the temple by things "unfit" for sacrifice—clearly a case

of ritual impurity; 3 Maccabees 4:16 tells of Antiochus "uttering *improper* words against the supreme God"—possibly *impure*, but possibly a case of proud defiance, which is *morally* reprehensible.

[38]Diogenes Laertius *Vitae* 7.108-9; see also 3.24; Epictetus *Discourses* 2.7.1; 2.14.18; 3.7.25; 4.12.16; *Enchiridion* 30.1; Cicero *De Officiis* 3.3. Philo follows this sense, on one occasion equating *kathēkonta* with virtue (*Legum Allegoriae* 1.56), on another occasion opposing it to unrighteousness (*adikia*, *Legum Allegoriae* 3.165). In general terms, Philo uses the word group to designate the responsibilities of everyday life: *Legum Allegoriae* 3.18, 126, 210; *De Cherubim* 14; *De Sacrificiis Abelis et Caini* 43; *De Plantatione* 95, 100.

[39]H. Schlier, "καθήκω," in *Theological Dictionary of the New Testament*, ed. Gerhard Kittel (Grand Rapids, Mich.: Eerdmans, 1965), 3:438.

[40]Boswell, *Christianity, Social Tolerance and Homosexuality*, pp. 110-12.

[41]Countryman (*Dirt, Greed and Sex*, p. 114), citing Romans 2:14; 2:27; 11:24; Galatians 2:15, but rejecting 1 Corinthians 11:13-15, since it pertains only to "widespread social usage"—a sense that would not serve Paul's purpose in Romans 1.

[42]Boswell, *Christianity, Social Tolerance and Homosexuality*, pp. 109-13. For further response to this point, see Hays, "Relations Natural and Unnatural," pp. 196-99.

[43]I will treat this subject more fully in chapter seven. For now it is enough to point out that Boswell's position depends on a distinction between "natures" or "orientations" that is utterly foreign to Paul and simplistic from an ethical standpoint. To affirm that same-sex intimacy occurs in nature (that is, people do it) does not automatically make it natural in the sense of moral acceptability; and to call an inclination a "nature" neither justifies nor renders inevitable the behavior toward which that person is inclined. Consider these statements in relation to alcoholism.

[44]See, for example, Hays, "Relations Natural and Unnatural," pp. 190, 200; Cranfield, *Romans 1-8*, p. 104; Dunn, *Romans 1-8*, pp. 53, 74-75.

[45]P. B. Jung and R. F. Smith, *Heterosexism: An Ethical Challenge* (Albany: State University of New York Press, 1993), pp. 80-81.

[46]Hays, "Relations Natural and Unnatural," pp. 192-95; J. B. DeYoung, "The Meaning of 'Nature' in Romans 1 and Its Implications for Biblical Perspectives of Homosexual Behavior," *Journal of the Evangelical Theological Society* 31 (1988): 429-47.

[47]Later, in *Laws* 839a, Plato reveals that by *natural* he does not refer to active-passive sex roles but to reproductive capacity.

[48]My translation. The Loeb Classical Library translation here reads "without respect for the sex nature which the active partner shares with the passive."

[49]See further examples, both pagan and Jewish, in Hays, "Relations Natural and Unnatural"; DeYoung, "Meaning of 'Nature' "; R. Scroggs, *The New Testament and Homosexuality* (Philadelphia: Fortress, 1983), pp. 59-60; V. P. Furnish, *The Moral Teaching of Paul* (Nashville: Abingdon, 1979), pp. 58-67.

[50]S. Dresner ("Homosexuality and the Order of Creation," *Judaism* 40 [Summer 1991]: 311) discusses a number of rabbinic texts condemning homosexuality, including *Genesis Rabbah* 26:5 and *Leviticus Rabbah* 23:9. R. Kirschner ("Halakah and Homosexuality:

A Reappraisal," *Judaism* 37 [Fall 1988]: 450) adds *b. Sanhedrin* 58a; *Mishnah Torah Melakhim* 9:5-6; *m. Qiddušin* 4:14; *b. Qiddušin* 82a; *Shulhan Arukh Even ha-Ezer* 24; *Sefer ha-Hinnukh* 209; *Asheri, Ned* 21a; and *Mishnah Torah Issurei Biah* 21:8. See also *b. Sanhedrin* 58a as quoted above, note 14.

[51]For a detailed treatment of the relation of Romans 1 to the creation account and to the contemporary Jewish Wisdom tradition, see K. W. Huggins, "An Investigation of the Jewish Theology of Sexuality Influencing the References to Homosexuality in Romans 1:18-32," Ph.D. dissertation, Southwestern Baptist Theological Seminary, 1986, pp. 200-44.

[52]One rare exception is the Plato reference quoted above. Another is in Plutarch's *Whether Beasts Are Rational*, in which he asserts that "until now the desires of animals have involved intercourse neither of male with male nor of female with female" (990D), and that to do so would be a "violation of nature" (990F). I have been able to locate no other joint reference to male and female homosexuality. Pseudo-Phocylides *Sentences* 190-92 probably refers not to homosexuality but to the assumption of an active role on the part of the woman in heterosexual intercourse: "Do not transgress with unlawful sex the limits set by nature. For even animals are not pleased by intercourse of male with male. And let women not imitate the sexual role of men."

[53]D. F. Wright, "Homosexuality: The Relevance of the Bible," *Evangelical Quarterly* 61 (1989): 295.

[54]This point is made by Countryman (*Dirt, Greed and Sex*, pp. 115-16), who in this instance is supported by a long scholarly tradition; see references in Cranfield, *Romans 1-8*, p. 127 n. 1.

[55]In the Pauline writings see 1 Corinthians 6:9; 15:33; Galatians 6:7; Ephesians 4:14; 1 Thessalonians 2:3; 2 Thessalonians 2:11; 2 Timothy 3:13; Titus 3:3.

[56]Dunn (*Romans 1-8*, p. 65) suggests that the "reciprocal nature of the transaction" is indicated by the prefixes *anti-* and *apo-* (*apolambanontes*), and he makes reference to *m. 'Abot* 4.2, "The reward of one transgression is [another] transgression."

[57]Countryman, *Dirt, Greed and Sex*, p. 115.

[58]Ibid., p. 110.

Chapter 5: From Sodom to Sodom

[1]It is, however, used several times in a sexual sense near both the relevant passages: Genesis 4:1, 17, 25; 24:16; 38:16; Judg 11:39; 21:12.

[2]The power of repetition among revisionists (for example, J. Boswell, *Christianity, Social Tolerance and Homosexuality* [New Haven, Conn.: Yale University Press, 1980], pp. 92-97; L. William Countryman, *Dirt, Greed and Sex* [Philadelphia: Fortress, 1988], pp. 30-32; J. J. McNeill, *The Church and the Homosexual* [Boston: Beacon, 1976; 4th ed. 1993], pp. 42-50) leads to the remarkable assertion of R. Williams (*Just As I Am: A Practical Guide to Being Out, Proud and Christian* [New York: Crown, 1992], pp. 47-48) that "virtually all mainstream biblical scholars" agree. A survey of the major commentaries on Genesis (see J. R. Wright, "Boswell on Homosexuality: A Case Undemonstrated,"

Anglican Theological Review 66 [Winter 1985]: 82) suggests that Williams defines *mainstream* as "mainstream *revisionist.*"

[3]S. Niditch, "The 'Sodomite' Theme in Judges 19-20: Family, Community and Social Disintegration," *Catholic Biblical Quarterly* 44 (1982): 369; see pp. 367-69 for a thorough discussion of the relationship between homosexuality and social disintegration in Genesis and Judges.

[4]See the explanation of M. Pope, *Job* (Garden City, N.Y.: Doubleday, 1973), p. 267. Pope argues persuasively (p. 236) that *flesh (bāśār)* here pertains to sex rather than food, as in Ezekiel 16:26; 23:20; and Leviticus 15:2-15 (probably a description of gonorrhea).

[5]For probable examples of euphemism, see J. B. DeYoung, "A Critique of Prohomosexual Interpretations of the Old Testament Apocrypha and Pseudepigrapha," *Bibliotheca Sacra* 147 (1990): 437-54, especially 453.

[6]See A. Phillips, "Uncovering the Father's Skirt," *Vetus Testamentum* 30 (1980): 38-43. Supporting evidence includes the fact that Ham is the father of Canaan, the nation associated with same-sex vices in Leviticus, and the supposition that this incident led to the otherwise obscure references to "uncovering the father's skirts" in Leviticus 18:7 and Deuteronomy 23:1. The absence of explicit reference to this story in subsequent condemnations of same-sex acts, however, requires that we leave in doubt the question of its familiarity in Paul's day.

[7]D. S. Bailey (*Homosexuality and the Western Christian Tradition* [London: Archon Books, 1975], p. 10) and G. A. Edwards (*Gay/Lesbian Liberation: A Biblical Perspective* [New York: Pilgrim, 1984], pp. 51-54) argue that *abominations* equals idolatry without implications for sexual sin, but the language of the chapter is so sexual that it requires a monumental effort of imagination to suppose that the original audience would so limit its interpretation of the passage.

[8]See D. F. Wright, "Early Christian Attitudes to Homosexuality," *Studia Patristica* 18, no. 2 (1989): 329-34.

[9]Edwards, *Gay/Lesbian Liberation*, pp. 35-39.

[10]See also *2 Enoch* 10:4-5 and 34:1-3 ms. P, which may represent early Christian revision; *Jubilees* 13:17; 20:5-6; *Testament of Levi* 17:11; *Epistle of Aristeas* 152; probably Wisdom of Solomon 14:26 ("confusion of sex"). In addition, the Septuagint of Genesis 19 uses terms that imply that the translators understood the same-sex connotation of the passages; see J. B. DeYoung, "The Contributions of the Septuagint to Biblical Sanctions Against Homosexuality," *Journal of the Evangelical Theological Society* 34 (June 1991): 161-65.

[11]*De Abrahamo* 133-41; *Specialibus Legibus* 3.37-39; *De Ebrietate* 222; *De Fuga et Inventione* 144; *De Vita Contemplativa* 59-62; compare *De Confusione Linguarum* 27.

[12]*Antiquities of the Jews* 1.11.3 §200; compare 1.11.1 §194-95.

[13]For example, laws against sodomy apply variously to homosexual intercourse, nonvaginal heterosexual intercourse, oral sex (fellatio) and some or all of the above, whether forced or voluntary. This bewildering situation results from regional varieties

of traditional definitions, some of which remained in laws and some of which were redefined as the term fell out of popular use. What the popular definition is now is anybody's guess.

[14]Boswell, *Christianity, Social Tolerance and Homosexuality*, p. 102; Countryman, *Dirt, Greed and Sex*, pp. 86, 107-9, 123.

[15]G. J. Wenham, "The Old Testament Attitude to Homosexuality," *Expository Times* 102 (Spring 1991): 362.

[16]In terms of the relative severity of penalty as an indication of distinctions between laws, it is notable that the violation of Levitical food laws causes one day of ritual uncleanness, and sex during menstruation incurs seven days' uncleanness; but sex between males—like adultery, bestiality and incest in the same context—carries the penalty of death.

[17]Deuteronomy 23:17; 1 Kings 14:24; 15:12; 22:46; 2 Kings 23:7; Job 36:14.

[18]Bailey, *Homosexuality and the Western Christian Tradition*, pp. 52-53; Boswell, *Christianity, Tolerance and Homosexuality*, p. 99; R. Scroggs, *The New Testament and Homosexuality* (Philadelphia: Fortress, 1983), p. 71.

[19]Edwards, *Gay/Lesbian Liberation*, p. 58; McNeill, *The Church and the Homosexual*, p. 57. Edwards also regards the Leviticus texts as references to cult prostitution, which would of course clinch his argument. There may be a connection, but since the Leviticus passage is not so specific, the question must remain open.

[20]W. Deming, "Mark 9.42—10.12, Matthew 5.27-32 and *b. Nid.* 13b: A First Century Discussion of Male Sexuality," *New Testament Studies* 36 (1990): 130-41.

[21]Quoting ibid., p. 133, my italics.

[22]Ibid., p. 141.

[23]*Sibylline Oracles* 2:73-75 (third century A.D.), where it is clearly connected to Leviticus: "Do not steal seeds. Whoever takes for himself is accursed [to generations of generations, to the scattering of life. Do not practice *homosexuality*, do not betray information, do not murder]. Give to one who has labored his wage. Do not oppress a poor man."

[24]See especially Scroggs, *The New Testament and Homosexuality*, pp. 62-65, 101-9, 127. Scroggs sees the origin of the term in Hellenistic Judaism, arguing that *arsenokoitēs* is a translation of the rabbinic designation *miškāḇ zākûr*, "lying of a male."

[25]Boswell, *Christianity, Social Tolerance and Homosexuality*, pp. 106-7, and app. 1, pp. 338-53. In Boswell's view, *malakoi* are probably masturbators.

[26]Countryman, *Dirt, Greed and Sex*, p. 119. Later Countryman argues that the *arsenokoitais* in 1 Timothy 1:10 are prostitutes because of the presence nearby of *pornois* ("fornicators," NRSV), which implies the use of prostitutes (p. 128). This, however, requires a shift from the user of a prostitute to the prostitute himself; and since it is less likely that Paul would envision former prostitutes than users of prostitutes among his audience, it is more plausible to see a transition from those who break the marriage bond with *females* to those who break it with *males*. Scroggs (*The New Testament and Homosexuality*, p. 120) contends that in 1 Timothy 1:10 the *pornois* are the male prostitutes (the equivalent of *malakoi* in 1 Cor 6:9) and the *arsenokoitai* are the men

who engage in sex with them, but this appears to strain the meaning of *pornois*. His thesis would be stronger, I believe, if he argued that only the adult male *solicitors* of sex *(pornois, arsenokoitai)* are addressed either as a general designation for all participants in the vice or because they are the ones far more likely to make up part of the immediate audience of such a letter ("this is what some of you used to be," 1 Cor 6:11).

[27]D. F. Wright, "Homosexuals or Prostitutes? The Meaning of *Arsenokoitai* (1 Cor. 6:9, 1 Tim. 1:10)," *Vigiliae Christianae* 38 (1984): 125-53, especially 126-29. See also P. Zaas, "1 Corinthians 6:9ff.: Was Homosexuality Condoned in the Corinthian Church?" *Society of Biblical Literature Seminar Papers* 17 (1979): 205-12, for the argument (against Scroggs) that the elements of Paul's vice list were actual practices in Corinth and not merely adoptions of standard Jewish Hellenistic material. See also E. Cantarella, *Bisexuality in the Ancient World* (New Haven, Conn.: Yale University Press, 1972), pp. 192-93.

[28]See also Philo *Hypothetica* 7.1-2 §357-8: "If you are guilty of pederasty or adultery or rape of a young person, even of a female, for I need not mention the case of a male . . . So too if you commit an outrage on the person of a slave or a free man . . . the penalty is the same, death." Compare the connection between adultery and homosexuality in the opening lines of *Pseudo-Phocylides:* "Phocylides, the wisest of men, set forth these counsels of God by his holy judgments, gifts of blessing. Neither commit adultery nor rouse homosexual passion [literally, stir a man's penis]."

[29]The Jewish tradition of sinful liaisons between angels and humans, based on Genesis 6:1-4, is apparent in *Jubilees* 7:20-21 and *Testament of the Twelve Patriarchs, Testament of Naphthali* 3:4-5. The latter passage mentions these angels and the men of Sodom in the same context as beings who "changed the order of nature."

[30]See *Sibylline Oracles* 5:143-79 (especially line 166) and 5:429-40 (especially line 430), which name adultery and pederasty; 4 Ezra 16:46-63, especially 47, which names harlotry; compare *Psalms of Solomon* 2:15-25; *Apocalypse of Baruch* 39:5-7; *Sibylline Oracles* 3:300-14.

[31]See, for example, 2 Enoch 34:2: "And all the world will be reduced to confusion by iniquities and wickednesses and abominable fornications, that is, friend with friend in the anus, and every other kind of wicked uncleanness which it is disgusting to report"; 2 Enoch 10:4: "This place, Enoch, has been prepared for those who do not glorify God who practice on the earth the sin which is against nature, which is child corruption in the anus in the manner of Sodom." The date of origin of 2 Enoch is debated, but the style here is entirely consistent with that of other Jewish writings within two hundred years either way of the time of Christ.

[32]Matthew 7:6; 15:26-27; Mark 7:27-28; Philippians 3:2.

[33]This connection was noted by R. H. Charles, *The Revelation of St. John* (Edinburgh: T & T Clark, 1920), 2:178. Charles makes the equation with "the polluted" in 21:8 but does not clearly make the equation of both with homosexuality. That equation is made by several commentators, including J. M. Ford, *Revelation* (Garden City, N.Y.:

Doubleday, 1975), p. 345.

Chapter 6: The Price of Love

[1]See, for example, P. Painton, "The Shrinking Ten Percent," *Time*, April 26, 1993, pp. 27-29; P. Rogers, "How Many Gays Are There?" *Newsweek*, February 15, 1993, p. 46.

[2]A. C. Kinsey, W. B. Pomeroy and C. E. Martin, *Sexual Behavior in the Human Male* (Philadelphia: W. B. Saunders, 1948); compare A. C. Kinsey, W. B. Pomeroy, C. E. Martin and P. H. Gebhard, *Sexual Behavior in the Human Female* (Philadelphia: W. B. Saunders, 1953).

[3]For a detailed critique, see J. H. Court and J. G. Muir, eds., *Kinsey, Sex and Fraud: The Indoctrination of a People* (Lafayette, La.: Huntington House, 1990).

[4]D. A. Dawson, *AIDS Knowledge and Attitudes for January-March 1990: Provisional Data from the National Health Interview Survey,* Advance Data from Vital and Health Statistics 193 (Hyattsville, Md.: National Center for Health Statistics, September 26, 1990), p. 11; J. E. Fitti and M. Cynamon, *AIDS Knowledge and Attitudes for April-June 1990: Provisional Data from the National Health Interview Survey,* Advance Data from Vital and Health Statistics 195 (Hyattsville, Md.: National Center for Health Statistics, December 18, 1990), p. 11; P. F. Adams and A. M. Hardy, *AIDS Knowledge and Attitudes for July-September 1990: Provisional Data from the National Health Interview Survey,* Advance Data from Vital and Health Statistics 198 (Hyattsville, Md.: National Center for Health Statistics, April 1, 1991), p. 11.

[5]Robert Fay et al., "Prevalence and Patterns of Same-Gender Contact Among Men," *Science* 243 (January 20, 1989): 338-48; S. M. Rogers and C. F. Turner, "Male-Male Sexual Contact in the U.S.A.: Findings from Five Sample Surveys, 1970-1990," *Journal of Sex Research* 28 (November 1991): 491-519. The fifth study reported by Rogers and Turner is for the city of Dallas and reports higher percentages: 8.1 percent male-to-male contact in the previous year, 4.6 percent lifetime.

[6]M. Diamond, "Homosexuality and Bisexuality in Different Populations," *Archives of Sexual Behavior* 22, no. 4 (1993): 291-310 (summary on p. 306). Diamond also reports city studies of San Francisco (1984) and New York (1985) that yielded numbers of 9.9 percent and 9 percent, respectively, who identified themselves as homosexual or bisexual. See also the review article by S. N. Seidman and R. O. Rieder, "A Review of Sexual Behavior in the United States," *American Journal of Psychiatry* 151 (March 1994): 330-41, which mentions several other corroborating studies unavailable to me.

[7]E. O. Laumann et al., *The Social Organization of Sexuality* (Chicago: University of Chicago Press, 1994), p. 294.

[8]See the discussion of the interrelation between practice, self-identification and reported desire in ibid., pp. 298-301. In that study 2.8 percent of the men and 1.4 percent of the women reported some level of homosexual or bisexual identity (p. 293), but these numbers did not perfectly overlap with the numbers indicating same-sex experience.

[9]See Rogers and Turner, "Male-Male Sexual Contact," pp. 508-9, table 8 (males only)

and discussion. See also Laumann et al., *Social Organization of Sexuality,* table 8.3A (p. 311) and discussion (pp. 310-13).

[10]Kinsey instituted a seven-point scale for self-reported orientation, from 0 for exclusively heterosexual to 6 for exclusively homosexual. For a discussion of the possibilities and limitations of this scale, see, for example, E. Coleman, "Toward a Synthetic Understanding of Sexual Orientation," in *Homosexuality/Heterosexuality: Concepts of Sexual Orientation,* ed. D. P. McWhirter, S. A. Sanders and J. M. Reinisch, Kinsey Institute Series 2 (New York: Oxford University Press, 1990), pp. 267-76, and F. Klein, "The Need to View Sexual Orientation as a Multivariable Dynamic Process: A Theoretical Perspective," in the same volume, pp. 277-82.

[11]See M. S. Weinberg, C. J. Williams and D. W. Pryor, *Dual Attraction: Understanding Bisexuality* (New York: Oxford University Press, 1994). This study is the most detailed to date, but it is flawed by the narrowness of the data, which are drawn from a rather small sample, recruited from a bisexual organization in a single location (San Francisco).

[12]T. W. Smith, "Adult Sexual Behavior in 1989: Number of Partners, Frequency of Intercourse and Risk of AIDS," *Planning Perspectives* 23 (May/June 1991): 102-7. See p. 104, table 2. Smith is director of the General Social Survey Project at the NORC (University of Chicago).

[13]G. Remafedi et al., "Demography of Sexual Orientation in Adolescents," *Pediatrics* 89, no. 4, pt. 2 (April 1992): 714-21. The statistics do not overlap: only 27.1 percent of students with homosexual experience identified themselves as homosexual or bisexual (p. 719). The apparent implication is that most adolescents who try it do not like it.

[14]L. Ku, F. L. Sonenstein and J. H. Pleck, "Patterns of HIV Risk and Preventive Behaviors Among Teenage Men," *Public Health Reports* 107 (March/April 1992): 131-38.

[15]A. M. Johnson et al., "Sexual Lifestyles and HIV Risk," *Nature* 360 (December 3, 1992): 410-12. The earlier pilot study of one thousand British adults yielded a higher result, 9 percent male, 4 percent female homosexual experience over the course of a lifetime, with 5 percent male, 1 percent female having had a homosexual partner: K. Wellings et al., "Sexual Lifestyles Under Scrutiny," *Nature* 348 (November 22, 1990): 276-78. Another British study of 480 subjects yielded a lower result, 1.7 percent who had ever had had a homosexual experience, and half of those had only had one such experience: D. Forman and C. Chilvers, "Sexual Behaviour of Young and Middle Aged men in England and Wales," *British Medical Journal* 298 (April 29, 1989): 1137-42.

[16]Reported in Diamond, "Homosexuality and Bisexuality," p. 295, table 1.

[17]A. Spira et al., "AIDS and Sexual Behavior in France," *Nature* 360 (December 3, 1992): 407-9; P. Aldous, "French Venture Where U.S. Fears to Tread," *Science* 257 (July 3, 1992): 25. This study involved 20,055 subjects.

[18]The studies all describe evidence-gathering and reporting techniques; see especially the discussions in Diamond, "Homosexuality and Bisexuality," pp. 303-6, and Lau-

mann et al., *Social Organization of Sexuality*, pp. 35-73.

[19]The number two is taken from Smith, "Adult Sexual Behavior," p. 104, table 2, which estimates orientation based on exclusive practice. The most liberal number possible would be fourteen: Fay et al. ("Prevalence and Patterns," pp. 346-47) estimate that various unknowns might allow for a doubling of their adjusted numbers of 3.0 percent for men (and I add 1.5 percent of women, based on the consistent finding of researchers: see Diamond, "Homosexuality and Bisexuality," p. 306) who had adult homosexual contacts "fairly often" (1.2 percent) or "frequently" (1.8 percent). This of course assumes that "fairly often" reflects constant rather than periodic or episodic experience and that such contact is always homosexual in motivation.

[20]A. P. Bell and M. S. Weinberg, *Homosexualities: A Study of Diversity Among Men and Women* (New York: Simon & Schuster, 1978).

[21]Ibid., p. 132.

[22]Ibid., p. 346, table 13.5.

[23]U.S. Department of Commerce, *1990 Census of Population: Social and Economic Characteristics* (September 1993), volumes by state. These statistics, incidentally, may provide independent verification of the overall homosexual population estimate given above. Since an additional 20 percent of male homosexuals and an additional 50 percent of female homosexuals are more loosely "coupled" at any given time (Bell and Weinberg, *Homosexualities*, pp. 91, 97), we might begin with the census number base of about 300,000, generously double it to account for reluctance to fill out the census form honestly, and then multiply the males by three and the females by 1.2: the total comes out to about 1.5 million.

[24]Ibid. California contains 23,275 male and 13,327 female same-sex partners. Other locales of interest, where the information is given by county in table 151 of the relevant state volumes, include Los Angeles County (male/female 8,080/3,977), Chicago (2,942/1,747), Washington, D.C. (1,822/479), Seattle (1,781/1,347), San Diego (1,918/949), Boston (1,264/691), Minneapolis-St. Paul (1,244/1,167) Dallas (1,150/412), Philadelphia (888/761) and Atlanta (852/325). The relevant volume on New York was unavailable at the time of writing; I estimate the numbers at 10,000/5,000 to reach the 33 percent figure for the twelve cities.

[25]Ibid., 2/6:984, table 151.

[26]Bell and Weinberg, *Homosexualities*, p. 308, table 7.

[27]Ibid., pp. 308-9, table 7. For females, the corresponding numbers are 6 percent who reported more than half their partners as strangers, and 8 percent who reported they had sex with more than half their partners only once.

[28]Ibid., p. 312, table 7.

[29]Ibid. These numbers match the results of a survey of 962 female homosexuals in K. Jay and A. Young, *The Gay Report* (New York: Summit, 1979), p. 324, which reports the number of partners lifetime at under ten for 62 percent of subjects, and more than twenty-five for just 13 percent. Laumann et al. (*Social Organization of Sexuality*, pp. 178-79, tables 5.1B-C) report that among the general population, 8.6 percent (12.0

percent male, 5.9 percent female) report five to ten partners in the previous five years; 2.7 percent (4.2 percent male, 1.4 percent female) report eleven to twenty; and 1.7 percent (3.3 percent male, 0.4 percent female) report more than twenty-one. Among those who have never married, these figures are 19.7 percent, 6.4 percent and 3.9 percent, respectively. In the previous year, 3.2 percent report more than five partners (5.1 percent male, 1.7 percent female); among those never married, 9.0 percent report more than five partners. The study gives no comparative data for same-sex partners.

[30]M. T. Saghir and E. Robins, *Male and Female Homosexuality: A Comprehensive Investigation* (Baltimore: Williams Wilkins, 1973), pp. 56-57.

[31]Ibid., p. 57, table 4.14; p. 226, table 12.11.

[32]Ibid., p. 226.

[33]This number is not reported by Saghir and Robins *(Male and Female Homosexuality)* but is derived from the numbers in tables 4.10, 4.14, 12.7 and 12.11.

[34]Ibid., pp. 339-40. Jay and Young surveyed 4,329 male homosexuals and 962 female homosexuals *(The Gay Report).*

[35]J. Harry, *Gay Couples* (New York: Praeger Books, 1984), p. 115, table 6.1. A smaller 1980 study found that 76.5 percent of male homosexuals in closed relationships had at least one additional partner, 40 percent at least six: D. Blasband and L. A. Peplaw, "Sexual Exclusivity," *Archives of Sexual Behavior* 14 (October 1985): 406, table 4.

[36]L. Linn et al., "Recent Sexual Behaviors Among Homosexual Men Seeking Primary Medical Care," *Archives of Internal Medicine* 149 (December 1989): 2685-90. The authors acknowledge the possibility that results are unrepresentative of all homosexual men, since their 823 subjects were drawn from those seeking medical help, who may be more promiscuous. But, they counter, most other studies, which recruit subjects from gay organizations and publications, are unrepresentative in other ways (p. 2689).

[37]G. R. Seage III et al., "The Relation Between Nitrite Inhalants, Unprotected Anal Intercourse and the Risk of Immunodeficiency Virus Infection," *American Journal of Epidemiology* 135 (January 1, 1992): 5, table 1. A 1990 British study found 28.4 percent of 387 subjects in "close-coupled" relationships, a result higher than that of Bell and Weinberg *(Homosexualities):* F. C. I. Hickson et al., "Maintenance of Open Gay Relationships: Some Strategies for Protection Against HIV," *AIDS Care* 4, no. 4 (1992): 412. The authors conclude, however, that this result is consistent with earlier studies and does not represent a trend toward exclusivity (p. 409). An Australian study that interviewed 145 subjects in 1986-1987 and again in 1991 found that the percentage who described their homosexual practice as "monogamous" rose from 22.8 to 25.5: S. Kippax et al., "Sustaining Safe Sex: A Longitudinal Study of a Sample of Homosexual Men," *AIDS* 7 (February 1993): 260, table 2. The combined result of two 1992 Dutch studies showed that 78 percent of 577 randomly selected male subjects reported more than five partners in the past year, 45 percent more than twenty partners: P. J. Veugelers et al., "Estimation of the Magnitude of the HIV Epidemic Among Homosexual Men: Utilization of Survey Data in Predictive Models," *European Journal of Epidemiology* 9 (July 1993): 438, table 1

[38]C. Leigh, M. T. Temple and K. F. Trocki, "The Sexual Behavior of U.S. Adults: Results from a Nation Survey," *American Journal of Public Health* 83 (October 1993): 1404, table 3.

[39]P. Blumstein and P. Schwartz, "Intimate Relationships and the Creation of Sexuality," in *Homosexuality/Heterosexuality: Concepts of Sexual Orientation*, ed. D. P. McWhirter, S. A. Sanders and J. M. Reinisch, Kinsey Institute Series 2 (New York: Oxford University Press, 1990), p. 317, table 18.2; compare Seidman and Rieder, "Review of Sexual Behavior," p. 336. Laumann et al. (*Social Organization of Sexuality*, p. 216, table 5.15) report that 85 percent of women and 75.5 percent of men report no extramarital affairs lifetime. In that study 14.9 percent of cohabiting people and 3.8 percent of married people reported more than one partner in the previous year. The study gives no comparative data for same-sex partners.

[40]D. P. McWhirter and A. M. Mattison (*The Male Couple: How Relationships Develop* [Englewood Cliffs, N.J.: Prentice-Hall, 1984]) found that of the 156 couples in their study, none of the relationships that lasted more than five years was monogamous, and only seven couples in the study were maintaining exclusivity (p. 253, table 34). Hickson et al. confirm this finding in relation to their more recent British study ("Maintenance of Open Gay Relationships," p. 412).

[41]Bell and Weinberg (*Homosexualities*, pp. 70-71, 298, table 5) report approximately 1.5 times the sexual activity on the part of males. They do not give an overall average, but approximately 50 percent of their sample of 685 men, and approximately 40 percent of their sample of 282 women, reported having sex more than twice per week. The average frequency of sexual intercourse for heterosexuals is just over once per week for men, just under once per week for women (Smith, "Adult Sexual Behavior," p. 103, table 1). Several studies have discovered that the frequency of sex among homosexual women declines rapidly as the relationship lengthens, to the point that many are treated for sexual desire disorder: M. Nichols, "Lesbian Relationships: Implications for the Study of Sexuality and Gender," in *Homosexuality/Heterosexuality: Concepts of Sexual Orientation*, ed. D. P. McWhirter, S. A. Sanders and J. M. Reinisch, Kinsey Institute Series 2 (New York: Oxford University Press, 1990), pp. 357-59.

[42]Bell and Weinberg, *Homosexualities*, pp. 107-11, and pp. 327-30, table 9. I give approximate percentages without distinguishing between white and black subjects as do Bell and Weinberg.

[43]J. Agnew, "Some Anatomical and Physiological Aspects of Anal Sexual Practices," *Journal of Homosexuality* 12 (Fall 1985): 75-90.

[44]Jay and Young, *The Gay Report*, pp. 456, 464, 480.

[45]Ibid., pp. 488, 491, 555.

[46]Ibid., p. 556. More specifically, 39 percent had a history of sadomasochism, 27 percent bondage/discipline, 23 percent water sports, 11 percent enemas, 22 percent fisting. Fourteen percent expressed a very or somewhat positive attitude toward sadomasochism, 15 percent toward bondage/discipline, 12 percent toward water sports, 7 percent toward enemas, and 11 percent toward fisting.

[47]Ibid., p. 587.

[48]Saghir and Robins, *Male and Female Homosexuality*, p. 83.

[49]Ibid., p. 82.

[50]J. Marmor, "Clinical Aspects of Male Homosexuality," in *Homosexual Behavior: A Modern Reappraisal*, ed. J. Marmor (New York: Basic Books, 1980), p. 270. This number seems unbelievable given the inability of most heterosexual men to reach orgasm more than three or four times per day, but I have read this number repeatedly and have heard it confirmed anecdotally. Part of the explanation lies in the use of sexual performance-enhancing drugs, described below.

[51]Jay and Young, *The Gay Report*, pp. 510, 512, 519. More specifically, 2.5 percent engaged in sadomasochism and 2.5 percent in bondage/discipline; 9 percent had a positive view of sadomasochism, 11 percent of bondage/discipline, and 8 percent of fisting.

[52]Ibid., pp. 544, 388, 414. It might be noted that 12-17 percent report positive attitudes toward hand-held or strap-on dildos. Interestingly, almost one-fourth of male homosexuals use dildos (W. Winkelstein et al., "Sexual Practices and Risk of Infection by the Human Immunodeficiency Virus," *Journal of the American Medical Association* 257 [January 16, 1987]: 323, table 2).

[53]Kippax et al., "Sustaining Safe Sex," pp. 260-61; Winkelstein et al., "Sexual Practices and Risk," pp. 321-25; K. L. Schmidt et al., "Sexual Behavior Related to Psycho-social Factors in a Population of Danish Homosexual and Bisexual Men," *Social Science and Medicine* 34 (May 15, 1992): 1119-27. Saghir and Robins (*Male and Female Homosexuality*, p. 54, table 4.9; p. 222, table 12.6) found similar numbers, with the exception of a significantly lower incidence of mutual masturbation among men (around 40 percent).

[54]Kippax et al. ("Sustaining Safe Sex," pp. 260-61), in a longitudinal study of 134 men between 1986 and 1991, report approximate percentages during the previous six months of 1991 who had engaged in rimming (40 percent), fingering the rectum (60 percent), fisting (40 percent) and ingestion of semen (40 percent). The percentage of fisting in this sample is far higher than that reported in other studies. L. McKusick et al. ("AIDS and Sexual Behaviors Reported by Gay Men in San Francisco," *American Journal of Public Health* 75 [1985]: 493-96) conducted a nonrandom study of 655 San Francisco men without AIDS and reported percentages of those who in one month in 1983 (p. 495, table 3), had engaged in rimming (25 percent), receptive fisting (5 percent), water sports (5 percent), anal receptive intercourse without a condom (40 percent) and ingestion of semen (40 percent). Winkelstein et al. ("Sexual Practices and Risk," p. 323, table 2) reported a 1984-1985 random study of 1,034 San Francisco men in key neighborhoods. They found the percentage of sexually active subjects who in the past two years had engaged in rimming (57 percent); and of the 70 percent who had engaged in receptive anal intercourse, 88 percent had engaged in fingering the rectum, 7.4 percent in fisting and 27 percent in the use of dildos. The study of B. R. Simon Rosser (*Male Homosexual Behavior and the Effects of AIDS Education* [New York: Praeger Books, 1991], p. 28, table 3.1), a 1988 survey of 159 New Zealand male

homosexuals, found percentages who in the past two months had engaged in rimming (30 percent), fingering the rectum (64 percent), fisting (4 percent) and anal receptive intercourse without a condom (79 percent). McWhirter and Mattison, in *The Male Couple* (p. 277, table 44), a survey of 312 male homosexuals in relationships, reported percentages of those who during the past year engaged in rimming (41 percent) and various sadomasochistic practices (7 percent). L. Corey and K. K. Holmes ("Sexual Transmission of Hepatitis A in Homosexual Men," *New England Journal of Medicine* 302 [February 21, 1980]: 437, table 3) found that 40 percent of a group of 102 Seattle male homosexuals frequently engaged in rimming. J. Elford et al. ("Kaposi's Sarcoma and Insertive Rimming," *Lancet* 339 [April 11, 1992]: 938, a longitudinal study of 1,085 Australian men from 1984 to 1991) found a fairly constant 30 percent who reported insertive rimming during the previous six months. M. T. Schechter et al. ("Changes in Sexual Behavior and Fear of AIDS," *Lancet* 1984 [June 9, 1984]: 1293, a two-year follow-up survey of 388 male homosexuals in Vancouver) reported receptive rimming among 90 percent of subjects, active rimming among 80 percent and receptive fisting among 20 percent.

The frequency of the most disease-prone practices appears to be much higher among subjects who are HIV positive: see, for example, V. Beral et al., "Risk of Kaposi's Sarcoma and Sexual Practices Associated with Faecal Contact in Homosexual and Bisexual Men with AIDS," *Lancet* 339 (March 14, 1992): 633, table 1, which shows the percentage of subjects who reported "at least once a month" for insertive oral-anal contact (67 percent), receptive oral contact (98 percent) and receptive anal contact (97 percent). See further discussion in the section on AIDS below.

Little direct comparative data is available with regard to practices in the heterosexual population. Laumann et al. (*Social Organization of Sexuality*, pp. 98-99, table 3.6) report lifetime experience of oral sex at about 70 percent and about 22 percent for the last event, but did not report occurrence for the previous year. About 9 percent experienced anal sex in the previous year, 23 percent lifetime. No figures were available on the practice of fingering the rectum, but 26 percent of men and 16 percent of women considered the idea "somewhat appealing" or "very appealing" (pp. 152, 162-63, tables 4.2-4.3).

[55]Linn et al., "Recent Sexual Behaviors," p. 2688.

[56]C. Vourakis, "Homosexuals in Substance Abuse Treatment," in *Substance Abuse: Pharmacologic, Developmental and Clinical Perspectives*, ed. C. Vourakis and D. S. Woolf (New York: John Wiley & Sons, 1983), p. 407; a similar description of the effect is given by B. J. Klamecki, "Medical Perspective of the Homosexual Issue," in *The Crisis of Homosexuality*, ed. J. I. Yamamoto (Wheaton, Ill.: Victor Books, 1990), p. 119.

[57]E. A. Holly et al., "Anal Cancer Incidence: Genital Warts, Anal Fissure or Fistural, Hemorrhoids and Smoking," *Journal of the National Cancer Institute* 81 (1989): 1728, table 2.

[58]Seage et al., "Relation Between Nitrite Inhalants," p. 6, table 2.

[59]T. Myers et al., "HIV, Substance Use and Related Behavior of Gay and Bisexual Men:

An Examination of the Talking Sex Project Cohort," *British Journal of Addiction* 87 (February 1992): 209. The most popular drug used regularly was marijuana (35.3 percent), followed by poppers (19.1 percent) and cocaine (5.5 percent). Compared to the general population, this study found 1.5 times the alcohol use, 3.6 times the marijuana use, 4 times the tranquilizer use, 2.3 times the cocaine use and 58 times the popper use. "This study's findings show a clear association between general substance use, particularly drug use, and number of sexual partners and sexual activity" (p. 212).

[60]C. Ryan and J. Bradford, "The National Lesbian Health Care Survey: An Overview," in *Psychological Perspectives on Lesbian and Gay Male Experiences*, ed. L. D. Garnets and D. C. Kimmel (New York: Columbia University Press, 1993), p. 551.

[61]See, for example, Myers et al., "HIV, Substance Abuse," p. 212 and bibliography; Linn et al., "Recent Sexual Behaviors," p. 2686, table 1; A. Messiah et al., "Factors Correlated with Homosexually Acquired Human Immunodeficiency Virus Infection in the Era of 'Safer Sex,' " *Sexually Transmitted Diseases* 20 (January/February 1993): 57; M. McCusker et al., "Use of Drugs and Alcohol by Homosexually Active Men in Relation to Sexual Practices," *Journal of Acquired Immunodeficiency Syndrome* 3, no. 7 (1990): 734.

[62]J. McCusker et al., "Maintenance of Behavioral Change in a Cohort of Homosexually Active Men," *AIDS* 6, no. 8 (1992): 864, table 1. See also Jay and Young, *The Gay Report*, pp. 431, 496, which reports that 44 percent of male subjects regularly used alcohol with sex, 32 percent marijuana and 21 percent poppers, while 29 percent of female subjects regularly used alcohol with sex, and 29 percent marijuana. Simon Rosser (*Male Homosexual Behavior*, p. 28, table 3.1) reports that 25 percent of male subjects had used poppers, and 21 percent other drugs, with sex in the previous two months.

[63]Laumann et al., *Social Organization of Sexuality*, p. 116, table 3.7. The percentages were somewhat higher among those who had never married and were not cohabiting (14.0 percent alcohol use with sex, 1.4 percent any drug) and among those who were divorced or separated and not cohabiting (12.2 percent and 3.3 percent).

[64]Linn et al., "Recent Sexual Behaviors," p. 2689.

[65]Bell and Weinberg, *Homosexualities*, p. 216.

[66]For example, Saghir and Robins, *Male and Female Homosexuality*, pp. 136, 294; L. A. Peplau and S. D. Cochran, "A Relationship Perspective on Homosexuality," in *Homosexuality/Heterosexuality: Concepts of Sexual Orientation*, ed. D. P. McWhirter, S. A. Sanders and J. M. Reinisch, Kinsey Institute Series 2 (New York: Oxford University Press, 1990), pp. 332-34; L. Diamant and R. B. Simono, "The Relationship of Homosexuality to Mental Disorders," in *Male and Female Homosexuality: Psychological Approaches*, ed. L. Diamant (Washington, D.C.: Hemisphere, 1987), pp. 171-72.

[67]Bell and Weinberg, *Homosexualities*, p. 346, table 13.5.

[68]See J. C. Gonsiorek, "An Introduction to Mental Health Issues and Homosexuality," *American Behavioral Scientist* 25, no. 4 (1982): 367-84.

[69]J. B. W. Williams et al., "Multidisciplinary Baseline Assessment of Homosexual Men with and Without Human Immunodeficiency Virus Infection: Part 2, Standardized Clinical Assessment of Current and Lifetime Psychopathology," *Archives of General*

Psychiatry 48 (February 1991): 129.

[70]N. Breslow, L. Evans and J. Langley, "Comparisons Among Heterosexual, Bisexual and Homosexual Male Sado-masochists," *Journal of Homosexuality* 13 (Fall 1986): 106.

[71]See articles and bibliographies by G. P. Jones and R. Bauserman in *Journal of Homosexuality* 20, nos. 1/2 (1990).

[72]Williams et al., "Multidisciplinary Baseline Assessment," p. 127, table 2; P. H. Rosenberger et al., "Psychopathology in Human Immunodeficiency Virus Infection: Lifetime and Current Assessment," *Comprehensive Psychiatry* 34 (May/June 1993): 153, table 1; 154, table 2. It should be noted that none of the subjects were referred to the study because of psychiatric difficulties (p. 151).

[73]Saghir and Robins, *Male and Female Homosexuality*, p. 274, table 14.4. The drug abuse history in this study was 5 percent for female homosexuals and 0 percent for females generally. See also C. E. Lewis, M. T. Saghir and E. Robins, "Drinking Patterns in Homosexual and Heterosexual Women," *Journal of Clinical Psychiatry* 43 (July 1982): 277-79.

[74]Compare, for example, the current psychiatric diagnoses in Rosenberger et al., "Psychopathology," p. 154, table 2, and Williams et al., "Multidisciplinary Baseline Assessment," p. 126, table 1, which reveal a rate similar to that of the general male population, to the comparable information in Saghir and Robins, *Male and Female Homosexuality*, p. 273, table 14.3, which reveals a rate ten times that of the female control group.

[75]For a summary of studies, see Vourakis, "Homosexuals in Substance Abuse Treatment," pp. 404-5, and J. M. Hall, "Lesbians and Alcohol: Patterns and Paradoxes in Medical Notions and Lesbians' Beliefs," *Journal of Psychoactive Drugs* 25 (April-June 1993): 110.

[76]Two excellent surveys of theories about the relation between homosexuality and alcoholism are S. Israelstam and S. Lambert, "Homosexuality as a Cause of Alcoholism: A Historical Overview," *International Journal of the Addictions* 18, no. 8 (1983): 1085-107; and Hall, "Lesbians and Alcohol," pp. 110-14. Both articles also contain extensive bibliographies.

[77]Williams et al., "Multidisciplinary Baseline Assessment," p. 127, table 2; Rosenberger et al., "Psychopathology," p. 153, table 1; 154, table 2. Rosenberger et al. found that 45 percent had a history of both affective (depression, etc.) and substance use disorders.

[78]Bell and Weinberg, *Homosexualities*, pp. 200-201, 444, table 21.9.

[79]Ryan and Bradford, "National Lesbian Health Care Survey," p. 550.

[80]For example, Bell and Weinberg, *Homosexualities*, pp. 215, 444, table 21.9; Saghir and Robins, *Male and Female Homosexuality*, pp. 273-78, tables 14.3-5.

[81]Bell and Weinberg, *Homosexualities*, p. 450, table 21.12.

[82]Jay and Young, *The Gay Report*, p. 728.

[83]Saghir and Robins, *Male and Female Homosexuality*, p. 288; G. Remafedi et al., "Risk Factors for Attempted Suicide in Gay and Bisexual Youth," *Pediatrics* 87 (January 1,

1987): 869-75; S. G. Schneider, N. L. Farberow and G. N. Kruks, "Suicidal Behavior in Adolescent and Young Adult Gay Men," *Suicide and Life Threatening Behavior* 19 (Winter 1989): 381-90; S. G. Schneider et al., "Factors Influencing Suicide Intent in Gay and Bisexual Suicide Ideators: Differing Models for Men with and Without Human Immunodeficiency Virus," *Journal of Personality and Social Psychology* 61 (November 1991): 776-88.

[84]Ryan and Bradford, "National Lesbian Health Care Survey," p. 550.

[85]The studies of Bell and Weinberg *(Homosexualities)*, Saghir and Robins *(Male and Female Homosexuality)*, Rosenberger et al. ("Psychopathology"), Williams et al. ("Multidisciplinary Baseline Assessment") and Ryan and Bradford ("National Lesbian Health Care Survey") detail various other psychiatric affective disorders that occur with greater frequency among homosexuals, including anxiety, tension, loneliness, paranoia and eating disorders. On the latter see D. B. Herzog et al., "Body Image Dissatisfaction in Homosexual and Heterosexual Males," *Journal of Nervous and Mental Disorders* 179 (June 1991): 356-59.

[86]K. Freund et al., "Pedophilia and Heterosexuality vs. Homosexuality," *Journal of Sex and Marital Therapy* 10 (Fall 1984): 197; P. Cameron, "Homosexual Molestation of Children: Sexual Interaction of Teacher and Pupil," *Psychological Reports* 57 (1985): 27-36.

[87]K. Freund and R. I. Watson, "The Proportions of Heterosexual and Homosexual Pedophiles Among Sex Offenders Against Children: An Exploratory Study," *Journal of Sex and Marital Therapy* 18 (Spring 1992): 34-43.

[88]The only prevalence study of which I am aware is that of J. M. Siegal et al., "The Prevalence of Childhood Sexual Assault," *American Journal of Epidemiology* 126 (December 1987): 1141-53. The number of victims per homosexual is derived from the fact that 3.8 percent of 3,132 adult subjects in this study were males who reported childhood sexual contact with an adult, 93 percent of those with an adult male. If we multiply the U.S. adult male population by 3.8 percent and then by 93 percent, we arrive at 3.2 million. The number may of course be higher if large numbers of adults repress, or do not report, the painful experience of molestation.

[89]If we take the total number of victims and divide it by the mean number of victims per pedophile (150), we arrive at 21,333. But this is not an accurate number, because it is based only on pedophiles who have been caught. The majority are probably never caught—perhaps in part because they molest fewer boys. If we lower the victimization rate to, say, twenty-five boys per pedophile, we arrive at the very disturbing number of 128,000, which is over 10 percent of the practicing male homosexual population.

[90]See *Journal of Homosexuality* 20, nos. 1/2 (1990), especially the articles by Bauserman, Brongersma and Jones.

[91]See, for example, G. D. Goss, *Jesus Acted Up: A Gay and Lesbian Manifesto* (San Francisco: Harper, 1993), pp. 28-29; P. B. Jung and R. F. Smith, *Heterosexism: An Ethical Challenge* (Albany, N.Y.: State University of New York Press, 1993), p. 185.

⁹²Since this section involves fewer statistics, I will reduce the frequency of notes in the text by acknowledgment of principal sources here: J. Agnew, "Some Anatomical and Physiological Aspects of Anal Sexual Practices," *Journal of Homosexuality* 12 (Fall 1985): 75-90; R. A. Bush and W. F. Owen, "Trauma and Other Non-infectious Problems in Homosexual Men," *The Medical Clinics of North America* 70, no. 3 (1986): 549-66; R. D. Catterall, "Sexually Transmitted Diseases of the Anus and Rectum," *Clinical Gastroenterology* 4 (1975): 659-69; Y. M. Felman, "Homosexual Hazards," *Practitioner* 224 (1980): 1151-56; H. L. Kazal et al., "The Gay Bowel Syndrome: Clinico-pathologic Correlation in 260 Cases," *Annals of Clinical Laboratory Science* 6 (1976): 184-92; A. I. Miles et al., "Effect of Anoreceptive Intercourse on Anorectal Function," *Journal of the Royal Society of Medicine* 86 (March 1993): 144-47; D. G. Ostrow, "Homosexuality and Sexually Transmitted Diseases," in *Sexually Transmitted Diseases,* ed. K. K. Holmes et al., 2nd ed. (New York: McGraw-Hill, 1989), pp. 61-69; W. F. Owen, "The Clinical Approach to the Male Homosexual Patient," *The Medical Clinics of North America* 70, no. 3 (1986): 499-535; T. C. Quinn, "Clinical Approach to Intestinal Infections in Homosexual Men," *The Medical Clinics of North America* 70, no. 3 1986): 611-34; T. Quinn and W. E. Stamm, "Proctitis, Proctocolitis and Enteritis in Homosexual Men," in *Sexually Transmitted Diseases,* ed. K. K. Holmes et al., 2nd ed. (New York: McGraw-Hill, 1989), pp. 663-83; M. F. Rein, "Clinical Approach to Urethritis, Mucotaneous Lesions and Inguinal Lymphadenopathy in Homosexual Men," *The Medical Clinics of North America* 70, no. 3 (1986): 587-610; and R. L. Rowan and P. I. Gillette, *The Gay Health Guide* (Boston: Little, Brown, 1978).

⁹³See, for example, Owen, "Clinical Approach to the Male Homosexual," pp. 505-17; Ostrow, "Homosexuality and Sexually Transmitted Diseases," pp. 104-5; Quinn, "Clinical Approach to Intestinal Infections," p. 628; Rowan and Gillette, *Gay Health Guide* (which devotes eight *chapters* to common diseases among male homosexuals not covered here).

⁹⁴Miles, "Effect of Anoreceptive Intercourse," p. 146.

⁹⁵Quinn, "Clinical Approach to Intestinal Infections," p. 615.

⁹⁶Bell and Weinberg, *Homosexualities,* p. 336, table 11; compare C. M. Surawicz et al., "Anal Dysplasia in Homosexual Men: Role of Anoscopy and Biopsy," *Gastroenterology* 105 (1993): 662, table 1. Prevalence figures for each disease, or percentages with a history of each disease, where available, are given below.

⁹⁷I base this estimate on McKusick et al., "AIDS and Sexual Behaviors," p. 494, table 1, which gives prevalence per disease figures for common afflictions of 20-30 percent.

⁹⁸Quinn, "Clinical Approach to Intestinal Infections," p. 621; compare D. I. Abrams, "The Relationship Between Kaposi's Sarcoma and the Intestinal Parasites Among Homosexual Males in the United States," *Journal of Acquired Immune Deficiency Syndrome* 3, supp. 1 (1990): 545, table 1, which shows the presence of amebiasis and other infectious pathogens at four to ten times that of the heterosexual population.

⁹⁹Ibid., pp. 615, 622.

¹⁰⁰Jay and Young, *The Gay Report,* p. 691. Messiah et al. report 53 percent over the

previous ten years ("Factors Correlated with Homosexually Acquired Human Immunodeficiency Virus," p. 53, table 2). McKusick et al., "AIDS and Sexual Behaviors," gives the figure 25 percent for the previous year alone (p. 494).

[101]See Quinn and Stamm, "Proctitis, Proctocolitis and Enteritis," p. 675; Holly et al., "Anal Cancer Incidence," p. 1728, table 2; Surawicz et al., "Anal Dysplasia," p. 662, table 1; J. B. F. de Wit et al., "Increase in Unprotected Anogenital Intercourse Among Homosexual Men," *American Journal of Public Health* 83 (October 1993): 1451-53; V. C. Riley, "Resurgent Gonorrhea in Homosexual Men," *Lancet* 337, no. 8733 (1991): 183; M. Young et al., "Rectal Gonorrhea and Unsafe Sex," *Lancet* 337, no. 8745 (1991): 853.

[102]Quinn, "Clinical Approach to Intestinal Infections," pp. 615, 620-21.

[103]Ibid., p. 618.

[104]Holly et al., "Anal Cancer Incidence," p. 1728, table 2; McKusick et al., "AIDS and Sexual Behaviors," p. 494, table 1, reports 25 percent with either gonorrhea or syphilis in the past year. Jay and Young, *The Gay Report*, p. 691, reports 12 percent with a history of syphilis in the late 1970s.

[105]S. A. Billstein, "Human Lice," and M. Orkin and H. Maibach, "Scabies," in *Sexually Transmitted Diseases*, ed. K. K. Holmes et al., 2nd ed. (New York: McGraw-Hill, 1989), pp. 467-71, 473-79.

[106]Jay and Young, *The Gay Report*, pp. 691-92.

[107]Ibid.

[108]Quinn, "Clinical Approach to Intestinal Infections," pp. 615, 619; Holly et al., "Anal Cancer Incidence," p. 1728, table 2; Surawicz et al., "Anal Dysplasia," p. 662, table 1; Messiah et al., "Factors Correlated with Homosexually Acquired Human Immunodeficiency Virus," p. 53, table 2; C. L. H Law et al., "Factors Associated with Clinical and Sub-clinical Anal Human Papillomavirus Infection in Homosexual Men." *Genitourinary Medicine* 67 (April 1991): 94. Again, the numbers are up from Jay and Young's late 1970s report of 17 percent with a history of warts (*The Gay Report*, pp. 691-92).

[109]Law et al., "Factors Associated," p. 94.

[110]J. Daling et al., "Sexual Practices, Sexually Transmitted Diseases and the Incidence of Anal Cancer," *New England Journal of Medicine* 317 (1987): 973-77; Holly et al., "Anal Cancer Incidence"; Law et al., "Factors Associated"; Surawicz et al., "Anal Dysplasia," pp. 658-66; D. Wexner, J. W. Milsom and T. H. Dailey, "The Demographics of Anal Cancers Are Changing: Identification of a High-Risk Population," *Diseases of Colon and Rectum* 30 (1987): 942-46.

[111]Jay and Young (*The Gay Report*, pp. 691-92) report 10 percent with a history of herpes. Messiah et al. ("Factors Correlated with Homosexually Acquired Human Immunodeficiency Virus," p. 53, table 2) show 20 percent over the previous ten years; McKusick et al. ("AIDS and Sexual Behaviors," p. 494, table 1) report 30 percent with a history of the disease. Surawicz et al. ("Anal Dysplasia," p. 662, table 1) report 10 percent.

[112]K. Schomer et al., "Hepatitis A Among Homosexual Men—U.S., Canada and Australia," *Morbidity and Mortality Weekly Report* 41 (March 6, 1992): 155, 161-64; J. Kani et

al., "Hepatitis A Virus Infection Among Homosexual Men," *British Medical Journal* 302 (June 8, 1991): 1399. [113]E. B. Keeffe, "Clinical Approach to Viral Hepatitis in Homosexual Men," *The Medical Clinics of North America* 70, no. 3 (1986): 567-73, 582.
[114]S. M. Lemon and J. E. Newbold, "Viral Hepatitis," in *Sexually Transmitted Diseases*, ed. K. K. Holmes et al., 2nd ed. (New York: McGraw-Hill, 1989), pp. 449-66; compare Keeffe, "Clinical Approach to Viral Hepatitis," pp. 571-73. An active vaccine may soon be available. As of this writing, the only preventative measure available is a monthly injection of gamma globulin.
[115]L. A. Kingsley et al., "Sexual Transmission Efficiency of Hepatitis B Virus and Human Immunodeficiency Virus Among Homosexual Men," *Journal of the American Medical Association* 264 (July 11, 1990): 230-34.
[116]Keeffe, "Clinical Approach to Viral Hepatitis," pp. 573-82.
[117]Laumann et al., *Social Organization of Sexuality*, pp. 381, 385-86, tables 11.4-11.5. For specific infections, see p. 382, table 11.1: for example, the general population lifetime incidence of gonorrhea is 6.6 percent, syphilis 0.8 percent, chlamydia 3.2 percent, genital warts 4.7 percent, herpes 2.1 percent, hepatitis 1.1 percent.
[118]For the history of AIDS, see M. Essex, "Origin of AIDS," J. M. Mann and S. L. Welles, "Global Aspects of the HIV Epidemic," and S. Y. Chu, R. L. Berkelman and J. W. Curran, "Epidemiology of HIV in the United States," in *AIDS: Etiology. Diagnosis, Treatment and Prevention*, ed. V. T. DeVita et al. (Philadelphia: J. B. Lippincott, 1992), pp. 3-12, 89-98, 99-108. A comprehensive treatment of the subject from a Christian perspective is G. G. Wood and J. E. Dietrich, *The Aids Epidemic: Balancing Compassion and Justice* (Portland, Ore.: Multnomah Press, 1990).
[119]Centers for Disease Control, "Projections of the Numbers of Persons Diagnosed with AIDS and the Number of Immunosuppressed HIV-Infected Persons—United States, 1992-94," *Morbidity and Mortality Weekly Report* 41 (December 25, 1992): 1-29; Centers for Disease Control, "Update: Acquired Immunodeficiency Syndrome—U.S. 1991," *Morbidity and Mortality Weekly Report* 41 (July 3, 1992): 463-68.
[120]A. J. Silvestre et al., "Changes in HIV Rates and Sexual Behavior Among Homosexual Men, 1984 to 1988/92," *American Journal of Public Health* 83 (April 1993): 578-80; Winkelstein et al., "Sexual Practices and Risk," pp. 321-25. The latter study also showed significant variation according to number of sexual partners: 32 percent for those with two to nine partners in the previous two years, 54 percent for those with ten to forty-nine partners, and 71 percent for those with more than fifty partners. The figure of 30 percent is given by T. A. Peterman, D. C. Des Jarlais, and J. N. Wasserheit, "Prevention of the Sexual Transmission of HIV," in *AIDS: Etiology, Diagnosis, Treatment and Prevention*, ed. V. T. DeVita et al. (Philadelphia: J. B. Lippincott, 1992), pp. 444, table 23-1, based on Centers for Disease Control, "National HIV Seroprevalence Serosurveys: Summary of Results—Data from Serosurveillance Activities Through 1989" (Washington, D.C.: U.S. Government Printing Office, 1990). Compare the Dutch study by P. J. Veugelers et al., "Estimation of the Magnitude of the HIV Epidemic Among Homosexual Men: Utilization of Survey Data in Predictive Models," *European*

Journal of Epidemiology 9 (July 1993): 436-41.

[121]I limit the discussion here to homosexual transmission. Thirty to thirty-five percent of AIDS cases have been traced to intravenous drug use, blood transfusions and perinatal transmission (20-30 percent of infected women pass on the disease to their infants). Heterosexual intercourse accounts for only about 5 percent of U.S. cases, many of which also involve suspicion of drug use or homosexual behavior. See, for example, M. A. Fumento, "AIDS: Are Heterosexuals at Risk?" *Commentary*, November 1987, pp. 21-27. The virus is not spread by inhalation, ingestion or insects. The transmission from mother to child is particularly tragic: not only do the vast majority of these children become orphans soon after birth, but they die within two years. There are now approximately twenty thousand such babies in the United States, and perhaps twenty times that number in Africa. See, for example, H. B. Peterson and M. F. Rogers, "Perinatal Transmission of HIV," in *AIDS: Etiology, Diagnosis, Treatment and Prevention*, ed. V. T. DeVita et al. (Philadelphia: J. B. Lippincott, 1992), pp. 471-78.

[122]I. P. Keet et al., "Orogenital Sex and the Transmission of HIV Among Homosexual Men," *Acquired Immunodeficiency Syndrome* 6 (February 1992): 223-26; A. R. Lifson et al., "HIV Seroconversion in Two Homosexual Men After Receptive Oral Intercourse with Ejaculation: Implications for Counseling Concerning Safe Sex Practices," *American Journal of Public Health* 80 (1990): 1509-11; A. B. Murray et al., "Coincident Acquisition of Neisseria Gonorrhea and HIV from Fellatio," *Lancet* 338 (September 28, 1991): 830; M. Quatro et al., "HIV Transmission by Fellatio," *European Journal of Epidemiology* 6, no. 3 (1990): 339-40; W. Rozenbaum et al., "HIV Transmission by Oral Sex," *Lancet* 1988, no. 1 (1988): 1395; S. K. Gill, C. Loveday and R. I. Gibson, "Transmission of HIV-1 Infection by Oroanal Intercourse," *Genitourinary Medicine* 68 (August 1992): 254-57.

[123]The main sources of information about HIV/AIDS for the following description are R. E. Chaisson, J. L. Gerberding and M. A. Sande, "Opportunistic Infections in AIDS," A. T. Haase, "Biology of Human Immunodeficiency Virus and Related Viruses," and P. A. Volberding, "AIDS-Related Malignancies," in *Sexually Transmitted Diseases*, ed. K. K. Holmes et al., 2nd ed. (New York: McGraw-Hill, 1989), pp. 691-701, 305-15, 685-90; A. R. Lifson, "Transmission of the Human Immunodeficiency Virus," A. M. Levine, "Lymphoma and Other Miscellaneous Cancers," B. Safai and J. J. Schwartz, "Kaposi's Sarcoma and the Acquired Immunodeficiency Syndrome," and P. A. Volberding, "Clinical Spectrum of HIV Disease," all in *AIDS: Etiology, Diagnosis, Treatment and Prevention*, ed. V. T. DeVita et al. (Philadelphia: J. B. Lippincott, 1992), pp. 111-22, 225-36, 209-24, 123-40; R. J. Biggar et al., "Risk of Other Cancers Following Kaposi's Sarcoma: Relation to Acquired Immunodeficiency Syndrome," *American Journal of Epidemiology* 139 (February 15, 1994): 362-68; L. P. Jacobsen et al., "Changes in Survival After Acquired Immunodeficiency Syndrome (AIDS): 1984-91," *American Journal of Epidemiology* 183 (December 1, 1993): 952-64.

[124]In addition to the sources listed above, see A. Wald et al., "Influence of HIV Infection on Manifestations and Natural History of Other Sexually Transmitted Diseases,"

Annual Review of Public Health 14 (1993): 19-42.

[125]S. M. Adib and D. G. Ostrow, "Trends in HIV/AIDS Behavioural Research Among Homosexual and Bisexual Men in the United States: 1981-1991," *AIDS Care* 3, no. 3 (1991): 281-87; S. M. Abib et al., "Relapse in Sexual Behavior Among Homosexual Men: A Two-Year Follow-up from the Chicago MACS/CCS," *Acquired Immunodeficiency Syndrome* 5 (June 1991): 757-60; Centers for Disease Control, "Patterns of Sexual Behavior Change Among Homosexual/Bisexual Men—Selected U.S. Sites, 1987-90," *Morbidity and Mortality Weekly Report* 40 (1991): 792-94; P. M. Davies et al., "Risk of HIV Infection in Homosexual Men," *British Medical Journal* 307 (September 11, 1993): 681; J. B. F. de Wit et al., "Increase in Unprotected Anogenital Intercourse Among Homosexual Men," *American Journal of Public Health* 83:10 (October 1993): 1451-53; L. S. Doll et al., "Homosexual Men Who Engage in High-Risk Sexual Behavior: A Multicenter Comparison," *Sexually Transmitted Diseases* 18 (July-September 1991): 67-75; M. L. Ekstrand and T. J. Coates, "Maintenance of Safer Sexual Behavior and Predictors of Risky Sex: The San Francisco Men's Health Study," *American Journal of Public Health* 80 (1990): 973-77; A. J. Hunt et al., "Changes in Sexual Behavior in a Large Cohort of Homosexual Men in England and Wales, 1988-89," *British Medical Journal* 302 (March 2, 1991): 505-6; Kippax et al., "Sustaining Safe Sex," pp. 257-63; M. McCusker et al., "Maintenance of Behavioral Change in a Cohort of Homosexually Active Men," *AIDS* 6 (1992): 861-68; K. L. Schmidt et al., "Sexual Behavior Related to Psycho-social Factors in a Population of Danish Homosexual and Bisexual Men," *Social Science and Medicine* 34 (May 15, 1992): 1119-27.

[126]Silvestre et al., "Changes in HIV Rates," p. 579.

[127]Linn et al., "Recent Sexual Behaviors," pp. 2685-90: 64 percent engaged in at least one unsafe act, including approximately half of those who had already tested HIV-positive.

[128]J. B. F. de Wit et al., "Safe Sexual Practices Not Reliably Maintained by Homosexual Men," *American Journal of Public Health* 82 (April 1992): 615-16.

[129]W. W. Darrow and K. Siegel, "Preventive Health Behavior and STD," in *Sexually Transmitted Diseases*, ed. K. K. Holmes et al., 2nd ed. (New York: McGraw-Hill, 1989), pp. 85-92; J. B. F. de Wit et al., "Why Do Homosexual Men Relapse into Unsafe Sex? Predictors of Resumption of Unprotected Anogenital Intercourse with Casual Partners," *AIDS* 7 (August 1993): 1113-18; M. L. Ekstrand et al., "Safer Sex Among Gay Men: What Is the Ultimate Goal?" *AIDS* 7 (February 1993): 281-82; M. L. Ekstrand, "Safer Sex Maintenance Among Gay Men: Are We Making Any Progress?" *AIDS* 6 (August 1992): 875-76; R. S. Gold and M. J. Skinner, "Situational Factors and Thought Processes Associated with Unprotected Intercourse in Young Gay Men," *AIDS* 6 (September 1992): 1021-30; F. C. I. Hickson et al., "Maintenance of Open Gay Relationships: Some Strategies for Protection Against HIV," *AIDS Care* 4, no. 4 (1992): 409-19; J. A. Kelly and D. A. Murphy, "Some Lessons Learned About Risk Reduction After Ten Years of the HIV/AIDS Epidemic," *AIDS Care* 3, no. 3 (1991): 251-57; L. Ku et al., "Patterns of HIV Risk and Preventive Behaviors Among Teenage Men," *Public*

Health Reports 107 (March/April 1992): 131-38; G. Marks et al., "HIV-Infected Men's Practices in Notifying Past Sexual Partners of Infection Risk," *Public Health Reports* 107 (January/February 1992): 100-105; R. Stall et al., "Relapse from Safer Sex: The Next Challenge for AIDS Prevention Efforts," *Journal of Acquired Immunodeficiency Syndrome* 3 (1990): 1181-87.

[130]On condom use problems see J. A. Catania et al., "Changes in Condom Use Among Homosexual Men in San Francisco," *Health Psychology* 10, no. 3 (1991): 190-99; Centers for Disease Control, "Update: Barrier Protection Against HIV Infection and Other Sexually Transmitted Diseases," *Morbidity and Mortality Weekly Report* 42 (August 6, 1993): 589-91; J. B. F. de Wit et al., "The Effectiveness of Condom Use Among Homosexual Men," *AIDS* 7 (May 1993): 751-52; D. J. Martin, "Inappropriate Lubricant Use with Condoms by Homosexual Men," *Public Health Reports* 107 (July/August 1992): 468-73; J. L. Peterson et al., "High Risk Sexual Behavior and Condom Use Among Gay and Bisexual African-American Men," *American Journal of Public Health* 82 (November 1992): 1490-94; J. L. P. Thompson et al., "Estimated Condom Failure and Frequency of Condom Use among Gay Men," *American Journal of Public Health* 83 (October 1993): 1409-13; P. Weatherburn et al., "Condom Use in a Large Cohort of Homosexually Active Men in England and Wales," *AIDS Care* 3, no. 3 (1991): 31-41.

[131]L. William Countryman, *Dirt, Greed and Sex* (Philadelphia: Fortress, 1988), p. 257.

Chapter 7: The Great Nature-Nurture Debate

[1]R. H. Denniston, "Homosexuality in Animals," in *Homosexual Behavior: A Modern Reappraisal,* ed. J. Marmor (New York: Basic Books, 1980), pp. 25-40. There may be some examples of same-sex pairing among birds, but some "promiscuity" is required for eggs: J. D. Weinrich, "The Kinsey Scale in Biology," in *Homosexuality/Heterosexuality: Concepts of Sexual Orientation,* ed. D. P. McWhirter, S. A. Sanders and J. M. Reinisch, Kinsey Institute Series 2 (New York: Oxford University Press, 1990), pp. 133-34.

[2]R. D. Nadler, "Homosexual Behavior in Nonhuman Primates," in *Homosexuality/Heterosexuality: Concepts of Sexual Orientation,* ed. D. P. McWhirter, S. A. Sanders and J. M. Reinisch, Kinsey Institute Series 2 (New York: Oxford University Press, 1990), pp. 138-70.

[3]L. A. Rosenblum, "Primates, *Homo sapiens* and Homosexuality," in *Homosexuality/Heterosexuality: Concepts of Sexual Orientation,* ed. D. P. McWhirter, S. A. Sanders and J. M. Reinisch, Kinsey Institute Series 2 (New York: Oxford University Press, 1990), pp. 172-73.

[4]A. Karlen, "Homosexuality in History," in *Homosexual Behavior: A Modern Reappraisal,* ed. J. Marmor (New York: Basic Books, 1980), pp. 75-90; and D. Greenberg, *The Construction of Homosexuality* (Chicago: University of Chicago Press, 1988), pp. 89-396.

[5]John Boswell, *Same-Sex Unions in Premodern Europe* (New York: Villard Books, 1994). For an excellent, detailed review, see B. D. Shaw, "A Groom of One's Own?" *The New*

Republic, July 18-25, 1994, pp. 33-41.

⁶See J. M. Carrier, "Homosexual Behavior in Cross-Cultural Perspective," in *Homosexual Behavior: A Modern Reappraisal,* ed. J. Marmor (New York: Basic Books, 1980), pp. 100-22; *Homosexuality and the World Religions,* ed. A. Swidler (Valley Forge, Penn.: Trinity Press International, 1993); and Greenberg, *Construction of Homosexuality,* pp. 25-88.

⁷See relevant articles and bibliography on each religious tradition in Swidler, *Homosexuality and the World Religions.*

⁸S. LeVay, "A Difference in Hypothalamic Structure Between Heterosexual and Homosexual Men," *Science* 258 (August 30, 1991): 1034-37.

⁹For the criticisms advanced here, see especially W. Byne and B. Parsons, "Human Sexual Orientation: The Biologic Theories Reappraised," *Archives of General Psychiatry* 50 (March 1993): 228-29, 234-35; R. C. Friedman and J. Downey, "Neurobiology and Sexual Orientation: Current Relationships," *Journal of Neuropsychiatry and Clinical Neurosciences* 5 (Spring 1993): 148; and M. Barinaga, "Is Homosexuality Biological?" *Science* 253 (August 30, 1991): 956-57.

¹⁰See D. F. Swaab, L. J. G. Gooren and M. A. Hofman, "Gender and Sexual Orientation in Relation to Hypothalamic Structures," *Hormone Research* 38, supp. 2 (1992): 51-61; Byne and Parsons, "Human Sexual Orientation," pp. 229, 236; A. Gibbons, "The Brain as 'Sexual Organ,' " *Science* 253 (August 30, 1991): 957-59. Swaab, Gooren and Hofman did not attempt to replicate LeVay's finding, but they found that another region of the hypothalamus, the sexually dimorphic nucleus, was identical in homosexual and heterosexual men, while the suprachiasmatic nucleus (function unknown) was larger in homosexual men.

¹¹L. S. Allen and R. A. Gorski, "Sexual Orientation and the Size of the Anterior Commissure in the Human Brain," *Proceedings of the National Academy of Sciences of the United States of America* 89 (August 1, 1992): 7199-202.

¹²K. O. Götestam, T. J. Coates and M. Ekstrand, "Handedness, Dyslexia and Twinning in Homosexual Men," *International Journal of Neuroscience* 63 (1992): 179-86.

¹³S. Demeter, J. L. Ringo and R. W. Doty, "Morphometric Analysis of the Human Corpus Callosum and Anterior Commissure," *Human Neurobiology* 6 (1988): 219-26.

¹⁴Byne and Parsons, "Human Sexual Orientation," p. 235.

¹⁵B. A. Gladue, "Psychobiological Contributions," in *Male and Female Homosexuality: Psychological Approaches,* ed. L. Diamant, Series in Clinical and Community Psychology (Washington, D.C.: Hemisphere, 1987), pp. 132-34; Byne and Parsons, "Human Sexual Orientation," pp. 231-32.

¹⁶See L. Gooren, "Biomedical Theories of Sexual Orientation: A Critical Examination," in *Homosexuality/Heterosexuality: Concepts of Sexual Orientation,* ed. D. P. McWhirter, S. A. Sanders and J. M. Reinisch, Kinsey Institute Series 2 (New York: Oxford University Press, 1990), pp. 71-87; Byne and Parsons, "Human Sexual Orientation," pp. 230-34; Friedman and Downey, "Neurobiology and Sexual Orientation," pp. 134-36.

¹⁷Gladue, "Psychobiological Contributions," p. 143, compare pp. 134-43. See also

J. Bancroft, "Commentary: Biological Contributions to Sexual Orientation," in *Homosexuality/Heterosexuality: Concepts of Sexual Orientation*, ed. D. P. McWhirter, S. A. Sanders and J. M. Reinisch, Kinsey Institute Series 2 (New York: Oxford University Press, 1990), p. 109; J. Money, "Sin, Sickness or Status? Homosexual Gender Identity and Psychoneuroendocrinology," in *Psychological Perspectives on Lesbian and Gay Male Experiences*, ed. L. D. Garnets and D. C. Kimmel (New York: Columbia University Press, 1993), pp. 162-63.

[18]"A Genetic Study of Male Sexual Orientation," *Archives of General Psychiatry* 48 (1991): 1089-96; J. M. Bailey et al., "Heritable Factors Influence Sexual Orientation in Women," *Archives of General Psychiatry* 50 (March 1993): 217-23.

[19]In the female study there were also thirty-five adoptive sisters, two of whom (6 percent) were homosexual.

[20]A 65 percent concordance rate for thirty-four monozygotic pairs and 30 percent concordance rate for twenty-three dizygotic pairs was reported by F. L. Whitam, M. Diamond and J. Martin, "Homosexual Orientation in Twins: A Report on Sixty-one Pairs and Three Triplet Sets," *Archives of Sexual Behavior* 22, no. 3 (1993): 187-206. Compare similar concordance figures for a smaller sample reported by N. Buhrich, J. M. Bailey and N. G. Martin, "Sexual Orientation, Sexual Identity and Sex-Dimorphic Behaviors in Male Twins," *Behavior Genetics* 21 (January 1991): 75-96.

[21]M. King and E. McDonald, "Homosexuals Who Are Twins: A Study of Forty-six Probands," *British Journal of Psychiatry* 160 (1992): 407-9; see further bibliography in Byne and Parsons, "Human Sexual Orientation," p. 229.

[22]N. Risch, E. Squires-Wheeler and B. J. B. Keats, "Male Sexual Orientation and Genetic Evidence," *Science* 262 (December 24, 1993): 2063.

[23]Some speculation in this direction which preserves biologic causation is provided by W. J. Turner, "Comments on Discordant Monozygotic Twinning in Homosexuality," *Archives of Sexual Behavior* 23 (February 1994): 115-19. Turner suggests the possibility of unequal blood supply in the womb and genetic changes following separation of the twins within the womb.

[24]D. Hamer et al., "A Linkage Between DNA Markers on the X Chromosome and Male Sexual Orientation," *Science* 261 (July 16, 1993): 321-27.

[25]M. Baron, "Genetic Linkage and Male Homosexual Orientation: Reasons to Be Cautious," *British Medical Journal* 307 (August 7, 1993): 337; compare M. King, "Sexual Orientation and the X," *Nature* 364 (July 22, 1993): 288. King is in other respects favorable toward Hamer's research.

[26]A. Fausto-Sterling and E. Balaban, "Genetics and Male Sexual Orientation," *Science* 261 (September 3, 1993): 1257.

[27]J. Maddox, "Wilful Public Misunderstanding of Genetics," *Nature* 364 (July 22, 1993): 281.

[28]Baron, "Genetic Linkage," p. 338; L. Pool, "Evidence for Homosexuality Gene," *Science* 261 (July 16, 1993): 291-2.

[29]Fausto-Sterling and Balaban, "Genetics and Male Sexual Orientation," p. 1257.

[30]Byne and Parsons, "Human Sexual Orientation," pp. 236-37.

[31]Maddox, "Wilful Public Misunderstanding," p. 281. Specialists will appreciate the exchange on several technical points of genetic research between N. Risch et al. and D. Hamer in *Science* 262 (December 24, 1993): 2063-65. I confess my incompetence to declare a winner in that debate.

[32]Byne and Parsons, "Human Sexual Orientation," p. 228.

[33]Lest there be any doubt that public opinion of morality is swayed by biologic causation studies, one study proved it with a group of students: J. Piskur and D. Degelman, "Effect of Reading a Summary of Research About Biological Bases of Homosexual Orientation on Attitudes Toward Homosexuality," *Psychological Reports* 71, no. 3, pt. 2 (December 1992): 1219-25.

[34]D. Y. Rist, "Are Homosexuals Born That Way?" *The Nation*, October 19, 1992, pp. 424-29.

[35]The best explanations of social construction theory in relation to the individual are R. C. Troiden, "The Formation of Homosexual Identities," in *Psychological Perspectives on Lesbian and Gay Male Experiences*, ed. L. D. Garnets and D. C. Kimmel (New York: Columbia University Press, 1993), pp. 191-217 and V. C. Cass, "The Implications of Homosexual Identity Formation for the Kinsey Model and Scale of Sexual Preference," in *Homosexuality/Heterosexuality: Concepts of Sexual Orientation*, ed. D. P. McWhirter, S. A. Sanders and J. M. Reinisch, Kinsey Institute Series 2 (New York: Oxford University Press, 1990), pp. 239-66. For a direct comparison to biological theories see J. P. De Cecco and J. P. Elia, "A Critique and Synthesis of Biological Essentialism and Social Constructionist Views of Sexuality and Gender," *Journal of Homosexuality* 24, nos 3/4 (1993): 1-26. On the historical dimension see D. F. Greenberg, *The Construction of Homosexuality* (Chicago: University of Chicago Press, 1988), pp. 1-21, 482-99, and M. Foucault, *The History of Sexuality*, vol. 1, *An Introduction* (New York: Vintage, 1980).

[36]This is Foucault's position, and presumably that of G. D. Goss (see above, chapters two and three); for a critique by another constructionist, see Greenberg, *Construction of Homosexuality*, pp. 489-99.

[37]The best of these, in my opinion, are Lawrence J. Hatterer, *Changing Homosexuality in the Male: Treatment for Men Troubled by Homosexuality* (New York: McGraw-Hill, 1970), and E. Moberly, "Homosexuality: Restating the Conservative Case," *Salmagundi* 58/59 (Fall 1982/Winter 1983): 281-99. Other important works reflecting variety within the developmental perspective include R. T. Barnhouse, *Homosexuality: A Symbolic Confusion* (New York: Seabury Press, 1977); I. Bieber et al., *Homosexuality: A Psychoanalytic Study* (New York: Basic Books, 1962), pp. 44-117; B. Burch, "Heterosexuality, Bisexuality and Lesbianism: Rethinking Psychoanalytic Views of Women's Sexual Object Choice," *Psychoanalytic Review* 80 (Spring 1993): 83-89; R. Fine, "Psychoanalytic Theory," in *Male and Female Homosexuality: Psychological Approaches*, ed. L. Diamant, Series in Clinical and Community Psychology (Washington, D.C.: Hemisphere, 1987), pp. 81-95; R. C. Friedman, "Contemporary Psychoanalysis and Homosexuality," *Experimental and Clinical Endocrinology* 98, no. 2 (1991): 155-60; E. Moberly, *Psychogenesis: The*

Early Development of Gender Identity (Longdon: Routledge & Kegan Paul, 1983); F. Morgenthaler, *Homosexuality, Heterosexuality, Perversion* (Hillsdale, N.J.: Analytic, 1988); C. W. Socarides, "The Homosexualities: A Psychoanalytic Classification," in *The Homosexualities: Reality, Fantasy and the Arts,* ed. C. W. Socarides and V. D. Volkan (Madison, Conn.: International Universities Press, 1991), pp. 9-46 (see also Socarides's books in my general bibliography); and M. Sternlicht, "The Neo-Freudians," in *Male and Female Homosexuality: Psychological Approaches,* ed. L. Diamant, Series in Clinical and Community Psychology (Washington, D.C.: Hemisphere, 1987), pp. 97-107.

[38]Twenty-three studies are cited by M. Siegelman, "Kinsey and Others: Empirical Input," in *Male and Female Homosexuality: Psychological Approaches,* ed. L. Diamant, Series in Clinical and Community Psychology (Washington, D.C.: Hemisphere, 1987), p. 51. See especially the large sample studies of M. T. Saghir and E. Robins, *Male and Female Homosexuality: A Comprehensive Investigation* (Baltimore: Williams Wilkins, 1973); Bieber et al., *Homosexuality,* pp. 79, 114; and A. Bell, M. Weinberg and S. Hammersmith, *Sexual Preference: Its Development in Men and Women* (Bloomington: Indiana University Press, 1981), pp. 41-62, 117-34.

[39]Saghir and Robins, *Male and Female Homosexuality,* pp. 139, 296-97, compared to 9 percent and 4 percent of heterosexual controls, respectively; compare D. K. Peters and P. J. Cantrell, "Factors Distinguishing Samples of Lesbian and Heterosexual Women," *Journal of Homosexuality* 21, no. 4 (1991): 10. Peters and Cantrell also found an unusual incidence of protracted absence during childhood on the part of fathers of homosexual women.

[40]See, for example, Saghir and Robins, *Male and Female Homosexuality,* pp. 17-31, 191-203; R. Green, *The "Sissy Boy" Syndrome and the Development of Homosexuality* (New Haven, Conn.: Yale University Press, 1987); G. Phillips and R. Over, "Adult Sexual Orientation in Relation to Memories of Childhood Gender Conforming and Gender Nonconforming Behaviors," *Archives of Sexual Behavior* 21, no. 6 (1992): 543-58; and Bell, Weinberg and Hammersmith, *Sexual Preference,* pp. 74-81, 145-52. It should be noted that Bell et al. do not use this finding in support of classic psychoanalytic theory.

[41]For further documentation on father relationships in relation to female homosexuals, see the summary of ten studies in G. J. M. van den Aardweg, *On the Origins and Treatment of Homosexuality* (New York: Praeger, 1986), pp. 183-84.

[42]Peters and Cantrell ("Factors Distinguishing Samples," pp. 2-3) cite ten former studies that document high rates of incest, rape and molestation; but their survey did not confirm the pattern.

[43]This argument of course cuts both ways: since developmental theory is now out of fashion, homosexuals are either not asked about or no longer "remember" early childhood problems. It is certainly suspicious that, to my knowledge, not a single study of early childhood among homosexuals has been conducted since the early 1980s. Is no one interested, or is grant money for research tied to political concerns? For extended arguments that developmental theory is an expression of homophobia see

K. Lewes, *The Psychoanalytic Theory of Homosexuality* (New York: Simon & Schuster, 1988), and the review by R. C. Friedman in *Archives of Sexual Behavior* 19 (June 1990): 293-301. In the same issue (pp. 303-7) Lewes reviews Friedman's published defense of developmental theory: *Male Homosexuality: A Contemporary Psychoanalytic Perspective* (New Haven, Conn.: Yale University Press, 1988).

⁴⁴For example, Siegelman, "Kinsey and Others," pp. 53-54; Bell, Weinberg and Hammersmith, *Sexual Preference*, p. 218.

⁴⁵Burch, "Heterosexuality, Bisexuality and Lesbianism," p. 97.

⁴⁶J. Greenspoon and P. A. Lamal, "A Behaviorist Approach," in *Male and Female Homosexuality: Psychological Approaches*, ed. L. Diamant, Series in Clinical and Community Psychology (Washington, D.C.: Hemisphere, 1987), pp. 109-28. See also M. Storms, "A Theory of Erotic Orientation Development," *Psychological Review* 88 (1981): 340-53.

⁴⁷See, for example, Goss, *Jesus Acted Up*, p. 44; J. J. McNeill, *The Church and the Homosexual* (Boston: Beacon, 1976; 4th ed. 1993), pp. 122-23.

⁴⁸L. S. Doll et al., "Self-Reported Childhood and Adolescent Sexual Abuse Among Adult Homosexual and Bisexual Men," *Child Abuse and Neglect* 16 (1992): 855-64. The study was conducted among one thousand adults in Chicago, Denver and San Francisco during 1989-1990.

⁴⁹D. P. McWhirter and A. M. Mattison, *The Male Couple: How Relationships Develop* (Englewood Cliffs, N.J.: Prentice-Hall, 1984), p. 269, table 41 (312 subjects); p. 271 for heterosexuals. It should be noted that the experiences reported by this study most often involved intimacy with other boys rather than men, and we must acknowledge that heterosexual men may be less likely to report such experiences. Obviously any statistics based on reports of childhood memories must be used very cautiously.

⁵⁰*Sexuality*, as I noted in chapter three, is indeed central to a person's being, but sexuality is broader and deeper than sexual activity, and it does not have to be expressed by sexual activity.

⁵¹Byne and Parsons ("Human Sexual Orientation," pp. 236-37) call this an "interactionist model"; De Cecco and Elia ("Critique and Synthesis," pp. 1-19) describe a "synthesis" of biological essentialism and social constructionism; and most developmental theorists acknowledge the possibility of an underlying biological factor.

⁵²This does happen: see K. Siegel and V. H. Raveis, "AIDS-Related Reasons for Gay Men's Adoption of Celibacy," *AIDS Education and Prevention* 5 (Fall 1993): 302-10.

⁵³See L. Diamant, introduction to *Male and Female Homosexuality: Psychological Approaches*, ed. L. Diamant, Series in Clinical and Community Psychology (Washington, D.C.: Hemisphere, 1987), pp. 1-15.

⁵⁴See, for example, R. A. Isay, "Psychoanalytic Theory and the Therapy of Gay Men," in *Homosexuality/Heterosexuality: Concepts of Sexual Orientation*, ed. D. P. McWhirter, S. A. Sanders and J. M. Reinisch, Kinsey Institute Series 2 (New York: Oxford University Press, 1990), pp. 283-303.

⁵⁵See, for example, D. C. Haldeman, "Sexual Orientation Conversion Therapy for Gay Men and Lesbians: A Scientific Examination," in *Homosexuality: Implications for Public*

Policy, ed. J. C. Gonsiorek and J. D. Weinrich (Newbury Park, Calif.: Sage, 1991), pp. 149-60. Haldeman is particularly critical of Christian ministries to homosexuals, which he considers unprofessional and ineffective gimmicks hiding under "the formidable auspices of the Christian church."

⁵⁶C. W. Socarides and B. Kaufman, "Reparative Therapy" (letter and replies), *American Journal of Psychiatry* 151 (January 1994): 157-59.

⁵⁷For a general discussion of treatment efforts and success rates see F. S. Berlin et al., "Media Distortion of the Public's Perception of Recidivism and Psychiatric Rehabilitation," *American Journal of Psychiatry* 148 (November 1991): 1572-76; L. Diamant, "The Therapies," in *Male and Female Homosexuality: Psychological Approaches,* ed. L. Diamant, Series in Clinical and Community Psychology (Washington, D.C.: Hemisphere, 1987), pp. 199-217 (I stole Diamant's clever subtitle for this section); and J. Marmor, "Clinical Aspects of Male Homosexuality," in *Homosexual Behavior: A Modern Reappraisal,* ed. J. Marmor (New York: Basic Books, 1980), pp. 275-79. For detailed reports of techniques and change results, see J. Bieber et al., *Homosexuality: A Psychoanalytic Study* (New York: Basic Books, 1962); L. Birk, "The Myth of Classical Homosexuality: Views of a Behavioral Psychotherapist," in *Homosexual Behavior: A Modern Reappraisal,* ed. J. Marmor (New York: Basic Books, 1980), pp. 376-90; A. Ellis, "The Effectiveness of Psychotherapy with Individuals Who Have Severe Homosexual Problems," in *The Problem of Homosexuality in Modern Society,* ed. H. M. Ruienbeck (New York: E. P. Dutton, 1965), pp. 175-82; M. P. Feldman and M. J. MacCulloch, *Homosexual Behavior: Therapy and Assessment* (Oxford: Pergamon, 1971); Hatterer, *Changing Homosexuality in the Male,* pp. 465-83 (and preceding discussion of technique, 49-387); H. E. Kaye et al., "Homosexuality in Women," *Archives of General Psychology* 17 (1967): 626-34.

⁵⁸W. H. Masters and V. E. Johnson, *Homosexuality in Perspective* (Boston: Little, Brown, 1979). Conversion candidates were those who had little or no prior heterosexual experience; reversion candidates were those with considerable prior heterosexual experience who were currently practicing homosexuality (p. 333). On the therapy technique, see especially pp. 255-60.

⁵⁹Ibid., p. 401. For criticism of this study, which centers on the incompleteness of the information supplied by Masters and Johnson, see Haldeman, "Sexual Orientation Conversion Therapy," pp. 154-55.

⁶⁰See, for example, Goss, *Jesus Acted Up,* p. 44; McNeill, *The Church and the Homosexual,* pp. 122-23. Both make explicit comparisons between aversion therapy and Nazi death camps. See Birk, "Myth of Classical Homosexuality," pp. 378-79, Diamant, "The Therapies," pp. 208-9, and Greenspoon and Lamal, "Behaviorist Approach," pp. 122-23, on the abandonment of physical aversion techniques.

⁶¹Greenspoon and Lamal, "Behaviorist Approach," pp. 124-26; Birk, "Myth of Classical Homosexuality," pp. 380-9.

⁶²Moberly, "Homosexuality: Restating the Conservative Case," pp. 291-93.

⁶³Hatterer (*Changing Homosexuality in the Male,* pp. 445-64) provides the most detailed catalog of variables. See also D. S. Sanders, "A Psychotherapeutic Approach to Ho-

mosexual Men," in *Homosexual Behavior: A Modern Reappraisal*, ed. J. Marmor (New York: Basic Books, 1980), pp. 342-56, especially p. 346; Marmor, "Clinical Aspects of Male Homosexuality," pp. 277-8; J. R. Cavanaugh, *Counseling the Homosexual* (Huntington, Ind.: Our Sunday Visitor, 1977), p. 240.

[64]The umbrella organization for such ministries to homosexuals is Exodus International, which provides a monthly update of referral and affiliate agencies by region to inquirers: P.O. Box 2121, San Rafael, CA 94912.

[65]This is the method of P. B. Jung and R. F. Smith (*Heterosexism: An Ethical Challenge* [Albany, N.Y.: State University of New York Press, 1993]), who dispute one study (Masters and Johnson) and one outdated method (behaviorist shock therapy), conclude that there has been "no documented success in reorienting homosexuals" (p. 19) and later feel free to generalize about "what we know scientifically about human sexuality" (p. 83). I trust that the authors know more than they reveal, but their method of argument is irresponsible. It is objectionable enough for these authors to deny the burden of proof at nearly every point, but in this case their apparent acceptance of the burden is a mirage. It appears that what they describe as lack of evidence is in fact an assertion that they are not convinced (read: not convinceable) by evidence contrary to their assumptions.

[66]Leanne Payne, *The Broken Image* (Westchester, Ill.: Crossway, 1981); see also Leanne Payne, *The Healing of the Homosexual* (Westchester, Ill.: Crossway, 1984), which is essentially a condensation of the earlier book.

[67]Andrew Comiskey, *Pursuing Sexual Wholeness* (Lake Mary, Fla.: Creation House, 1989). A study guide for small groups is also available.

[68]Bob Davies and Lori Rentzel, *Coming Out of Homosexuality* (Downers Grove, Ill.: InterVarsity Press, 1993).

[69]Michael Saia, *Counseling the Homosexual* (Minneapolis: Bethany House, 1988).

[70]J. R. Cavanaugh, *Counseling the Homosexual* (Huntington, Ind.: Our Sunday Visitor, 1977).

[71]G. J. M. van den Aardweg, *Homosexuality and Hope* (Ann Arbor, Michigan: Servant, 1985). Van den Aardweg has also written a clinical book, cited above (n. 41), which contains a helpful appendix (pp. 269-77) giving parents guidelines for the encouragement of heterosexuality in their children.

[72]J. Arterburn, *How Do I Tell My Mother?* (Nashville: Oliver-Nelson, 1988; rev. 1990).

[73]M. White, *Stranger at the Gate* (New York: Simon & Schuster, 1994); G. D. Comstock, *Gay Theology Without Apology* (New York: Pilgrim, 1993); R. Williams, *Just As I Am: A Practical Guide to Being Out, Proud and Christian* (New York: Crown, 1992); J. J. McNeill, *The Church and the Homosexual* (Boston: Beacon, 1976; 4th ed. 1993).

[74]Arterburn, *How Do I Tell My Mother?* pp. 127, 181.

Bibliography

For ease of reference I divide the bibliography by topic. Section 1, "Theology and Ethics," covers chapters two through five. Section 2, "Prevalence and Health," covers chapter six. Section 3, "Causation and Change," covers chapter seven. "For Further Reading" lists nontechnical sources that are similar in perspective to this book.

Throughout the bibliography, an asterisk (*) indicates a source of particular importance, either because it is representative of an influential position or because it contains a broad review of subject matter.

Section 1: Theology and Ethics

*Bailey, S. *Homosexuality and the Western Christian Tradition.* London: Green, 1955.

Barth, K. *Church Dogmatics* 3/4. Edinburgh: T & T Clark, 1961.

Bauserman, R. "Objectivity and Ideology: Criticism of Theo Sandfort's Research of Man-Boy Sexual Relations," *Journal of Homosexuality* 20, nos. 1/2 (1990): 297-312.

*Boswell, J. *Christianity, Social Tolerance and Homosexuality.* New Haven, Conn.: Yale University Press, 1980.

Brongersma, E. "Boy-Lovers and Their Influence on Boys: Distorted Research and Anecdotal Observations." *Journal of Homosexuality* 20, nos. 1/2 (1990): 145-73.

Brooten, B. J. "Patristic Interpretations of Romans 1:26," *Studia Patristica* 18:2 (1985) 287-91.

————. "Paul and the Law: How Complete Was the Departure?" *Princeton Seminary Bulletin* supp. 1 (1990): 83.

————. "Paul's Views on the Nature of Women and Female Homoeroticism." In *Immaculate and Powerful: The Female in Sacred Image and Social Reality.* Edited by C. W. Atkinson, C. H. Buchanan and M. R. Miles. Boston: Beacon, 1985.

Bruce, F. F. *1 & 2 Thessalonians.* Waco, Tex.: Word, 1982.

Cahill, L. S. "Moral Methodology: A Case Study." In *A Challenge to Love: Gay and Lesbian Catholics in the Church.* Edited by R. Nugent. New York: Crossroad, 1983.

Cantarella, E. *Bisexuality in the Ancient World.* New Haven, Conn.: Yale University Press, 1972.

Charles, R. H. *The Revelation of St. John.* Edinburgh: T & T Clark, 1920.

Charlesworth, J. H., ed. *The Old Testament Pseudepigrapha.* 2 vols. Garden City, N.Y.: Doubleday, 1983-1985.

Christ, C. P. "Why Women Need the Goddess: Phenomenological, Psychological and Political Reflections." In *Womanspirit Rising: A Feminist Reader in Religion.* Edited by C. P. Christ and J. Plaskow. San Francisco: Harper & Row, 1979.

Comstock, G D. *Gay Theology Without Apology.* New York· Pilgrim, 1993.

*Countryman, L William. *Dirt, Greed and Sex.* Philadelphia: Fortress, 1988.

Cranfield, C. E. B. *The Epistle to the Romans.* Edinburgh: T & T Clark, 1975.

Deming, W. "Mark 9.42-10.12, Matthew 5.27-32 and *b. Nid.* 13b: A First Century Discussion of Male Sexuality." *New Testament Studies* 36 (1990): 130-41.

DeYoung, J. B. "The Contributions of the Septuagint to Biblical Sanctions Against Homosexuality." *Journal of the Evangelical Theological Society* 34 (June 1991): 157-77.

————. "A Critique of Prohomosexual Interpretations of the Old Testament Apocrypha and Pseudepigrapha." *Bibliotheca Sacra* 147 (1990): 437-54.

————. "The Meaning of 'Nature' in Romans 1 and Its Implications for Biblical Perspectives of Homosexual Behavior." *Journal of the Evangelical Theological Society* 31 (1988): 429-47.

Dover, K. *Greek Homosexuality.* 2nd ed. Cambridge, Mass.: Harvard University Press, 1989.

Dresner, S. "Homosexuality and the Order of Creation." *Judaism* 40 (Summer 1991): 309-21.

Dunn, J. D. G. *Romans 1-8.* Waco, Tex.: Word, 1988.

Edwards, G. A. *Gay/Lesbian Liberation: A Biblical Perspective* New York: Pilgrim, 1984.

Elshtain, J. B. "Homosexual Politics." *Salmagundi* 58/59 (Fall 1982/Winter 1983): 252-80.

Farley, M. A. "An Ethic for Same-Sex Relations." In *A Challenge to Love: Gay and Lesbian Catholics in the Church.* Edited by R. Nugent. New York: Crossroad, 1983.

Fiorenza, E. Schüssler. "Toward a Feminist Biblical Hermeneutics: Biblical Interpretation and Liberation Theology." In *The Challenge of Liberation Theology.* Edited by B. Mahan and L. D. Richesin. Maryknoll, N.Y.: Orbis, 1981.

Ford, J. M. *Revelation.* Garden City, N.Y.: Doubleday, 1975.

Foucault, M. *The History of Sexuality.* Vol. 1, *An Introduction.* New York: Vintage, 1980.

————. *Language, Counter-Memory, Practice.* Ithaca, N.Y. Cornell University Press, 1977.

Furnish, V. P. *The Moral Teaching of Paul.* Nashville: Abingdon, 1979.

Goss, R. *Jesus Acted Up: A Gay and Lesbian Manifesto.* San Francisco: Harper, 1993.

Grenz, S. *Sexual Ethics.* Dallas: Word, 1990.

Guinan, M. D. "Homosexuals: A Christian Pastoral Response Now." In *A Challenge to Love: Gay and Lesbian Catholics in the Church.* Edited by R. Nugent. New York: Crossroad, 1983.

Hampson, M. D. *Theology and Feminism.* Cambridge, Mass.: Blackwell, 1990.

Hanigan, J. P. *Homosexuality: The Test Case for Christian Ethics.* New York: Paulist, 1988.

*Hays, R. B. "Relations Natural and Unnatural: A Response to John Boswell's Exegesis of Romans 1." *Journal of Religious Ethics* 14 (1986): 186-95.

Huggins, K. W. "An Investigation of the Jewish Theology of Sexuality Influencing the References to Homosexuality in Romans 1:18-32." Ph.D. diss., Southwestern Baptist Theological Seminary, 1986.

Jones, G. P. "The Study of Intergenerational Intimacy in North America: Beyond Politics and Pedophilia." *Journal of Homosexuality* 20, nos. 1/2 (1990): 275-95.

Jung, P. B., and R. F. Smith. *Heterosexism: An Ethical Challenge.* Albany: State University of New York Press, 1993.

Kirk, M., and H. Madsen. *After the Ball: How America Will Conquer Its Fear and Hatred of Gays in the 90s.* New York: Plume Books, 1989.

Kirschner, R. "Halakah and Homosexuality: A Reappraisal." *Judaism* 37 (Fall 1988): 450-58.

Lance, D. "The Anthropological Context of Genesis 19 and Judges 19." Paper presented at the 1992 annual meeting of the Society of Biblical Literature, San Francisco, 1992.

Li, C. " 'The Main Thing Is Being Wanted': Some Case Studies on Adult Sexual Experiences with Children." *Journal of Homosexuality* 20, nos. 1/2 (1990): 129-43.

McNeill, J. J. *The Church and the Homosexual.* 4th ed. Boston: Beacon, 1993 (1st ed. 1976).

Maguire, D. "The Morality of Homosexual Marriage." In *A Challenge to Love: Gay and Lesbian Catholics in the Church.* Edited by R. Nugent. New York: Crossroad, 1983.

Niditch, S. "The 'Sodomite' Theme in Judges 19-20: Family, Community and Social Disintegration." *Catholic Biblical Quarterly* 44 (1982): 365-78.

Novak, D. "Before Revelation: The Rabbis Paul, and Karl Barth." *Journal of Religion* 71 (January 1991): 50-66.

O'Donovan, O. "Transsexualism and Christian Marriage." *Journal of Religious Ethics* 11 (Spring 1983): 135-62.

Petersen, W. L. "Can *ΑΡΣΕΝΟΚΟΙΤΑΙ* Be Translated by 'Homosexuals'? (1 Cor. 6.9; 1 Tim 1.10)," *Vigiliae Christianae* 40 (1986): 187-91.

Phillips, A. "Uncovering the Father's Skirt." *Vetus Testamentum* 30 (1980): 38-43.

Pope, M. *Job.* Garden City, N.Y.: Doubleday, 1973.

*Pronk, P. *Against Nature? Types of Moral Argumentation Regarding Homosexuality.* Grand Rapids, Mich.: Eerdmans, 1993.

Sandfort, T. "Pedophilia and the Gay Movement." *Journal of Homosexuality* 13 (Winter 1986/Spring 1987): 89-110.

Scott, D. A. "The Hermeneutics of Marriage." *Anglican Theological Review* 72 (Spring 1990): 168-71.

Scroggs, R. *The New Testament and Homosexuality.* Philadelphia: Fortress, 1983.

Scruton, R. *Sexual Desire: A Moral Philosophy of the Erotic.* New York: Free Press, 1986.

Swidler, A., ed. *Homosexuality and World Religions.* Valley Forge, Penn.: Trinity Press International, 1993.

Thorstad, D. "Man/Boy Love and the American Gay Movement." *Journal of Homosexuality* 20, nos. 1/2 (1990): 251-74.

Ukleja, P. M. "The Bible and Homosexuality, pt. 2: Homosexuality in the New Testament." *Bibliotheca Sacra* 140 (1983): 350-58.

————. "Homosexuality and the Old Testament." *Bibliotheca Sacra* 140 (1983): 259-66.

van Zessen, G. "A Model for Group Counseling with Male Pedophiles." *Journal of Homosexuality* 20, nos. 1/2 (1990): 189-98.

Wannamaker, C. A. *The Epistles to the Thessalonians.* Grand Rapids, Mich.: Eerdmans, 1990.

Wenham, G. J. "The Old Testament Attitude to Homosexuality." *Expository Times* 102 (Spring 1991): 359-63.

Westermann, C. *Genesis 1-11.* Minneapolis: Augsburg, 1984.

White, M. *Stranger at the Gate.* New York: Simon & Schuster, 1994.

Williams, R. *Just As I Am: A Practical Guide to Being Out, Proud and Christian.* New York: Crown, 1992.

———. "Toward a Theology for Lesbian and Gay Marriage." *Anglican Theological Review* 72 (Spring 1990): 134-57.

Wright, D. F. "Early Christian Attitudes to Homosexuality." *Studia Patristica* 18, no. 2 (1989): 329-34.

———. "Homosexuality: The Relevance of the Bible." *Evangelical Quarterly* 61 (October 1989): 291-300.

*———. "Homosexuals or Prostitutes? The Meaning of *Arsenokoitai* (1 Cor 6:9, 1 Tim 1:10)." *Vigiliae Christianae* 38 (1984): 125-53.

Wright, J. R. "Boswell on Homosexuality: A Case Undemonstrated." *Anglican Theological Review* 66 (Winter 1985): 79-94.

Zaas, P. "Catalogues and Context: 1 Corinthians 5 and 6." *New Testament Studies* 34 (October 1988): 622-29.

———. "1 Corinthians 6:9ff.: Was Homosexuality Condoned in the Corinthian Church?" *Society of Biblical Literature Seminar Papers* 17 (1979): 205-12.

Section 2: Prevalence and Health

Abib, S. M., et al. "Relapse in Sexual Behavior Among Homosexual Men: a Two-Year Follow-up from the Chicago MACS/CCS." *Acquired Immunodeficiency Syndrome* 5 (June 1991): 757-60.

Abib, S. M., and D. G. Ostrow. "Trends in HIV/AIDS Behavioural Research Among Homosexual and Bisexual Men in the United States: 1981-1991." *AIDS Care* 3, no. 3 (1991): 281-87.

Abrams, D. I. "The Relationship Between Kaposi's Sarcoma and the Intestinal Parasites Among Homosexual Males in the United States." *Journal of Acquired Immune Deficiency Syndrome* 3, supp. 1 (1990): 544-46.

Adams, P. F., and A. M. Hardy. *AIDS Knowledge and Attitudes for July-September 1990: Provisional Data from the National Health Interview Survey.* Advance Data from Vital and Health Statistics 198. Hyattsville, Md.: National Center for Health Statistics, April 1, 1991.

*Agnew, J. "Some Anatomical and Physiological Aspects of Anal Sexual Practices." *Journal of Homosexuality* 12 (1986): 75-96.

Aldous, P. "French Venture Where U.S. Fears to Tread." *Science* 257 (July 3, 1992): 25.

Bauserman, R. "Objectivity and Ideology: Criticism of Theo Sandfort's Research of Man-Boy Sexual Relations." *Journal of Homosexuality* 20, nos. 1/2 (1990): 297-312.

*Bell, A. P., and M. S. Weinberg. *Homosexualities: A Study of Diversity Among Men and Women.* New York: Simon & Schuster, 1978.

Beral, V., et al. "Risk of Kaposi's Sarcoma and Sexual Practices Associated with Faecal Contact in Homosexual and Bisexual Men with AIDS." *Lancet* 339 (March 14, 1992): 632-35.

Berkelman, R. L., et al. "Epidemiology of Human Immunodeficiency Virus Infection and Acquired Immunodeficiency Syndrome." *The American Journal of Medicine* 86 (1989): 761-70.

Biggar, R. J. "Risk of Other Cancers Following Kaposi's Sarcoma: Relationship to Acquired Immunodeficiency Syndrome." *American Journal of Epidemiology* 139 (February 15, 1994): 362-68.

Billstein, S. A. "Human Lice." In *Sexually Transmitted Diseases.* Edited by K. K. Holmes et al. 2nd ed. New York: McGraw-Hill, 1989.

Blasband, D., and L. A. Peplaw. "Sexual Exclusivity." *Archives of Sexual Behavior* 14 (October 1985): 395-412.

Bloomfield, K. "A Comparison of Alcohol Consumption Between Lesbians and Heterosexual Women in an Urban Population." *Drug and Alcohol Dependence* 33 (October 1993): 257-69.

Blumstein, P., and P. Schwartz. "Intimate Relationships and the Creation of Sexuality." In *Homosexuality/Heterosexuality: Concepts of Sexual Orientation.* Edited by D. P. McWhirter, S. A. Sanders and J. M. Reinisch. Kinsey Institute Series 2. New York: Oxford University Press, 1990.

Breslow, N., L. Evans and J. Langley. "Comparisons Among Heterosexual, Bisexual and Homosexual Male Sado-masochists." *Journal of Homosexuality* 13 (Fall 1986): 83-107.

Brongersma, E. "Boy-Lovers and Their Influence on Boys: Distorted Research and Anecdotal Observations." *Journal of Homosexuality* 20, nos. 1/2 (1990): 145-73.

Bush, R. A., and W. F. Owen. "Trauma and Other Non-infectious Problems in Homosexual Men." *The Medical Clinics of North America* 70, no. 3 (1986): 549-66.

Butler, K. M., and P. A. Pizzo. "HIV Infection in Children." In *AIDS: Etiology, Diagnosis, Treatment and Prevention.* Edited by V. T. DeVita et al. Philadelphia: J. B. Lippincott, 1992.

Cameron, P. "Homosexual Molestation of Children: Sexual Interaction of Teacher and Pupil." *Psychological Reports* 57 (1985): 1227-36.

Catania, J. A., et al. "Changes in Condom Use Among Homosexual Men in San Francisco." *Health Psychology* 10, no. 3 (1991): 190-99.

Catterall, R. D. "Sexually Transmitted Diseases of the Anus and Rectum." *Clinical Gastroenterology* 4 (1975): 659-69.

Centers for Disease Control. "Patterns of Sexual Behavior Change Among Homosexual/Bisexual Men—Selected U.S. Sites, 1987-90." *Morbidity and Mortality Weekly Report* 40 (November 22, 1991): 792-94.

————. "Projections of the Numbers of Persons Diagnosed with AIDS and the Number of Immunosuppressed HIV-Infected Persons—United States, 1992-94." *Mor-*

bidity and Mortality Weekly Report 41 (December 25, 1992): 1-29.

———. "Update: Acquired Immunodeficiency Syndrome—U.S. 1991." *Morbidity and Mortality Weekly Report* 41 (July 3, 1992): 463-68.

———. "Update: Barrier Protection Against HIV Infection and Other Sexually Transmitted Diseases." *Morbidity and Mortality Weekly Report* 42 (August 6, 1993): 589-91.

Chaisson, R. E., J. L. Gerberding and M. A. Sande. "Opportunistic Infections in AIDS." In *Sexually Transmitted Diseases.* Edited by K. K. Holmes et al. 2nd ed. New York: McGraw-Hill, 1989.

Chu, S. Y., R. L. Berkelman and J. W. Curran. "Epidemiology of HIV in the United States." In *AIDS: Etiology, Diagnosis, Treatment and Prevention.* Edited by V. T. DeVita et al. Philadelphia: J. B. Lippincott, 1992.

Coleman, E. "Toward a Synthetic Understanding of Sexual Orientation." In *Homosexuality/Heterosexuality: Concepts of Sexual Orientation.* Edited by D. P. McWhirter, S. A. Sanders and J. M. Reinisch. Kinsey Institute Series 2. New York: Oxford University Press, 1990.

Corey, L., and K. K. Holmes. "Sexual Transmission of Hepatitis A in Homosexual Men." *New England Journal of Medicine* 302 (February 21, 1980): 435-38.

Court, J. H., and J. G. Muir, eds. *Kinsey, Sex and Fraud: The Indoctrination of a People.* Lafayette, La.: Huntington House, 1990.

Daling, J. R., et al. "Sexual Practices, Sexually Transmitted Diseases and the Incidence of Anal Cancer." *New England Journal of Medicine* 317 (1987): 973-77.

Darrow, W. W., and K. Siegel. "Preventive Health Behavior and STD." In *Sexually Transmitted Diseases.* Edited by K. K. Holmes et al. 2nd ed. New York: McGraw-Hill, 1989.

Davies, P. M. "Safer Sex Maintenance Among Gay Men: Are We Moving in the Right Direction?" *AIDS* 7 (February 1993): 279-80.

Davies, P. M., et al. "Risk of HIV Infection in Homosexual Men." *British Medical Journal* 307 (September 11, 1993): 681.

Dawson, D. A. *AIDS Knowledge and Attitudes for January-March 1990: Provisional Data from the National Health Interview Survey.* Advance Data from Vital and Health Statistics 198. Hyattsville, Md.: National Center for Health Statistics, September 26, 1990.

de Wit, J. B. F., et al. "The Effectiveness of Condom Use Among Homosexual Men." *AIDS* 7 (May 1993): 751-52.

*———. "Increase in Unprotected Anogenital Intercourse Among Homosexual Men." *American Journal of Public Health* 83 (October 1993): 1451-53.

———. "Why Do Homosexual Men Relapse into Unsafe Sex? Predictors of Resumption of Unprotected Anogenital Intercourse with Casual Partners." *AIDS* 7 (August 1993): 1113-18.

Diamant, L., and R. B. Simono. "The Relationship of Homosexuality to Mental Disorders." In *Male and Female Homosexuality: Psychological Approaches.* Edited by L. Diamant. Washington, D.C.: Hemisphere, 1987.

Diamond, M. "Homosexuality and Bisexuality in Different Populations." *Archives of*

Sexual Behavior 22, no. 4 (1993): 291-310.

*Doll, L. S., et al. "Homosexual Men Who Engage in High-Risk Sexual Behavior: A Multicenter Comparison." *Sexually Transmitted Diseases* 18 (July-September 1991): 170-75.

Ekstrand, M. L. "Safer Sex Maintenance Among Gay Men: Are We Making Any Progress?" *AIDS* 6 (August 1992): 875-76.

Ekstrand, M. L., and T. J. Coates. "Maintenance of Safer Sexual Behavior and Predictors of Risky Sex: The San Francisco Men's Health Study." *American Journal of Public Health* 80 (1990): 973-77.

Ekstrand, M. L., et al. "Safer Sex Among Gay Men: What Is the Ultimate Goal?" *AIDS* 7 (February 1993): 281-82.

Elford, J., et al. "Kaposi's Sarcoma and Insertive Rimming." *Lancet* 339 (April 11, 1992): 938.

*Essex, M. "Origin of AIDS." In *AIDS: Etiology, Diagnosis, Treatment and Prevention.* Edited by V. T. DeVita et al. Philadelphia: J. B. Lippincott, 1992.

Fay, R., et al. "Prevalence and Patterns of Same-Gender Contact Among Men." *Science* 243 (January 20, 1989): 338-48.

Felman, Y. M. "Homosexual Hazards." *Practitioner* 224 (1980): 1151-56.

Fitti, J. E., and M. Cynamon. *AIDS Knowledge and Attitudes for April-June 1990: Provisional Data from the National Health Interview Survey.* Advance Data from Vital and Health Statistics 195. Hyattsville, Md.: National Center for Health Statistics, December 18, 1990.

Forman, D., and C. Chilvers. "Sexual Behaviour of Young and Middle Aged Men in England and Wales." *British Medical Journal* 298 (April 29, 1989): 1137-42.

*Freund, K., and R. J. Watson. "The Proportions of Heterosexual and Homosexual Pedophiles Among Sex Offenders Against Children: An Exploratory Study." *Journal of Sex and Marital Therapy* 18 (Spring 1992): 34-43.

Freund, K., et al. "Pedophilia and Heterosexuality vs. Homosexuality." *Journal of Sex and Marital Therapy* 10 (1984): 193-200.

Fumento, M. A. "AIDS: Are Heterosexuals at Risk?" *Commentary,* November 1987, pp. 21-27.

Gellin, B. G., and D. E. Rogers. "Technical Successes and Social Failures: Approaching the Second Decade of the AIDS Epidemic." In *AIDS: Etiology, Diagnosis, Treatment and Prevention.* Edited by V. T. DeVita et al. Philadelphia: J. B. Lippincott, 1992.

Gill, S. K., C. Loveday and R. J. Gibson. "Transmission of HIV-1 Infection by Oroanal Intercourse." *Genitourinary Medicine* 68 (August 1992): 254-57.

Gold, R. S., and M. J. Skinner. "Situational Factors and Thought Processes Associated with Unprotected Intercourse in Young Gay Men." *AIDS* 6 (September 1992): 1021-30.

Gonsiorek, J. C. "An Introduction to Mental Health Issues and Homosexuality." *American Behavioral Scientist* 25, no. 4 (1982): 367-84.

Haase, A. T. "Biology of Human Immunodeficiency Virus and Related Viruses." In

Sexually Transmitted Diseases. Edited by K. K. Holmes et al. 2nd ed. New York: McGraw-Hill, 1989.

Hall, J. M. "Lesbians and Alcohol: Patterns and Paradoxes in Medical Notions and Lesbians' Beliefs." *Journal of Psychoactive Drugs* 25 (April-June 1993): 109-19.

Harry, J. *Gay Couples.* New York: Praeger Books, 1984.

Herron, M. "Living with AIDS." *Whole Earth Review,* Fall 1985, pp. 34-53.

Herzog, D. B., et al. "Body Image Dissatisfaction in Homosexual and Heterosexual Males." *Journal of Nervous and Mental Disorders* 179 (June 1991): 356-59.

Hickson, F. C. I., et al. "Maintenance of Open Gay Relationships: Some Strategies for Protection Against HIV." *AIDS Care* 4, no. 4 (1992): 409-19.

Holly, E. A., et al. "Anal Cancer Incidence: Genital Warts, Anal Fissure or Fistural, Hemorrhoids and Smoking." *Journal of the National Cancer Institute* 81 (1989): 1726-31.

Hunt, A. J., et al. "Changes in Sexual Behavior in a Large Cohort of Homosexual Men in England and Wales, 1988-89." *British Medical Journal* 302 (March 2, 1991): 505-6.

*Israelstam, S., and S. Lambert. "Homosexuality as a Cause of Alcoholism: A Historical Overview." *International Journal of the Addictions* 18, no. 8 (1983): 1085-1107.

Jacobsen, L. P., et al. "Changes in Survival After Acquired Immunodeficiency Syndrome (AIDS): 1984-91." *American Journal of Epidemiology* 183 (December 1, 1993): 952-64.

Jacobsen, L. P., et al. "Incidence of Kaposi's Sarcoma in a Cohort of Homosexual Men Infected with the Human Immunodeficiency Virus Type I." *Journal of Acquired Immunodeficiency Syndrome* 3, supp. 1 (1990): S24-31.

*Jay, K., and A. Young. *The Gay Report.* New York: Summit, 1979.

Johnson, A. M., et al. "Sexual Lifestyles and HIV Risk." *Nature* 360 (December 3, 1992): 410-12.

Jones, G. P. "The Study of Intergenerational Intimacy in North America: Beyond Politics and Pedophilia." *Journal of Homosexuality* 20, nos. 1/2 (1990): 275-95.

Kani, J., et al. "Hepatitis A Virus Infection Among Homosexual Men." *British Medical Journal* 302 (June 8, 1991): 1399.

Kazal, H. L., et al. "The Gay Bowel Syndrome: Clinico-Pathologic Correlation in 260 Cases." *Annals of Clinical Laboratory Science* 6 (1976): 184-92.

Keeffe, E. B. "Clinical Approach to Viral Hepatitis in Homosexual Men." *The Medical Clinics of North America* 70, no. 3 (1986): 567-86.

Keet, I. P., et al. "Orogenital Sex and the Transmission of HIV Among Homosexual Men." *Acquired Immunodeficiency Syndrome* 6 (February 1992): 223-26.

Kelly, J. A., and D. A. Murphy. "Some Lessons Learned About Risk Reduction After Ten Years of the HIV/AIDS Epidemic." *AIDS Care* 3, no. 3 (1991): 251-57.

Kingsley, L. A., et al. "Sexual Transmission Efficiency of Hepatitis B Virus and Human Immunodeficiency Virus Among Homosexual Men." *Journal of the American Medical Association* 264 (July 11, 1990): 230-34.

Kinsey, A. C., W. B. Pomeroy and C. E. Martin. *Sexual Behavior in the Human Male.* Philadelphia: W. B. Saunders, 1948.

Kinsey, A. C., et al. *Sexual Behavior in the Human Female.* Philadelphia: W. B. Saunders, 1953.

Kippax, S., et al. "Sustaining Safe Sex: A Longitudinal Study of a Sample of Homosexual Men." *AIDS* 7 (February 1993): 257-63.

Klamecki, B. J. "Medical Perspective of the Homosexual Issue." In *The Crisis of Homosexuality.* Edited by J. I. Yamamoto. Wheaton, Ill.: Victor Books, 1990.

Klein, F. "The Need to View Sexual Orientation as a Multivariable Dynamic Process: A Theoretical Perspective." In *Homosexuality/Heterosexuality: Concepts of Sexual Orientation.* Edited by D. P. McWhirter, S. A. Sanders and J. M. Reinisch. Kinsey Institute Series 2. New York: Oxford University Press, 1990.

Ku, L., et al. "Patterns of HIV Risk and Preventive Behaviors Among Teenage Men." *Public Health Reports* 107 (March/April 1992): 131-38.

Laumann, E. O., et al. *The Social Organization of Sexuality.* Chicago: University of Chicago Press, 1994.

Law, C. L. H., et al. "Factors Associated with Clinical and Sub-clinical Anal Human Papillomavirus Infection in Homosexual Men." *Genitourinary Medicine* 67 (April 1991): 92-98.

Leigh, B. C., M. T. Temple and K. F. Trocki. "The Sexual Behavior of U.S. Adults: Results from a Nation Survey." *American Journal of Public Health* 83 (October 1993): 1400-8.

Lemon, S. M., and J. E. Newbold. "Viral Hepatitis." In *Sexually Transmitted Diseases.* Edited by K. K. Holmes et al. 2nd ed. New York: McGraw-Hill, 1989.

Levine, A. M. "Lymphoma and Other Miscellaneous Cancers." In *AIDS: Etiology, Diagnosis, Treatment and Prevention.* Edited by V. T. DeVita et al. Philadelphia: J. B. Lippincott, 1992.

Lewis, C. E., M. T. Saghir and E. Robins. "Drinking Patterns in Homosexual and Heterosexual Women." *Journal of Clinical Psychiatry* 43, no. 7 (1982): 83-95.

*Lifson, A. R. "Transmission of the Human Immunodeficiency Virus." In *AIDS: Etiology, Diagnosis, Treatment and Prevention.* Edited by V. T. DeVita et al. Philadelphia: J. B. Lippincott, 1992.

Lifson, A. R., et al. "HIV Seroconversion in Two Homosexual Men After Receptive Oral Intercourse with Ejaculation: Implications for Counseling Concerning Safe Sex Practices." *American Journal of Public Health* 80 (1990): 1509-11.

*Linn, L., et al. "Recent Sexual Behaviors Among Homosexual Men Seeking Primary Medical Care." *Archives of Internal Medicine* 149 (December 1989): 2685-90.

McCusker, M., et al. "Maintenance of Behavioral Change in a Cohort of Homosexually Active Men." *AIDS* 6 (August 1992): 861-68.

———. "Use of Drugs and Alcohol by Homosexually Active Men in Relation to Sexual Practices." *Journal of Acquired Immunodeficiency Syndrome* 3, no. 7 (1990): 729-36.

McKusick, L., et al. "AIDS and Sexual Behaviors Reported by Gay Men in San Francisco." *American Journal of Public Health* 75 (1985): 493-96.

McWhirter, D. P., and A. M. Mattison. *The Gay Couple: How Relationships Develop.* Englewood Cliffs, N.J.: Prentice-Hall, 1984.

Mann, J. M., and S. L. Welles. "Global Aspects of the HIV Epidemic." In *AIDS: Etiology, Diagnosis, Treatment and Prevention.* Edited by V. T. DeVita et al. Philadelphia: J. B. Lippincott, 1992.

Marks, G., et al. "HIV-Infected Men's Practices in Notifying Past Sexual Partners of Infection Risk." *Public Health Reports* 107 (January/February 1992): 100-105.

Marmor, J. "Clinical Aspects of Male Homosexuality." In *Homosexual Behavior: A Modern Reappraisal.* Edited by J. Marmor. New York: Basic Books, 1980.

Martin, D. J. "Inappropriate Lubricant Use with Condoms by Homosexual Men." *Public Health Reports* 107 (July/August 1992): 468-73.

Messiah, A., et al. "Factors Correlated with Homosexually Acquired Human Immunodeficiency Virus Infection in the Era of 'Safer Sex.' " *Sexually Transmitted Diseases* 20 (January/February 1993): 51-58.

Miles, A. J., et al. "Effect of Anoreceptive Intercourse on Anorectal Function." *Journal of the Royal Society of Medicine* 86 (March 1993): 144-47.

Murray, A. B., et al. "Coincident Acquisition of Neisseria Gonorrhea and HIV from Fellatio." *Lancet* 338 (September 28, 1991): 830.

Myers, T., et al. "HIV, Substance Use and Related Behavior of Gay and Bisexual Men: An Examination of the Talking Sex Project Cohort." *British Journal of Addiction* 87 (February 1992): 207-14.

Nichols, M. "Lesbian Relationships: Implications for the Study of Sexuality and Gender." In *Homosexuality/Heterosexuality: Concepts of Sexual Orientation.* Edited by D. P. McWhirter, S. A. Sanders and J. M. Reinisch. Kinsey Institute Series 2. New York: Oxford University Press, 1990.

Orkin, M., and H. Maibach. "Scabies." In *Sexually Transmitted Diseases.* Edited by K. K. Holmes et al. 2nd ed. New York: McGraw-Hill, 1989.

*Ostrow, D. G. "Homosexual Behavior and Sexually Transmitted Diseases." In *Sexually Transmitted Diseases.* Edited by K. K. Holmes et al. 2nd ed. New York: McGraw-Hill, 1989.

*Owen, W. F. "The Clinical Approach to the Male Homosexual Patient." *The Medical Clinics of North America* 70, no. 3 (1986): 499-535.

Parra, W., et al. "Patient Counseling and Behavior Modification." In *Sexually Transmitted Diseases.* Edited by K. K. Holmes et al. 2nd ed. New York: McGraw-Hill, 1989.

Peplau, L. A., and S. D. Cochran. "A Relationship Perspective on Homosexuality." In *Homosexuality/Heterosexuality: Concepts of Sexual Orientation.* Edited by D. P. McWhirter, S. A. Sanders and J. M. Reinisch. Kinsey Institute Series 2. New York: Oxford University Press, 1990.

Peterman, T. A., D. C. Des Jarlais and J. N. Wasserheit. "Prevention of the Sexual Transmission of HIV." In *AIDS: Etiology, Diagnosis, Treatment and Prevention.* Edited by V. T. DeVita et al. Philadelphia: J. B. Lippincott, 1992.

Peterson, H. B., and M. F. Rogers. "Perinatal Transmission of HIV." In *AIDS: Etiology,*

Diagnosis, Treatment and Prevention. Edited by V. T. DeVita et al. Philadelphia: J. B. Lippincott, 1992.

Peterson, J. L., et al. "High Risk Sexual Behavior and Condom Use Among Gay and Bisexual African-American Men." *American Journal of Public Health* 82 (November 1992): 1490-94.

Quatro, M., et al. "HIV Transmission by Fellatio." *European Journal of Epidemiology* 6, no. 3 (1990): 339-40.

*Quinn, T. C. "Clinical Approach to Intestinal Infections in Homosexual Men." *The Medical Clinics of North America* 70, no. 3 (1986): 611-34.

Quinn, T. C., and W. E. Stamm. "Proctitis, Proctocolitis and Enteritis in Homosexual Men." In *Sexually Transmitted Diseases.* Edited by K. K. Holmes et al. 2nd ed. New York: McGraw-Hill, 1989.

Rein, M. F. "Clinical Approach to Urethritis, Mucotaneous Lesions and Inguinal Lymphadenopathy in Homosexual Men." *The Medical Clinics of North America* 70, no. 3 (1986): 587-610.

Reisman, J. A., and E. W. Eichel. *Kinsey, Sex and Fraud.* Lafayette, La.: Lochinvar-Huntington House, 1990.

Remafedi, G., et al. "Demography of Sexual Orientation in Adolescents." *Pediatrics* 89, no. 4, pt. 2 (April 1992): 714-21.

Remafedi, G., et al. "Risk Factors for Attempted Suicide in Gay and Bisexual Youth." *Pediatrics* 87 (January 1, 1987): 869-75.

Riley, V. C. "Resurgent Gonorrhea in Homosexual Men." *Lancet* 337 (1991): 183.

*Rogers, S. M., and C. F. Turner. "Male-Male Sexual Contact in the U.S.A.: Findings from Five Sample Surveys, 1970-1990." *Journal of Sex Research* 28 (November 1991): 491-519.

Rosenberger, P. H., et al. "Psychopathology in Human Immunodeficiency Virus Infection: Lifetime and Current Assessment." *Comprehensive Psychiatry* 34 (May/June 1993): 150-58.

Rothenberg, R. B., and J. J. Potterat. "Strategies for Management of Sex Partners." In *Sexually Transmitted Diseases.* Edited by K. K. Holmes et al. 2nd ed. New York: McGraw-Hill, 1989.

Rowan, R. L., and P. J. Gillette. *The Gay Health Guide.* Boston: Little, Brown, 1978.

Rozenbaum, W., et al. "HIV Transmission by Oral Sex." *Lancet* 1988, no. 1 (1988): 1395.

Ryan, C., and J. Bradford. "The National Lesbian Health Care Survey: An Overview." In *Psychological Perspectives on Lesbian and Gay Male Experiences.* Edited by L. D. Garnets and D. C. Kimmel. New York: Columbia University Press, 1993.

Safai, B., and J. J. Schwartz. "Kaposi's Sarcoma and the Acquired Immunodeficiency Syndrome." In *AIDS: Etiology, Diagnosis, Treatment and Prevention.* Edited by V. T. DeVita et al. Philadelphia: J. B. Lippincott, 1992.

Saghir, M. T., and E. Robins. *Male and Female Homosexuality: A Comprehensive Investigation.* Baltimore: Williams and Wilkins, 1973.

Schechter, M. T., et al. "Changes in Sexual Behavior and Fear of AIDS." *Lancet* 1984 (June 9, 1984): 1293.

Schmidt, K. L., et al. "Sexual Behavior Related to Psycho-social Factors in a Population of Danish Homosexual and Bisexual Men." *Social Science and Medicine* 34 (May 15, 1992): 1119-27.

Schneider, S. G., N. L. Farberow and G. N. Kruks. "Suicidal Behavior in Adolescent and Young Adult Gay Men." *Suicide and Life Threatening Behavior* 19 (Winter 1989): 381-90.

Schneider, S. G., et al. "Factors Influencing Suicide Intent in Gay and Bisexual Suicide Ideators: Differing Models for Men with and Without Human Immunodeficiency Virus." *Journal of Personality and Social Psychology* 61 (November 1991): 776-88.

Schomer, K., et al. "Hepatitis A Among Homosexual Men—U.S., Canada and Australia." *Morbidity and Mortality Weekly Report* 41 (March 6, 1992): 155, 161-64.

Seage, G. R., III, et al. "The Relation Between Nitrite Inhalants, Unprotected Anal Intercourse and the Risk of Immunodeficiency Virus Infection." *American Journal of Epidemiology* 135 (January 1, 1992): 1-11.

Seidman, S. N., and R. O. Rieder. "A Review of Sexual Behavior in the United States." *American Journal of Psychiatry* 151 (March 1994): 330-41.

Siegal, J. M., et al. "The Prevalence of Childhood Sexual Assault." *American Journal of Epidemiology* 126 (1987): 1141-53.

*Silvestre, A. J., et al. "Changes in HIV Rates and Sexual Behavior Among Homosexual Men, 1984 to 1988/92." *American Journal of Public Health* 83 (April 1993): 578-80.

Simon Rosser, B. R. *Male Homosexual Behavior and the Effects of AIDS Education.* New York: Praeger Books, 1991.

Smith, T. W. "Adult Sexual Behavior in 1989: Number of Partners, Frequency of Intercourse and Risk of AIDS." *Family Planning Perspectives* 23 (May/June 1991): 102-7.

Spira, A., et al. "AIDS and Sexual Behavior in France." *Nature* 360 (December 3, 1992): 407-9.

*Stall, R., et al. "Relapse from Safer Sex: The Next Challenge for AIDS Prevention Efforts." *Journal of Acquired Immunodeficiency Syndrome* 3 (1990): 1181-87.

Surawicz, C. M., et al. "Anal Dysplasia in Homosexual Men: Role of Anoscopy and Biopsy." *Gastroenterology* 105 (1993): 658-66.

Task Force on Pediatric AIDS. "Perinatal Human Immunodeficiency Virus Infection." *Pediatrics* 82 (1988): 941-44.

Thompson, J. L. P., et al. "Estimated Condom Failure and Frequency of Condom Use among Gay Men." *American Journal of Public Health* 83 (October 1993): 1409-13.

U.S. Department of Commerce. *1990 Census of Population. Social and Economic Characteristics.* Washington, D.C.: Government Printing Office, September 1993.

———. *Statistical Abstract of the United States 1990.* Washington, D.C.: Government Printing Office, 1990.

Veugelers, P. J., et al. "Estimation of the Magnitude of the HIV Epidemic Among Homosexual Men: Utilization of Survey Data in Predictive Models." *European Journal of Epidemiology* 9 (July 1993): 436-41.

Volberding, P. A. "AIDS-Related Malignancies." In *Sexually Transmitted Diseases.* Edited by K. K. Holmes et al. 2nd ed. New York: McGraw-Hill, 1989.

————. "Clinical Spectrum of HIV Disease." In *AIDS: Etiology, Diagnosis, Treatment and Prevention.* Edited by V. T. DeVita et al. Philadelphia: J. B. Lippincott, 1992.

Vourakis, C. "Homosexuals in Substance Abuse Treatment." In *Substance Abuse: Pharmacologic, Developmental and Clinical Perspectives.* Edited by C. Vourakis and D. S. Woolf. New York: John Wiley & Sons, 1983.

Wald, A., et al. "Influence of HIV Infection on Manifestations and Natural History of Other Sexually Transmitted Diseases." *Annual Review of Public Health* 14 (1993): 19-42.

Weatherburn, P., et al. "Condom Use in a Large Cohort of Homosexually Active Men in England and Wales." *AIDS Care* 3, no. 3 (1991): 31-41.

Weinberg, M. S., C. V. Williams and D. W. Prior. *Dual Attraction: Understanding Bisexuality.* New York: Oxford University Press, 1994.

Wellings, K., et al. "Sexual Lifestyles Under Scrutiny." *Nature* 348 (November 22, 1990): 276-78.

Wexner, D., J. W. Milsom and T. H. Dailey. "The Demographics of Anal Cancers Are Changing: Identification of a High-Risk Population." *Diseases of Colon and Rectum* 30 (1987): 942-46.

Williams, J. B. W., et al. "Multidisciplinary Baseline Assessment of Homosexual Men with and Without Human Immunodeficiency Virus Infection: Part 2, Standardized Clinical Assessment of Current and Lifetime Psychopathology." *Archives of General Psychiatry* 48 (February 1991): 124-30.

Winkelstein, W., et al. "Sexual Practices and Risk of Infection by the Human Immunodeficiency Virus." *Journal of the American Medical Association* 257 (January 16, 1987): 321-25.

Wood, G. G., and J. E. Dietrich. *The Aids Epidemic: Balancing Compassion and Justice.* Portland, Ore.: Multnomah Press, 1990.

Young, M., et al. "Rectal Gonorrhea and Unsafe Sex." *Lancet* 337 (April 6, 1991): 853.

Section 3: Causation and Change

Allen, L. S., and R. A. Gorski. "Sexual Orientation and the Size of the Anterior Commissure in the Human Brain." *Proceedings of the National Academy of Sciences of the United States of America* 89 (August 1, 1992): 7199-202.

Arterburn, J. *How Will I Tell My Mother?* Nashville: Oliver-Nelson, 1988; rev. 1990.

*Bailey, J. M., and R. C. Pillard. "A Genetic Study of Male Sexual Orientation." *Archives of General Psychiatry* 48 (1991): 1089-96.

*Bailey, J. M., et al. "Heritable Factors Influence Sexual Orientation in Women." *Archives of General Psychiatry* 50 (March 1993): 217-23.

Bancroft, J. "Commentary: Biological Contributions to Sexual Orientation." In *Homosexuality/Heterosexuality: Concepts of Sexual Orientation.* Edited by D. P. McWhirter, S. A. Sanders and J. M. Reinisch. Kinsey Institute Series 2. New York: Oxford University Press, 1990.

Barinaga, M. "Is Homosexuality Biological?" *Science* 253 (August 30, 1991): 956-57.

Barnhouse, R. T. *Homosexuality: A Symbolic Confusion.* New York: Seabury Press, 1977.

Baron, M. "Genetic Linkage and Male Homosexual Orientation: Reasons to Be Cautious." *British Medical Journal* 307 (August 7, 1993): 337-38.

*Bell, A., M. Weinberg and S. Hammersmith. *Sexual Preference: Its Development in Men and Women.* Bloomington: Indiana University Press, 1981.

Berlin, F. S., et al. "Media Distortion of the Public's Perception of Recidivism and Psychiatric Rehabilitation." *American Journal of Psychiatry* 148 (November 1991): 1572-76.

Bieber, I. *Psychogenesis: The Early Development of Gender Identity.* London: Routledge & Kegan Paul, 1983.

*Bieber, I., et al. *Homosexuality: A Psychoanalytic Study.* New York: Basic Books, 1962.

Birk, L. "The Myth of Classical Homosexuality: Views of a Behavioral Psychotherapist." In *Homosexual Behavior: A Modern Reappraisal.* Edited by J. Marmor. New York: Basic Books, 1980.

Boswell, J. *Same-Sex Unions in Premodern Europe.* New York: Villard Books, 1994.

Buhrich, N., J. M. Bailey and N. G. Martin. "Sexual Orientation, Sexual Identity and Sex-Dimorphic Behaviors in Male Twins." *Behavior Genetics* 21 (January 1991): 75-96.

Burch, B. "Heterosexuality, Bisexuality and Lesbianism: Rethinking Psychoanalytic Views of Women's Sexual Object Choice." *Psychoanalytic Review* 80 (Spring 1993): 83-89.

*Byne, W., and B. Parsons. "Human Sexual Orientation: The Biologic Theories Reappraised." *Archives of General Psychiatry* 50 (March 1993): 228-39.

Carrier, J. M. "Homosexual Behavior in Cross-Cultural Perspective." In *Homosexual Behavior: A Modern Reappraisal.* Edited by J. Marmor. New York: Basic Books, 1980.

Cass, V. C. "The Implications of Homosexual Identity Formation for the Kinsey Model and Scale of Sexual Preference." In *Homosexuality/Heterosexuality: Concepts of Sexual Orientation.* Edited by D. P. McWhirter, S. A. Sanders and J. M. Reinisch. Kinsey Institute Series 2. New York: Oxford University Press, 1990.

Cavanaugh, J. R. *Counseling the Homosexual.* Huntington, Ind.: Our Sunday Visitor, 1977.

*Davies, B., and L. Rentzel. *Coming Out of Homosexuality.* Downers Grove, Ill.: InterVarsity Press, 1993.

De Cecco, J. P., and J. P. Elia. "A Critique and Synthesis of Biological Essentialism and Social Constructionist Views of Sexuality and Gender." *Journal of Homosexuality* 24, nos. 3/4 (1993): 1-26.

Demeter, S., J. L. Ringo and R. W. Doty. "Morphometric Analysis of the Human Corpus Callosum and Anterior Commissure." *Human Neurobiology* 6 (1988): 219-26.

Denniston, R. H. "Homosexuality in Animals." In *Homosexual Behavior: A Modern Reappraisal.* Edited by J. Marmor. New York: Basic Books, 1980.

Diamant, L. Introduction. In *Male and Female Homosexuality: Psychological Approaches.* Edited by L. Diamant. Series in Clinical and Community Psychology. Washington, D.C.: Hemisphere, 1987.

————. "The Therapies." In *Male and Female Homosexuality: Psychological Approaches.* Edited by L. Diamant. Series in Clinical and Community Psychology. Washington, D.C.: Hemisphere, 1987.

Doll, L. S., et al. "Self-Reported Childhood and Adolescent Sexual Abuse Among Adult Homosexual and Bisexual Men." *Child Abuse and Neglect* 16 (1992): 855-64.

Ellis, A. "The Effectiveness of Psychotherapy with Individuals Who Have Severe Homosexual Problems." In *The Problem of Homosexuality in Modern Society.* Edited by H. M. Ruienbeck. New York: E. P. Dutton, 1965.

Fausto-Sterling, A., and E. Balaban. "Genetics and Male Sexual Orientation." *Science* 261 (September 3, 1993): 1257.

Feldman, M. P., and M. J. MacCulloch. *Homosexual Behavior: Therapy and Assessment.* Oxford: Pergamon, 1971.

Fine, R. "Psychoanalytic Theory." In *Male and Female Homosexuality: Psychological Approaches.* Edited by L. Diamant. Series in Clinical and Community Psychology. Washington, D.C.: Hemisphere, 1987.

*Foucault, M. *The History of Sexuality.* Vol. 1, *An Introduction.* New York: Vintage, 1980.

Friedman, R. C. "Contemporary Psychoanalysis and Homosexuality." *Experimental and Clinical Endocrinology* 98, no. 2 (1991): 155-60.

————. *Male Homosexuality: A Contemporary Psychoanalytic Perspective.* New Haven, Conn.: Yale University Press, 1988.

————. Review of K. Lewes, *The Psychoanalytic Theory of Male Homosexuality* (New York: Simon & Schuster, 1988). *Archives of Sexual Behavior* 19 (June 1990): 293-301.

*Friedman, R. C., and J. Downey. "Neurobiology and Sexual Orientation: Current Relationships." *Journal of Neuropsychiatry and Clinical Neurosciences* 5 (Spring 1993): 131-53.

Gibbons, A. "The Brain as 'Sexual Organ.' " *Science* 253 (August 30, 1991): 957-59.

*Gladue, B. A. "Psychobiological Contributions." In *Male and Female Homosexuality: Psychological Approaches.* Edited by L. Diamant. Series in Clinical and Community Psychology. Washington, D.C.: Hemisphere, 1987.

Gooren, L. "Biomedical Theories of Sexual Orientation: A Critical Examination." In *Homosexuality/Heterosexuality: Concepts of Sexual Orientation.* Edited by D. P. McWhirter, S. A. Sanders and J. M. Reinisch. Kinsey Institute Series 2. New York: Oxford University Press, 1990.

Götestam, K. O., T. J. Coates and M. Ekstrand. "Handedness, Dyslexia and Twinning in Homosexual Men." *International Journal of Neuroscience* 63 (1992): 179-86.

Green, R. *The "Sissy Boy" Syndrome and the Development of Homosexuality.* New Haven, Conn.: Yale University Press, 1987.

*Greenberg, D. *The Construction of Homosexuality.* Chicago: University of Chicago Press, 1988.

*Greenspoon, J., and P. A. Lamal. "A Behaviorist Approach." In *Male and Female Homosexuality: Psychological Approaches.* Edited by L. Diamant. Series in Clinical and Community Psychology. Washington, D.C.: Hemisphere, 1987.

Haldeman, D. C. "Sexual Orientation Conversion Therapy for Gay Men and Lesbians: A Scientific Examination." In *Homosexuality: Implications for Public Policy*. Edited by J. C. Gonsiorek and J. D. Weinrich. Newbury Park, Calif.: Sage, 1991.

*Hamer, D., et al. "A Linkage Between DNA Markers on the X Chromosome and Male Sexual Orientation." *Science* 261 (July 16, 1993): 321-27.

*Hatterer, L. J. *Changing Homosexuality in the Male: Treatment for Men Troubled by Homosexuality*. New York: McGraw-Hill, 1970.

Isay, R. A. "Psychoanalytic Theory and the Therapy of Gay Men." In *Homosexuality/ Heterosexuality: Concepts of Sexual Orientation*. Edited by D. P. McWhirter, S. A. Sanders and J. M. Reinisch. Kinsey Institute Series 2. New York: Oxford University Press, 1990.

Karlen, A. "Homosexuality in History." In *Homosexual Behavior: A Modern Reappraisal*. Edited by J. Marmor. New York: Basic Books, 1980.

Kaye, H. E., et al. "Homosexuality in Women." *Archives of General Psychology* 17 (1967): 626-34.

King, M. "Sexual Orientation and the X." *Nature* 364 (July 22, 1993): 288-89.

King, M., and E. McDonald. "Homosexuals Who Are Twins: A Study of Forty-six Probands." *British Journal of Psychiatry* 160 (1992): 407-9.

*LeVay, S. "A Difference in Hypothalamic Structure Between Heterosexual and Homosexual Men." *Science* 258 (August 30, 1991): 1034-37.

Lewes, K. *The Psychoanalytic Theory of Homosexuality*. New York: Simon & Schuster, 1988.

————. Review of R. C. Friedman, *Male Homosexuality: A Contemporary Psychoanalytic Perspective* (New Haven, Conn.: Yale University Press, 1988). *Archives of Sexual Behavior* 19 (June 1990): 303-7.

McWhirter, D. P., and A. M. Mattison. *The Gay Couple: How Relationships Develop*. Englewood Cliffs, N.J.: Prentice-Hall, 1984.

Maddox, J. "Wilful Public Misunderstanding of Genetics." *Nature* 364 (July 22, 1993): 281.

Marmor, J. "Clinical Aspects of Male Homosexuality." In *Homosexual Behavior: A Modern Reappraisal*. Edited by J. Marmor. New York: Basic Books, 1980.

Masters, W. H., and V. E. Johnson. *Homosexuality in Perspective*. Boston: Little, Brown, 1979.

*Moberly, E. "Homosexuality: Restating the Conservative Case." *Salmagundi* 58/59 (Fall 1982/Winter 1983): 281-99.

————. *Psychogenesis: The Early Development of Gender Identity*. London: Routledge & Kegan Paul, 1983.

Money, J. "Sin, Sickness or Status? Homosexual Gender Identity and Psychoneuroendocrinology." In *Psychological Perspectives on Lesbian and Gay Male Experiences*. Edited by L. D. Garnets and D. C. Kimmel. New York: Columbia University Press, 1993.

Morgenthaler, F. *Homosexuality, Heterosexuality, Perversion*. Hillsdale, N.J.: Analytic, 1988.

Nadler, D. "Homosexual Behavior in Nonhuman Primates." In *Homosexuality/Heterosexuality: Concepts of Sexual Orientation*. Edited by D. P. McWhirter, S. A. Sanders and J. M. Reinisch. Kinsey Institute Series 2. New York: Oxford University Press, 1990.

Payne, L. *The Broken Image.* Westchester, Ill.: Crossway, 1981.

*―――. *The Healing of the Homosexual.* Westchester, Ill.: Crossway, 1984.

Peters, D. K., and P. J. Cantrell. "Factors Distinguishing Samples of Lesbian and Heterosexual Women." *Journal of Homosexuality* 21, no. 4 (1991): 1-15.

Peters, T. "On the Gay Gene: Back to Original Sin Again?" *Dialog* 33 (Winter 1994): 30-38.

Phillips, G., and R. Over. "Adult Sexual Orientation in Relation to Memories of Childhood Gender Conforming and Gender Nonconforming Behaviors." *Archives of Sexual Behavior* 21, no. 6 (1992): 543-58.

Piskur, J., and D. Degelman. "Effect of Reading a Summary of Research About Biological Bases of Homosexual Orientation on Attitudes Toward Homosexuality." *Psychological Reports* 71. no. 3, pt. 2 (December 1992): 1219-25.

Pool, L. "Evidence for Homosexuality Gene." *Science* 261 (July 16, 1993): 291-92.

Risch, N, E. Squires-Wheeler and B. J. B. Keats. "Male Sexual Orientation and Genetic Evidence." *Science* 262 (December 24, 1993): 2063-64.

Rist, D. Y. "Are Homosexuals Born That Way?" *The Nation,* October 19, 1992, pp. 424-29.

Rosenblum, L. A. "Primates, *Homo sapiens* and Homosexuality." In *Homosexuality/Heterosexuality: Concepts of Sexual Orientation.* Edited by D. P. McWhirter, S. A. Sanders and J. M. Reinisch. Kinsey Institute Series 2. New York: Oxford University Press, 1990.

Saghir, M. T., and E. Robins. *Male and Female Homosexuality: A Comprehensive Investigation.* Baltimore: Williams and Wilkins, 1973.

Saia, M. *Counseling the Homosexual.* Minneapolis: Bethany House, 1988.

Sanders, D. S. "A Psychotherapeutic Approach to Homosexual Men." In *Homosexual Behavior: A Modern Reappraisal.* Edited by J. Marmor. New York: Basic Books, 1980.

Shaw, B. D. "A Groom of One's Own?" *The New Republic,* July 18-25, 1994, pp. 33-41.

Siegel, K., and V. H. Raveis. "AIDS-Related Reasons for Gay Men's Adoption of Celibacy." *AIDS Education and Prevention* 5 (Fall 1993): 302-10.

Siegelman, M. "Kinsey and Others: Empirical Input." In *Male and Female Homosexuality: Psychological Approaches.* Edited by L. Diamant. Series in Clinical and Community Psychology. Washington, D.C.: Hemisphere, 1987.

Socarides, C. W., and B. Kaufman. "The Homosexualities: A Psychoanalytic Classification." In *The Homosexualities: Reality, Fantasy and the Arts.* Edited by C. W. Socarides and V. D. Volkan. Madison, Conn.: International Universities Press, 1991.

*―――. *Homosexuality.* New York: Jason Aronson, 1978.

―――. *Homosexuality: Psychoanalytic Therapy.* Northvale, N.J.: Jason Aronson, 1989.

―――. "Reparative Therapy" (letter and replies). *American Journal of Psychiatry* 151 (January 1994): 157-59.

Sternlicht, M. "The Neo-Freudians." In *Male and Female Homosexuality: Psychological Approaches.* Edited by L. Diamant. Series in Clinical and Community Psychology. Washington, D.C.: Hemisphere, 1987.

Storms, M. "A Theory of Erotic Orientation Development." *Psychological Review* 88

(1981): 340-53.

Swaab, D. F., L. J. G. Gooren and M. A. Hofman. "Gender and Sexual Orientation in Relation to Hypothalamic Structures." *Hormone Research* 38, supp. 2 (1992): 51-61.

Swidler, A., ed. *Homosexuality and the World Religions.* Valley Forge, Penn.: Trinity Press International, 1993.

*Troiden, R. C. "The Formation of Homosexual Identities." In *Psychological Perspectives on Lesbian and Gay Male Experiences.* Edited by L. D. Garnets and D. C. Kimmel. New York: Columbia University Press, 1993.

Turner, W. J. "Comments on Discordant Monozygotic Twinning in Homosexuality." *Archives of Sexual Behavior* 23 (February 1994): 115-19.

van den Aardweg, G. J. M. *Homosexuality and Hope.* Ann Arbor, Mich.: Servant, 1985.

————. *On the Origins and Treatment of Homosexuality.* New York: Praeger Books, 1986.

Weinberg, M. S., C. J. Williams and D. W. Pryor. *Dual Attraction: Understanding Bisexuality.* New York: Oxford University Press, 1994.

Weinrich, J. D. "The Kinsey Scale in Biology." In *Homosexuality/Heterosexuality: Concepts of Sexual Orientation.* Edited by D. P. McWhirter, S. A. Sanders and J. M. Reinisch. Kinsey Institute Series 2. New York: Oxford University Press, 1990.

Whitam, F. L., M. Diamond and J. Martin. "Homosexual Orientation in Twins: A Report on Sixty-one Pairs and Three Triplet Sets." *Archives of Sexual Behavior* 22, no. 3 (1993): 187-206.

Section 4: For Further Reading

Arterburn, J. *How Will I Tell My Mother?* Nashville: Oliver-Nelson, 1988; rev. 1990.

Bergner, M. *Setting Love in Order: Hope and Healing for the Homosexual.* Grand Rapids, Mich.: Baker Book House, 1995.

Comiskey, A. *Pursuing Sexual Wholeness.* Lake Mary, Fla.: Creation House, 1989.

Davies, B., and L. Rentzel. *Coming Out of Homosexuality.* Downers Grove, Ill.: InterVarsity Press, 1993.

Grenz, S. *Sexual Ethics.* Dallas: Word, 1990.

Hanigan, J. P. *Homosexuality: The Test Case for Christian Ethics.* New York: Paulist, 1988.

Hays, R. B. "Relations Natural and Unnatural: A Response to John Boswell's Exegesis of Romans 1." *Journal of Religious Ethics* 14 (1986): 186-95.

Klamecki, B. J. "Medical Perspective of the Homosexual Issue." In *The Crisis of Homosexuality.* Edited by J. I. Yamamoto. Wheaton, Ill.: Victor Books, 1990.

O'Donovan, O. "Transsexualism and Christian Marriage." *Journal of Religious Ethics* 11 (Spring 1983): 135-62.

Payne, L. *The Broken Image.* Westchester, Ill.: Crossway, 1981.

Saia, M. *Counseling the Homosexual.* Minneapolis: Bethany House, 1988.

Wood, G. G., and J. E. Dietrich. *The AIDS Epidemic: Balancing Compassion and Justice.* Portland, Ore.: Multnomah Press, 1990.

Wright, D. F. "Homosexuality: The Relevance of the Bible." *Evangelical Quarterly* 61 (October 1989): 291-300.

Index of Subjects

adultery 52-54, 67, 90-91, 93-94
AIDS. See HIV
alcohol 110-11, 113, 127-28
anal intercourse. See sexual practices
arsenokoitēs 33-34, 52, 94-96
behaviorism. See causation: behavioral
Bible, authority of. See Scripture
biology. See causation: biological
bisexuality 103
body
    relation to soul 43, 44, 47
    sin against 100-101, 130
causation 131-53, 163
    behavioral 147-48
    biological 137-42
    environmental 144-46
    cultural 142-44, 146-47
    volitional 149-50
celibacy 47, 53, 60, 165-68
change. See therapy
childhood. See causation
children. See pederasty, pedophilia
choice. See causation: volitional
civil rights 25-27
complementarity 35-36, 44-48, 51, 57-59, 81-82, 115-16
creation theology 39-48, 52-54, 80-83, 100-101
developmental. See causation: environmental
disease. See health
drug use 110-12, 127-28
environment. See causation: environmental
evangelical, description of 16-22
ex-gays. See therapy
experience, authority of 13-

14, 18, 41-42, 59-63, 83, 155-59
family 49-51
feminism 37, 58-59
fundamentalism 17-22
gay. See homosexuality: terminology
genes. See causation: biological
Gibeah 86-89
healing. See therapy
health 116-30, 162-63
heterosexism. See hypocrisy
HIV 116-17, 118, 121, 122-26, 127, 129
Holiness Code. See purity
homophobia. See hypocrisy
homosexuality
    animals and 134
    definition 29
    families 168-69
    health and 116-30, 162-63
    in history 135-37
    politics and 27-28
    practices 105-12, 127
    prevalence 101-5
    in religions 136
    terminology 23-24, 82
hormones. See causation: biological
hypocrisy 54-56, 172-73
idolatry 67, 78-81, 83-85, 89
intercourse. See sexual practices
law, biblical. See purity
lesbianism 37, 65-66, 79, 81, 96, 101-16
liberation theology 36-37, 49
marriage 43-44, 52-54, 56-58, 81-82, 85, 90, 93-94, 96, 98-99, 161-62
ministry 155-59, 163, 170-75
nature/natural 45-47, 77-83, 131-34
oral intercourse. See sexual

practices
orientation 82, 89, 131-53, 163-65
parents. See homosexuality: families
pederasty 32-33, 65-66, 81, 93-96
pedophilia 59-63, 83, 114-15, 127, 133, 148-49, 164
personhood 35-36, 43, 67, 81-83, 85, 100-101
practices. See sexual practices
prevalence 101-5
procreation. See reproduction
promiscuity 105-8, 120, 121, 124-26, 127, 128, 162
prostitutes, male 32-33, 92-93, 95-96, 98
psychopathology 112-16, 127-30, 163
purity 32, 35, 52, 56-57, 64-65, 72-76, 89-92, 96, 99
religions 136
reproduction 35-36, 42-48, 51, 53-54, 57-58, 65, 96, 115-16
sadomasochism. See sexual practices
Scripture
    authority of 18-19, 41-42, 58-59, 62-63, 161
    interpretation of 69-71
sexual practices 105-12, 127
sexually transmitted diseases. See health
sociology. See causation: cultural
Sodom 30-32, 34, 72, 80, 86-89, 96-97
suicide 114, 127
terminology 23-24, 82
therapy 153-59
tolerance 13, 25-26, 171-74
unnatural. See nature/natural
world religions. See religions

Index of Scripture References

Old Testament

Genesis
1—2 *39-44, 162*
1:27-28 *40-45, 81*
1:31 *42, 82*
2:18 *40, 44*
2:23-24 *40, 43-44*
2:24 *53*
4:1 *192*
4:7 *192*
4:25 *192*
6:1-4 *195*
9:20-27 *88*
13:10-13 *87*
13:13 *182*
14:21-24 *87*
18:16-33 *87*
18:20 *182*
16 *48*
17:2 *42*
19:1-8 *30-31, 34, 35, 86-89*
19:5 *30*
19:8 *87*
24:16 *192*
38:16 *192*

Exodus
15:26 *26*
20:1-17 *52*
20:3 *53*
20:13 *52*
20:14 *52 93*
22:21 *182*

Leviticus
15:2-15 *193*
17—26 *32*
18—20 *89-92*
18:7 *193*
18:22 *32, 88, 89-92, 95-96, 97*
20:13 *32, 88, 89-92, 94, 95-96, 97*

Deuteronomy
10:18-19 *182*
13:18 *26*
22:22-29 *90*
23:1 *193*
23:17-18 *90, 92-93, 182, 194*
29:23 *182*
32:32 *182*

Judges
11:39 *192*
21:12 *192*
19:16 *31*
19:16-30 *30-31, 35*
19:22 *30, 87*
19:22-24 *87*
21:25 *26, 87*

1 Kings
14:24 *182, 194*
15:12 *182, 194*
22:46 *182, 194*

2 Kings
23:7 *182, 194*

Job
18:15 *182*
31:31-32 *88*
36:14 *93, 182, 194*

Psalms
11:6 *182*
127:3 *42*
139 *55*
140:10 *182*

Song of Solomon
1—8 *43, 59*
2:6 *184*
4:5-6 *184*
5:2-5 *184*
7:7-8 *184*

8:1-3 *184*

Isaiah
1:9-10 *182*
1:15 *93*
3:9 *182*
13:19 *182*
34:9 *182*

Jeremiah
20:16 *182*
23:14 *182*
49:18 *88, 182*
50:40 *182*

Lamentations
4:6 *182*

Ezekiel
16:22 *88*
16:26 *193*
16:49 *31*
16:50 *88, 97*
16:58 *88*
23:20 *193*
38:22 *182*

Hosea
11:8 *182*

Amos
4:11 *182*

Zephaniah
2:9 *182*

New Testament

Matthew
1:24-25 *48*
5:3-12 *166*
5:27-30 *32, 53, 93-94, 186*
7:1-5 *54*
7:6 *195*

10:14-15 *31, 182*
11:23 *182*
11:28-30 *175*
13:57 *190*
15:26-27 *195*
19:1-12 *40-41, 53, 162*
19:10-12 *43, 48*
23:27 *75*
24:45-51 *190*

Mark
4:19 *188*
6:4 *190*
7 *35, 56*
7:22 *57*
7:27-28 *195*
9:42—10:12 *93-94*
12:4 *190*
12:25 *42*

Luke
10:10-12 *31, 174, 182*
17:22-27 *190*
17:29 *182*
20:11 *190*
21:34-36 *190*
22:15 *188*

John
8:1-11 *32*
8:11 *59, 172*
8:44 *188*
8:49 *190*

Acts
5:41 *190*
10 *35, 56*
10:14 *75*
10:28 *75*
11:8 *75*
22:22 *77*

Romans
1:18-32 *33, 66-67, 78, 162*

1:23 *78*
1:24 *71*
1:24-25 *67*
1:24-27 *70*
1:24-28 *68-69*
1:25 *78*
1:26 *71, 96*
1:26-27 *32-33, 35, 37,*
  65-85, 96, 161
1:26-32 *52, 98, 190*
1:27 *71, 122*
1:28-32 *66, 67*
1:29-31 *76, 81, 91*
1:32 *96*
2 *54, 56*
2:1-2 *54*
2:14-16 *165, 191*
2:21-24 *54*
2:22 *67, 85*
2:23 *76*
2:27 *191*
3:9 *67*
3:10-18 *77*
3:31 *57*
4:4 *84*
6:12 *71, 100*
6:15-16 *57*
6:19 *75*
7:5 *73*
7:7-8 *71*
7:7-25 *53*
7:12-13 *57*
8:18 *189*
9:21 *190*
11:24 *191*
12 *56*
12:1-2 *47*
13:14 *71*
14 *66*
14:14 *35*

1 Corinthians
3:8 *84*
4:10 *190*
5:11-13 *164*
6—7 *43-44*
6:9-10 *33-34, 35, 52,*
  66, 95-96, 97, 98,
  192, 194
6:11 *195*
6:12-20 *41, 52, 53,*
  162, 184
6:13, 18-19 *100*
6:20 *47*
7:2 *189*
7:4-5 *42, 59, 189*
7:8 *48*

7:9 *74, 165, 189*
7:14 *190*
7:25-38 *48*
7:39-40 *48*
9:17-18 *84*
10:6 *188*
11:11-12 *59*
11:13-15 *191*
11:14 *190*
12:23 *190*
15 *184*
15:33 *192*
15:43 *75*

2 Corinthians
1:3-11 *179-80*
1:5-7 *189*
6:8 *190*
6:13 *83*
6:14 *190*
6:17—7:1 *190*
7:1 *100, 190*
11:21 *190*
12:21 *75*

Galatians
2:15 *191*
3:28 *35, 57, 59*
5:16 *188*
5:17 *188*
5:19 *190*
5:24 *73, 188*
6:7 *192*

Ephesians
2:1-20 *55*
2:3 *188*
4:14 *192*
4:19 *189, 190*
4:22 *188*
4:24-32 *190*
5:3 *57, 189, 190*
5:5 *189, 190*
5:21-23 *53, 162*
5:29 *100*
6:14 *190*

Philippians
1:23 *71*
3:2 *195*
3:10 *189*

Colossians
1:9-10 *146*
1:21-23 *55*
1:24 *189*
2:5 *190*

2:20-23 *185*
3:5 *57, 73, 188, 189*
3:12-17 *190*
3:18-19 *186*

1 Thessalonians
2:3 *190, 192*
2:17 *71*
4:3 *72*
4:3-8 *48, 189*
4:5 *72, 73, 188*
4:6 *57, 72, 189*
4:7 *75, 189*

2 Thessalonians
2:11 *192*

1 Timothy
1:10 *33-34, 35, 95-96,*
  97, 98, 194
2:14 *81*
3:2 *186*
3:5 *98*
3:11-12 *186*
4:3 *186*
4:3-5 *185*
5:9-16 *48*
5:16 *186*
6:9 *188*
6:10 *73*

2 Timothy
2:20 *190*
2:22 *188*
3:1 *189*
3:6 *188*
3:13 *192*
4:3 *188*

Titus
2:3-6 *186*
2:12 *188*
3:3 *192*

Hebrews
2:9-10 *189*
5:14 *146*
6:18-19 *55*
9:14 *146*
9:22 *146*
10:32 *189*
13:2 *31*
13:4 *186*
13:9 *185*

James
1:14-15 *188*

2:6 *190*
2:18-26 *184*

1 Peter
1:11 *189*
1:14 *188*
2:11 *188*
3:1-7 *186*
3:21 *146*
4:1-6 *55*
4:2-3 *188*
4:13 *189*
5:1 *189*
5:5 *190*
5:9 *189*
5:10 *55*

2 Peter
1:4 *188*
2:6-7 *34, 35, 96-97,*
  184
2:10 *188*
2:14 *57, 98*
2:18 *188*
3:3 *188*

1 John
1:5—2:2 *55*
2:16-17 *188*
3—5 *184*
4:2 *42*

Jude
7 *34, 35, 86, 96-97,*
  184
8 *98*
16 *188*
18 *188*

Revelation
2:7 *97*
2:11 *97*
16:15 *76*
17—18 *97*
17:4 *98, 190*
18:3 *57*
18:9 *57*
18:14 *188*
21—22 *42*
21:8 *97-98, 195*
22:12 *84, 183*
22:15 *97-98, 183*

Index of Other Ancient Writings

Apocalypse of Baruch
  39:5-7 *195*
Cicero, *De Officiis*
  3.3 *191*
Dio Chrysostom, *Discourse*
  77/78.36 *188*
  7.151-52 *188*
Diodorus Siculus, *History*
  32.10.8-11 *79*
Diogenes Laertius, *Vitae*
  3.24 *191*
  7.108-9 *77, 191*
Dionysius of Halicarnassus,
  Roman Antiquities
  16.4.2-3 *79*
2 Enoch
  10:4-5 *193, 195*
  34:1-3 ms P *193,   95*
Epictetus, *Discourses*
  2.7.1 *191*
  2.14.18 *191*
  3.7.25 *191*
  4.12.16 *191*
Epictetus, *Enchiridion*
  30.1 *191*
Epistle of Aristeas
  152 *193*
4 Ezra
  16:46-63 *195*
Josephus, *Against Apion*
  2.199 *96*
  2.273-75 *80*
Josephus, *Antiquities*
  1.11.1, 3 *193*
Jubilees
  7:20-21 *195*
  13:17 *193*
  16:5 *89*
  20:5-6 *89, 193*
2 Maccabees
  6:4 *190*
3 Maccabees
  4:16 *191*
4 Maccabees
  1:33, 35 *73*
Philo, *De Abrahamo*
  96 *189*
  133-41 *193*
  135 *72, 80*
Philo *De Cherubim*
  14 *191*
Philo, *De Confusione*
  Linguarum
  27 *193*
Philo, *De Decalogo*
  49 *74*
  123 *189*

149 *189*
Philo, *De Ebrietate*
  214 *189*
  222 *189, 193*
Philo, *De Fuga et Inventione*
  144 *72, 193*
Philo, *De Gigantibus*
  34 *74*
  35 *189*
Philo, *De Migratione Abrahami*
  65 *190*
Philo, *De Opificio Mundi*
  80 *189*
Philo, *De Plantatione*
  95 *191*
  100 *191*
Philo, *De Posteriori Caini*
  26 *189*
  71 *189*
  116 *189*
  180 *188*
Philo, *De Praemiis et Poenis*
  77 *188*
Philo, *De Sacrificiis Abelis et*
  Caini
  43 *191*
Philo, *De Specialibus Legibus*
  1.150 *190*
  3.37-42 *80, 193*
Philo, *De Vita Contemplativa*
  59-62 *193*
Philo, *De Virtutibus*
  136 *189*
Philo, *Hypothetica*
  7.1-2 *195*
Philo, *Legum Allegoriae*
  1.56 *191*
  2.29 *190*
  2.66 *76*
  3.18 *191*
  3.126 *191*
  3.138 *189*
  3.139 *190*
  3.147 *190*
  3.155 *189*
  3.158 *76*
  3.165 *191*
  3.210 *191*
Philo, *Quod Deus Immutabilis*
  Sit
  113 *189*
Plato, *Laws*
  636C *79, 188*
  838E-839B *188, 191*
Plato, *Republic*
  2.366A *188*
  562-65 *26*

Plutarch, *Erotikos*
  751 C, E *79, 188*
Plutarch, *Whether Beasts Are*
  Rational
  990F *192*
Psalms of Solomon
  2:15-25 *195*
Pseudo-Phocylides, *Sentences*
  1-2 *195*
  190-92 *192*
Rabbinic writings
  Asheri, Nedarim 21a *192*
  Genesis Rabbah 26:5 *191*
  Leviticus Rabbah 23:9 *191*
  Mishnah 'Abot 4:2 *192*
  Mishnah Torah Issurei Biah
    21:8 *192*
  Mishnah Torah Melakhim
    9:5-6 *192*
  Mishnah Qiddusin 4:14 *192*
  Sefer ha-Hinnukh 209 *192*
  Talmud b. Niddah 13b *93*
  Talmud b. Qiddušin 82a *192*
  Talmud b. Sanhedrin 58a
    188, 192
Seneca, *Moral Epistles*
  47.7 *188*
Sibylline Oracles
  2:73-75 *193*
  3:300-14 *195*
  5:143-79 *195*
  5:429-40 *195*
Sirach
  16:8 *182*
  23:6 *73*
  23:16 *74*
  30:13 *76*
Sophocles, *Antigone*
  449, 481, 663 *188*
Testament of the
  Twelve Patriarchs
  Testament of Benjamin 9:1 *88*
  Testament of Joseph 4:6 *190*
  Testament of Judah 14:5 *190*
  Testament of Levi 17:11 *193*
  Testament of Naphthali 3:4
    88, 195
Wisdom of Solomon
  10:8 *182*
  12:23 *80*
  13:1 *80*
  14:12, 23-27 *80*
  14:26 *193*
  19:13-14 *182*